The Morgan Kaufmann Series in Data Management Systems
Series Editor, Jim Gray

The Object Database Standard: ODMG 2.0
R.G.G Cattell et al.

Introduction to Advanced Database Systems
Carlo Zaniolo, Stefano Ceri, Christos Faloutsos, Richar
V.S. Subrahmanian, and Roberto Zicari

Principles of Transaction Processing
Philip A. Bernstein and Eric Newcomer

Using the New DB2: IBM's Object-Relational Database System
Don Chamberlin

Distributed Algorithms
Nancy A. Lynch

Object-Relational DBMSs: The Next Great Wave
Michael Stonebraker with Dorothy Moore

Active Database Systems: Triggers and Rules For Advanced Database Processing
Edited by Jennifer Widom and Stefano Ceri

Joe Celko's SQL for Smarties: Advanced SQL Programming
Joe Celko

Migrating Legacy Systems: Gateways, Interfaces, and the Incremental Approach
Michael L. Brodie and Michael Stonebraker

Database: Principles, Programming and Performance
Patrick O'Neil

Database Modeling and Design: The Fundamental Principles, Second Edition
Toby J. Teorey

Readings in Database Systems, Second Edition
Edited by Michael Stonebraker

Atomic Transactions
Nancy Lynch, Michael Merritt, William Weihl, and Alan Fekete

Query Processing for Advanced Database Systems
Edited by Johann Christoph Freytag, David Maier, and Gottfried Vossen

Transaction Processing: Concepts and Techniques
Jim Gray and Andreas Reuter

Understanding the New SQL: A Complete Guide
Jim Melton and Alan R. Simon

Building an Object-Oriented Database System: The Story of O_2
Edited by François Bancilhon, Claude Delobel, and Paris Kanellakis

Database Transaction Models for Advanced Applications
Edited by Ahmed K. Elmagarmid

A Guide to Developing Client/Server SQL Applications
Setrag Khoshafian, Arvola Chan, Anna Wong, and Harry K.T. Wong

The Benchmark Handbook for Database and Transaction Processing Systems, Second Edition
Edited by Jim Gray

Camelot and Avalon: A Distributed Transaction Facility
Edited by Jeffrey L. Eppinger, Lily B. Mummert, and Alfred Z. Spector

Readings in Object-Oriented Database Systems
Edited by Stanley B. Zdonik and David Maier

AUTHORIZED

The Object Database Standard: ODMG 2.0

Edited by
R.G.G. Cattell
Douglas K. Barry

Contributors

Dirk Bartels
Mark Berler
Jeff Eastman
Sophie Gamerman
David Jordan
Adam Springer
Henry Strickland
Drew Wade

Morgan Kaufmann Publishers, Inc.
San Francisco, California

Senior Editor Diane D. Cerra
Production Manager Yonie Overton
Production Editor Cheri Palmer
Editorial Assistant Antonia Richmond
Cover Production (based on series design) Rob Upchurch/MacTemps
Proofreader Beverly McGuire
Printer Edwards Brothers, Inc.

This book has been author-typeset using FrameMaker.

Morgan Kaufmann Publishers, Inc.
Editorial and Sales Office
340 Pine Street, Sixth Floor
San Francisco, CA 94104-3205
USA
Telephone 415 / 392-2665
Facsimile 415 / 982-2665
E-Mail mkp@mkp.com
Web site http://www.mkp.com

01 00 99 98 97 5 4 3 2 1

Library of Congress Cataloging-in-Publication Data is available for this book.
ISBN 1-55860-463-4

Contents

Preface

This book defines the ODMG standard for object database management systems. It should be useful to engineers, managers, and students interested in object database systems. Although product documentation from ODMG member companies covers similar information, this book represents the definitive reference for writing code that will work with multiple products. The book has also proven useful in courses on object databases and as an overview of object database programming.

Release 2.0 differs from the previous Release 1.2 in a number of ways. With the wide acceptance of Java, we added a Java persistence standard in addition to the existing Smalltalk and C++ ones. We made the ODMG object model much more comprehensive, added a meta-object interface, defined an object interchange format, and worked to make the programming language bindings consistent with the common model. We made changes throughout the specification based on several years' experience implementing the standard in object database products.

With Release 2.0, the ODMG standard has reached a new level of maturity. Products now available comply reasonably well with the C++ binding, Smalltalk binding, OQL, and even the new Java binding. As with Release 1.2, we expect future work to be backward compatible with Release 2.0. Although we expect a few changes to come, for example, to the Java binding, the standard should now be reasonably stable. For any changes since publication of this book, please check the contact information at the end of Chapter 1, particularly the Web site www.odmg.org.

ODMG created a working group for each chapter of this book. The contributors listed on the cover of this book are the elected chairs and editors for those working groups. Work on standards is not always recognized as important to companies whose livelihood depends on next quarter's revenue, so these authors are to be commended on their personal dedication and cooperation in improving the usability and consistency of their technology. In addition, other people have made important contributions to the ODMG working groups and to previous releases of this standard. These people are acknowledged in Chapter 1.

Rick Cattell, March 1997

Chapter 1

Overview

1.1 Background

This document describes the continuing work on standards for object database management systems (ODBMSs) undertaken by the members of the Object Database Management Group (ODMG). This specification represents an enhancement to ODMG-93, Release 1.2.

We have worked outside of traditional standards bodies for our efforts in order to make quick progress. Standards groups are well suited to incremental changes to a proposal once a good starting point has been established, but it is difficult to perform substantial creative work in such organizations due to their lack of continuity, large membership, and infrequent meetings. It should be noted that relational database standards started with a database model and language implemented by the largest company involved (IBM); for our work, we have picked and combined the best features of implementations we had available to us.

1.1.1 Importance of a Standard

Before ODMG, the lack of a standard for object databases was a major limitation to their more widespread use. The success of relational database systems did not result simply from a higher level of data independence and a simpler data model than previous systems. Much of their success came from the standardization that they offer. The acceptance of the SQL standard allows a high degree of portability and interoperability between systems, simplifies learning new relational DBMSs, and represents a wide endorsement of the relational approach.

All of these factors are important for object DBMSs, as well. The scope of object DBMSs is more far-reaching than that of relational DBMSs, integrating the programming language and database system, and encompassing all of an application's operations and data. A standard is critical to making such applications practical.

The intense ODMG effort has given the object database industry a "jump start" toward standards that would otherwise have taken many years. ODMG enables many vendors to support and endorse a common object database interface to which customers write their applications.

1.1.2 Goals

Our primary goal is to put forward a set of standards allowing an ODBMS customer to write portable applications, i.e., applications that could run on more than one ODBMS product. The data schema, programming language binding, and data manipulation and query languages must be portable. Eventually, we hope our standards proposal will be helpful in allowing interoperability between the ODBMS products as well, e.g., for heterogeneous distributed databases communicating through the OMG Object Request Broker.

We are striving to bring programming languages and database systems to a new level of integration, moving the industry forward as a whole through the practical impetus of real products that conform to a more comprehensive standard than is possible with relational systems. We have gone further than the least common denominator of the first relational standards, and we want to provide portability for the entire application, not just the small portion of the semantics encoded in embedded SQL statements.

The ODMG member companies, representing almost the entire ODBMS industry, are supporting this standard. Thus, our proposal has become a de facto standard for this industry. We have also used our specification in our work with standards groups such as the OMG and the ANSI X3H2 (SQL) committee.

We do not wish to produce identical ODBMS products. Our goal is source code portability; there is a lot of room for future innovation in a number of areas. There will be differences between products in performance, languages supported, functionality unique to particular market segments (e.g., version and configuration management), accompanying programming environments, application construction tools, small versus large scale, multithreading, networking, platform availability, depth of functionality, suites of predefined type libraries, GUI builders, design tools, and so on.

Wherever possible, we have used existing work as the basis for our proposals, from standards groups and from the literature. But, primarily, our work is derived by combining the strongest features of the ODBMS products currently available. These products offer demonstrated implementations of our standards components that have been tried in the field.

1.1.3 Definition

It is important to define the scope of our efforts, since ODBMSs provide an architecture that is significantly different than other DBMSs — they are a revolutionary rather than an evolutionary development. Rather than providing only a high-level language such as SQL for data manipulation, an ODBMS transparently integrates database capability with the application programming language. This transparency makes it unnecessary to learn a separate DML, obviates the need to explicitly copy and translate data between database and programming language representations, and supports substantial performance advantages through data caching in applications. The ODBMS includes the query language capability of relational systems as well, and the query language model is more powerful; e.g., it incorporates lists, arrays, and results of any type. Figure 1-1 provides a comparison of DBMS architectures.

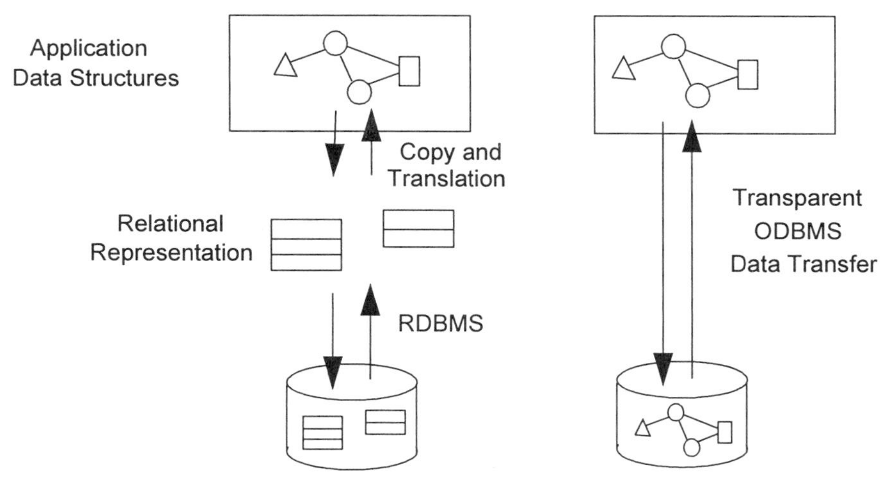

Figure 1-1. Comparison of DBMS Architectures

In summary, we define an *ODBMS* to be a DBMS that integrates database capabilities with object-oriented programming language capabilities. An ODBMS makes database objects appear as programming language objects, in one or more existing programming languages. The ODBMS extends the language with transparently persistent data, concurrency control, data recovery, associative queries, and other database capabilities. For more extensive definition and discussion of ODBMSs, the reader is referred to textbooks in this area (e.g., Cattell, *Object Data Management*).

1.2 Architecture

In order to understand the chapters of this book, it is necessary to understand the overall architecture of ODBMSs.

1.2.1 Major Components

The major components of ODMG 2.0 are described in subsequent chapters:

> *Object Model.* The common data model to be supported by ODBMSs is described in Chapter 2. We have used the OMG Object Model as the basis for

our model. The OMG core model was designed to be a common denominator for object request brokers, object database systems, object programming languages, and other applications. In keeping with the OMG Architecture, we have designed an ODBMS *profile* for their model, adding components (e.g., relationships) to the OMG core object model to support our needs. Release 2.0 introduces a meta model in this chapter.

Object Specification Languages. The specification languages for ODBMSs are described in Chapter 3. One is the object definition language, or ODL, to distinguish it from traditional database data definition languages, or DDLs. We use the OMG interface definition language (IDL) as the basis for ODL syntax. Release 2.0 adds another language, the object interchange format, or OIF, which can be used to exchange objects between databases, provide database documentation, or drive database test suites.

Object Query Language. We define a declarative (nonprocedural) language for querying and updating database objects. This object query language, or OQL, is described in Chapter 4. We have used the relational standard SQL as the basis for OQL, where possible, though OQL supports more powerful capabilities.

C++ Language Binding. Chapter 5 presents the standard binding of ODBMSs to C++; it explains how to write portable C++ code that manipulates persistent objects. This is called the C++ OML, or object manipulation language. The C++ binding also includes a version of the ODL that uses C++ syntax, a mechanism to invoke OQL, and procedures for operations on databases and transactions.

Smalltalk Language Binding. Chapter 6 presents the standard binding of ODBMSs to Smalltalk; it defines the binding in terms of the mapping between ODL and Smalltalk, which is based on the OMG Smalltalk binding for IDL. The Smalltalk binding also includes a mechanism to invoke OQL and procedures for operations on databases and transactions.

Java Language Binding. Chapter 7 defines the binding between the ODMG Object Model (ODL and OML) and the Java programming language as defined by Version 1.1 of the Java™ Language Specification. The Java language binding also includes a mechanism to invoke OQL and procedures for operations on databases and transactions.

It is possible to read and write the same database from C++, Smalltalk, and Java, as long as the programmer stays within the common subset of supported data types. More chapters may be added at a future date for other language bindings. Note that unlike SQL in relational systems, ODBMS data manipulation languages are tailored to specific application programming languages, in order to provide a single, integrated environment for programming and data manipulation. We don't believe exclusively in a universal DML syntax. We go further than relational systems, as we support a unified object model for sharing data across programming languages, as well as a common query language.

1.2.2 Additional Components

In addition to the object database standards, ODMG has produced some ancillary results aimed at forwarding the ODBMS industry. These are included as appendices:

> *OMG Object Model Profile.* Appendix A describes the differences between our object model and the OMG Object Model, so that Chapter 2 can stand alone. As just mentioned, we have defined the components in an ODBMS profile for OMG's model. This appendix delineates these components.
>
> *OMG ORB Binding.* Appendix B describes how ODBMS objects could participate as OMG objects, through an adaptor to an object request broker (ORB) that routes object invocations through object identifiers provided by an ODBMS. We also outline how ODBMSs can make use of the OMG ORB.

1.2.3 ODBMS Architecture Perspective

A better understanding of the architecture of an ODBMS will help put the components we have discussed into perspective.

Figure 1-2 illustrates the use of the typical ODBMS product that we are trying to standardize. The programmer writes declarations for the application schema (both data and interfaces) plus a source program for the application implementation. The source program is written in a programming language (PL) such as C++, using a class library that provides full database OML, including transactions and object query. The schema declarations may be written in an extension of the programming language syntax, labeled PL ODL in the figure, or in a programming language–independent ODL. The latter could be used as a higher-level design language, or to allow schema definition independent of programming language.

The declarations and source program are then compiled and linked with the ODBMS to produce the running application. The application accesses a new or existing database, whose types must conform to the declarations. Databases may be shared with other applications on a network; the ODBMS provides a shared service for transaction and lock management, allowing data to be cached in the application.

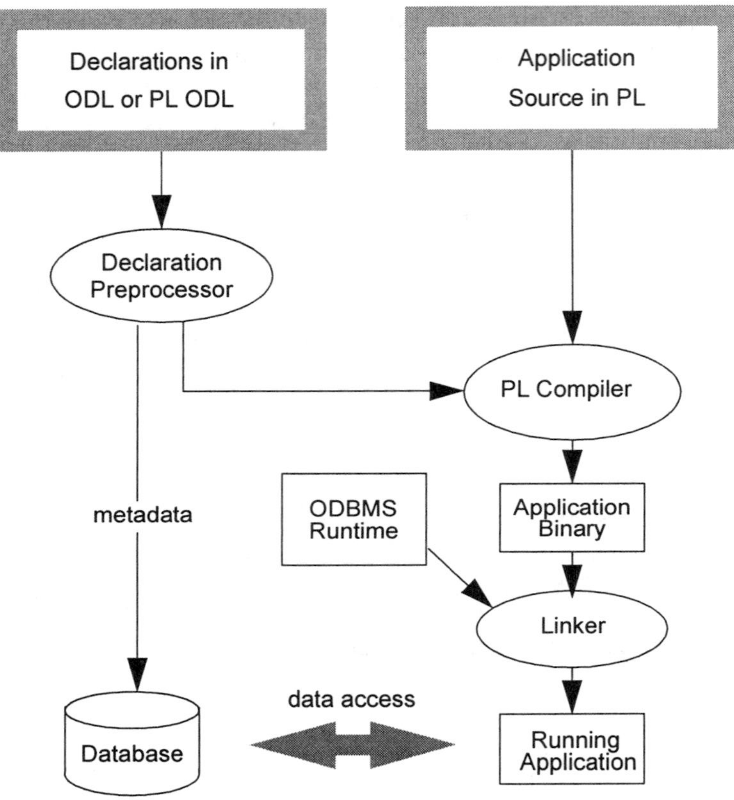

Figure 1-2. Using an ODBMS

1.3 Status

This document describes Release 2.0 of the ODMG standard. The ODMG voting member companies and many of the reviewer member companies are committed to support this standard in their products by the end of 1998.

1.3.1 Participants

As of March 1997, the participants in the ODMG are

- Rick Cattell (ODMG chair, Java workgroup chair, Release 1.0 editor), JavaSoft
- Jeff Eastman (ODMG vice-chair, object model workgroup chair, Smalltalk editor), Windward Solutions

- Douglas Barry (ODMG executive director, Release 1.1, 1.2, and 2.0 editor), Barry & Associates
- Mark Berler (object model and object specification languages editor), American Management Systems
- David Jordan (C++ editor), Lucent Technologies
- Francois Bancilhon, Sophie Gamerman (OQL editor), voting member, O_2 Technology
- Dirk Bartels (C++ workgroup chair), Olaf Schadow, voting member, POET Software
- William Kelly, voting member, UniSQL
- Paul Pazandak, voting member, IBEX
- Ken Sinclair, voting member, Object Design
- Adam Springer (Smalltalk workgroup chair), voting member, GemStone Systems
- Henry Strickland (Java editor), Craig Russell, voting member, Versant Object Technology
- Drew Wade (OQL workgroup chair), Jacob Butcher, Dann Treachler, voting member, Objectivity
- Michael Card, reviewer member, Lockheed Martin
- Edouard Duvillier, reviewer member, MATISSE Software
- Jean-Claude Franchitti, reviewer member, VMARK Software
- Marc Gille, reviewer member, MICRAM Object Technology
- William Herndon, reviewer member, MITRE
- Mamdouh Ibrahim, reviewer member, Electronic Data Systems
- Richard Jensen, reviewer member, Persistence Software
- Yutaka Kimura, reviewer member, NEC
- Shaun Marsh, reviewer member, Fujitsu Open Systems Solutions
- Richard Patterson, reviewer member, Microsoft
- Shirley Schneider, reviewer member, ONTOS
- Jamie Shiers, reviewer member, CERN
- John Shiner, reviewer member, Andersen Consulting
- Jacob Stein, reviewer member, Sybase
- Fernando Velez, reviewer member, Unidata
- Satoshi Wakayama, reviewer member, Hitachi

It is to the personal credit of all participants that the ODMG standard has been produced and revised expeditiously. All of the contributors put substantial time and personal investment into the meetings and this document. They showed remarkable dedication to our goals; no one attempted to twist the process to his or her company's advantage. The reviewers were also very helpful, always ready to contribute.

In addition to the regular ODMG participants above, we received valuable feedback from others in academia and industry. We would like to thank our academic reviewers, in particular Eliot Moss for his contribution to the object model chapter. We would also like to thank Joshua Duhl for his exhaustive review of Release 1.2 as part of the process to create certification test suites.

1.3.2 History

Some of the history and methodology of ODMG may be helpful in understanding our work and the philosophy behind it. We learned a lot about how to make quick progress in standards in a new industry while avoiding "design by committee."

ODMG was conceived at the invitation of Rick Cattell in the summer of 1991, in an impromptu breakfast with ODBMS vendors frustrated at the lack of progress toward ODBMS standards. Our first meeting was at SunSoft in the fall of 1991.

The group adopted rules that have been instrumental to our quick progress. We wanted to remain small and focused in our work, yet be open to all parties who are interested in our work. The structure evolved over time. Presently, we have established workgroups, one for each chapter of the specification. Each workgroup is intended to remain small, allowing for good discussion. The specifications adopted in each workgroup, however, must go before the ODMG Board for final approval. The Board usually holds open meetings for representatives from all members to attend and comment on our work.

The people who come to our meetings from our member companies are called Technical Representatives. They are required to have a technical background in our industry. We also have established rules requiring the same Technical Representatives come repeatedly to our meetings to maintain continuity of our work. Technical Representatives from voting member companies often contribute 25 percent of their time to the ODMG. Some of the Technical Representatives from our reviewer members contribute an equal amount of time while others are more in the range of 10 percent of their time.

Voting membership is open to organizations that have developed and commercially sell a currently shipping ODBMS as defined on page 3. Reviewer members are individuals or organizations having a direct and material interest in the work of the ODMG. Certification members, our newest group of members, are individuals or organizations having a direct and material interest in the certification work of the ODMG.

1.3.3 Accomplishments

Since the publication of Release 1.0, a number of activities have occurred.

1. Incorporation of the ODMG and the establishment of an office.
2. Affiliation with the Object Management Group (OMG), OMG adoption (February 1994) of a Persistence Service endorsing ODMG-93 as a standard interface for storing persistent state, and OMG adoption (May 1995) of a Query Service endorsing the ODMG OQL for querying OMG objects.
3. Establishment of liaisons with ANSI X3H2 (SQL), X3J16 (C++), and X3J20 (Smalltalk), and ongoing work between ODMG and X3H2 for converging OQL and SQL3.
4. Addition of reviewer membership to allow the user community to participate more fully in the efforts of the ODMG.
5. Addition of certification membership to allow the user community to participate in the development of our certification test suites.
6. Publication of articles written by ODMG participants that explain the goals of the ODMG and how they will affect the industry.
7. Collection of feedback on Release 1.0, 1.1, and 1.2, of which much was used in this release.

1.3.4 Next Steps

We now plan to proceed with several actions in parallel to keep things moving quickly.

1. Distribute Release 2.0 through this book.
2. Complete implementation of the specifications in our respective products.
3. Collect feedback and corrections for the next release of our standards specification.
4. Continue to maintain and develop our work.
5. Continue to submit our work to OMG or ANSI groups, as appropriate.

1.3.5 Suggestion and Proposal Process

If you have suggestions for improvements in future versions of our document, we welcome your input. We recommend that change proposals be submitted as follows:

1. State the essence of your proposal.
2. Outline the motivation and any pros/cons for the change.
3. State exactly what edits should be made to the text, referring to page number, section number, and paragraph.
4. Send your proposal to proposal@odmg.org.

1.3.6 Contact Information

For more information about the ODMG and the latest status of its work, send electronic mail to info@odmg.org. You will receive an automated response.

If you have questions on ODMG 2.0, send them to question@odmg.org.

If you have additional questions, or if you want membership information for the ODMG, please contact ODMG's executive director, Douglas Barry, at dbarry@odmg.org, or contact:

Object Database Management Group
14041 Burnhaven Drive, Suite 105
Burnsville, MN 55337 USA
voice: +1-612-953-7250
fax: +1-612-397-7146
email: info@odmg.org
Web: www.odmg.org

1.3.7 Related Standards

There are references in this book to ANSI X3 documents, including SQL specifications (X3H2), Object Information Management (X3H7), the X3/SPARC/DBSSG OODB Task Group Report (contact fong@ecs.ncsl.nist.gov), and the C++ standard (X3J16). ANSI documents can be obtained from:

X3 Secretariat, CBEMA
1250 Eye Street, NW, Suite 200
Washington, DC 20005-3922 USA

There are also references to Object Management Group (OMG) specifications, from the Object Request Broker (ORB) Task Force (also called CORBA), the Object Model Task Force (OMTF), and the Object Services Task Force (OSTF). OMG can be contacted at:

Object Management Group
Framingham Corporate Center
492 Old Connecticut Path
Framingham, MA 01701 USA
voice: +1-508-820-4300
fax: +1-508-820-4303
email: omg@omg.org
Web: www.omg.org

Chapter 2

Object Model

2.1 Introduction

This chapter defines the Object Model supported by ODMG-compliant object database management systems. The Object Model is important because it specifies the kinds of semantics that can be defined explicitly to an ODBMS. Among other things, the semantics of the Object Model determine the characteristics of objects, how objects can be related to each other, and how objects can be named and identified.

Chapter 3 defines programming language–independent object specification languages. One such specification language, Object Definition Language (ODL), is used to specify application object models and is presented for all of the constructs explained in this chapter for the Object Model. It is also used in this chapter to define the operations on the various objects of the Object Model. Chapters 5, 6, and 7, respectively, define the C++, Smalltalk, and Java programming language bindings for ODL and for manipulating objects. Programming languages have some inherent semantic differences; these are reflected in the ODL bindings. Thus some of the constructs that appear here as part of the Object Model may be modified slightly by the binding to a particular programming language. Modifications are explained in Chapters 5, 6, and 7.

The Object Model specifies the constructs that are supported by an ODBMS:

- The basic modeling primitives are the *object* and the *literal*. Each object has a unique identifier. A literal has no identifier.
- Objects and literals can be categorized by their *types*. All elements of a given type have a common range of states (i.e., the same set of properties) and common behavior (i.e., the same set of defined operations). An object is sometimes referred to as an *instance* of its type.
- The state of an object is defined by the values it carries for a set of *properties*. These properties can be *attributes* of the object itself or *relationships* between the object and one or more other objects. Typically the values of an object's properties can change over time.
- The behavior of an object is defined by the set of *operations* that can be executed on or by the object. Operations may have a list of input and output parameters, each with a specified type. Each operation may also return a typed result.
- A *database* stores objects, enabling them to be shared by multiple users and applications. A database is based on a *schema* that is defined in ODL and contains instances of the types defined by its schema.

The ODMG Object Model specifies what is meant by objects, literals, types, operations, properties, attributes, relationships, and so forth. An application developer uses the constructs of the ODMG Object Model to construct the object model for the application. The application's object model specifies particular types, such as Document, Author, Publisher, and Chapter, and the operations and properties of each of these types. The application's object model is the database's (logical) schema.

Analogous to the ODMG Object Model for object databases is the relational model for relational databases, as embodied in SQL. The relational model is the fundamental definition of a relational database management system's functionality. The ODMG Object Model is the fundamental definition of an ODBMS's functionality. It includes significantly richer semantics than does the relational model, by declaring relationships and operations explicitly.

2.2 Types: Specifications and Implementations

There are two aspects to the definition of a type. A type has an external *specification* and one or more *implementations*. The specification defines the external characteristics of the type. These are the aspects that are visible to users of the type: the *operations* that can be invoked on its instances, the *properties*, or state variables, whose values can be accessed, and any *exceptions* that can be raised by its operations. By contrast, a type's implementation defines the internal aspects of the objects of the type: the implementation of the type's operations and other internal details.

An external specification of a type consists of an abstract, implementation-independent description of the operations, exceptions, and properties that are visible to users of the type. An *interface* definition is a specification that defines only the abstract behavior of an object type. A *class* definition is a specification that defines the abstract behavior and abstract state of an object type. A *literal* definition defines only the abstract state of a literal type. Type specifications are illustrated in Figure 2-1.

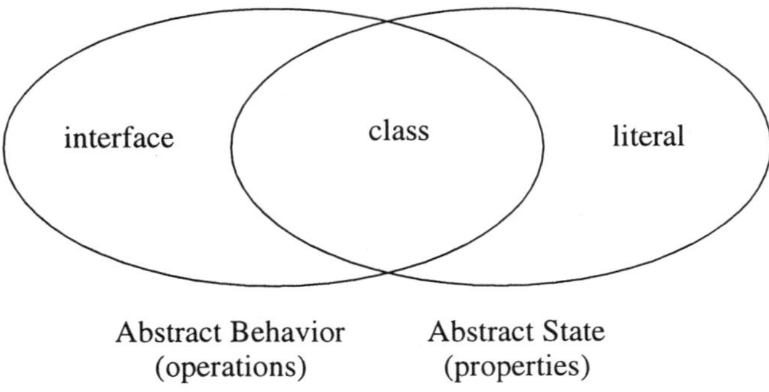

Figure 2-1. Type Specifications

For example, interface Employee defines only the abstract behavior of Employee objects. Class Person defines both the abstract behavior and the abstract state of Person objects. Finally, the struct Complex defines only the abstract state of Complex number literals. In addition to the struct definition and the primitive literal datatypes (boolean, char, short, long, float, double, octet, string, and any), ODL defines declarations for user-defined collection, union, and enumeration literal types.

```
interface Employee {...};
class Person {...};
struct Complex {float re; float im; };
```

An implementation of an object type consists of a *representation* and a set of *methods*. The representation is a data structure that is derived from the type's abstract state by a *language binding*: For each property contained in the abstract state there is an instance variable of an appropriate type defined. The methods are procedure bodies that are derived from the type's abstract behavior by the language binding: For each of the operations defined in the type's abstract behavior a method is defined. This method implements the externally visible behavior of an object type. A method might read or modify the representation of an object's state or invoke operations defined on other objects. There can also be methods in an implementation that have no direct counterpart to the operations in the type's specification. The internals of an implementation are not visible to the users of the objects.

Each language binding also defines an implementation mapping for literal types. Some languages have constructs that can be used to represent literals directly. For example, C++ has a structure definition that can be used to represent the above Complex literal directly using language features. Other languages, notably Smalltalk and Java, have no direct language mechanisms to represent structured literals. These language bindings map each literal type into constructs that can be directly supported using object classes. Further, since both C++ and Java have language mechanisms for directly handling floating point datatypes, these languages would bind the float elements of Complex literals accordingly. Finally, Smalltalk binds these fields to instances of the class Float. As there is no way to specify the abstract behavior of literal types, programmers in each language will use different operators to access these values.

The distinction between specification and implementation views is important. The separation between these two is the way that the Object Model reflects encapsulation. The ODL of Chapter 3 is used to specify the external specifications of types in application object models. The language bindings of Chapters 5, 6, and 7, respectively, define the C++, Smalltalk, and Java constructs used to specify the implementations of these specifications.

A type can have more than one implementation, although only one implementation is usually used in any particular program. For example, a type could have one C++ implementation and another Smalltalk implementation. Or a type could have one C++ implementation for one machine architecture and another C++ implementation for a different machine architecture. Separating the specifications from the implementations keeps the semantics of the type from becoming tangled with representation details. Separating the specifications from the implementations is a positive step toward multilingual access to objects of a single type and sharing of objects across heterogeneous computing environments.

Many object-oriented programming languages, including C++, Java, and Smalltalk, have language constructs called classes. These are implementation classes and are not to be confused with the *abstract classes* defined in the Object Model. Each language binding defines a mapping between abstract classes and its language's implementation classes.

2.2.1 Subtyping and Inheritance of Behavior

Like many object models, the ODMG Object Model includes inheritance-based type-subtype relationships. These relationships are commonly represented in graphs; each node is a type and each arc connects one type, called the *supertype*, and another type, called the *subtype*. The type/subtype relationship is sometimes called an *is-a* relationship, or simply an *ISA* relationship. It is also sometimes called a *generalization-specialization* relationship. The supertype is the more general type; the subtype is the more specialized.

```
interface Employee {...};
interface Professor : Employee {...};
interface Associate_Professor : Professor {...};
```

For example, Associate_Professor is a subtype of Professor; Professor is a subtype of Employee. An instance of the subtype is also logically an instance of the supertype. Thus an Associate_Professor instance is also logically a Professor instance. That is, Associate_Professor is a special case of Professor.

An object's *most specific type* is the type that describes all the behavior and properties of the instance. For example, the most specific type for an Associate_Professor object is the Associate_Professor interface; that object also carries type information from the Professor and Employee interfaces. An Associate_Professor instance conforms to all the behaviors defined in the Associate_Professor interface, the Professor interface, and any supertypes of the Professor interface (and their supertypes, ...). Where an object of type Professor can be used, an object of type Associate_Professor can be used instead, because Associate_Professor inherits from Professor.

A subtype's interface may define characteristics in addition to those defined on its supertypes. These new aspects of state or behavior apply only to instances of the subtype (and any of its subtypes). A subtype's interface also can be refined to specialize state and behavior. For example, the Employee type might have an operation for calculate_ paycheck. The Salaried_Employee and Hourly_Employee class implementations might each refine that behavior to reflect their specialized needs. The polymorphic nature of object programming would then enable the appropriate behavior to be invoked at run-time, dependent on the actual type of the instance.

```
class Salaried_Employee : Employee {...};
class Hourly_Employee : Employee {...};
```

The ODMG Object Model supports multiple inheritance of object behavior. Therefore it is possible that a type could inherit operations that have the same name, but different parameters, from two different interfaces. The model precludes this possibility by disallowing name overloading during inheritance.

Classes are types that are directly instantiable, meaning instances of these types may be created by the programmer. Interfaces are types that cannot be directly instantiated. For example, instances of the classes Salaried_Employee and Hourly_Employee may be created, but instances of their supertype interface Employee cannot. Subtyping pertains to the inheritance of behavior only; thus interfaces may inherit from other interfaces and classes may also inherit from interfaces. Due to the inefficiencies and ambiguities of multiple inheritance of state, however, interfaces may not inherit from classes, nor may classes inherit from other classes.

2.2.2 Inheritance of State

In addition to the ISA relationship that defines the inheritance of behavior between object types, the ODMG Object Model defines an EXTENDS relationship for the inheritance of state. The EXTENDS relationship also applies only to *object* types; thus only classes and not literals may inherit state. The EXTENDS relationship is a single inheritance relationship between two classes whereby the subordinate class inherits all of the properties and all of the behavior of the class that it extends.

```
class Person {
    attribute string name;
    attribute Date birthDate;
    };

// in the following, the colon denotes the ISA relationship
// the extends denotes the EXTENDS relationship
class EmployeePerson extends Person : Employee {
    attribute Date hireDate;
    attribute Currency payRate;
    relationship Manager boss inverse Manager::subordinates;
    };

class ManagerPerson extends EmployeePerson : Manager {
    relationship set<Employee> inverse Employee::boss;
    };
```

The EXTENDS relationship is transitive; thus in the example, every ManagerPerson would have a name, a birthDate, a hireDate, a payRate, and a boss. Note also that, since class EmployeePerson inherits behavior from (ISA) Employee, instances of EmployeePerson and ManagerPerson would all support the behavior defined within this interface.

The only legal exception to the name-overloading prohibition occurs when the same property declaration occurs in a class and in one of its inherited interfaces. Since the properties declared within an interface also have a procedural interface, such redundant declarations are useful in situations where it is desirable to allow relationships to cross distribution boundaries yet they also constitute part of the abstract state of the object (see section 2.6 on page 35 for information about the properties and behavior that can be defined for atomic objects). In the previous example, it would be permissible (and actually necessary) for the interfaces Employee and Manager to contain copies of the boss/subordinates relationship declarations, respectively. It would also be permissible for the interface Employee to contain the hireDate and/or payRate attributes if distributed access to these state variables was desired.

2.2.3 Extents

The *extent* of a type is the set of all instances of the type within a particular database. If an object is an instance of type **A**, then it will of necessity be a member of the extent of **A**. If type **A** is a subtype of type **B**, then the extent of **A** is a subset of the extent of **B**.

A relational DBMS maintains an extent for every defined table. By contrast, the object database designer can decide whether the ODBMS should automatically maintain the extent of each type. Extent maintenance includes inserting newly created instances in the set and removing instances from the set as they are deleted. It may also mean creating and managing indexes to speed access to particular instances in the extent. Index maintenance can introduce significant overhead, so the object model definer specifies that the extent should be indexed separately from specifying that the extent should be maintained by the ODBMS.

2.2.4 Keys

In some cases the individual instances of a type can be uniquely identified by the values they carry for some property or set of properties. These identifying properties are called *keys*. In the relational model, these properties (actually, just attributes in relational databases) are called *candidate keys*. A *simple key* consists of a single property. A *compound key* consists of a set of properties. The scope of uniqueness is the extent of the type; thus a type must have an extent to have a key.

2.3 Objects

This section considers each of the following aspects of objects:

- Creation, which refers to the manner in which objects are created by the programmer.
- Identifiers, which are used by an ODBMS to distinguish one object from another and to find objects.
- Names, which are designated by programmers or end users as convenient ways to refer to particular objects.
- Lifetimes, which determine how the memory and storage allocated to objects are managed.
- Structure, which can be either atomic or not, in which case the object is composed of other objects.

2.3.1 Object Creation

Objects are created by invoking creation operations on *factory interfaces* provided on factory objects supplied to the programmer by the language binding implementation. The new operation, defined below, causes the creation of a new instance of an object of the Object type.

```
interface ObjectFactory {
    Object        new();
};
```

All objects have the following ODL interface, which is implicitly inherited by the definitions of all user-defined objects:

```
interface Object {
    enum          Lock_Type{read, write, upgrade};
    exception     LockNotGranted{};
    void          lock(in Lock_Type mode) raises(LockNotGranted);
    boolean       try_lock(in Lock_Type mode);
    boolean       same_as(in Object anObject);
    Object        copy();
    void          delete();
};
```

Identity comparisons of objects are achieved using the same_as operation. The copy operation creates a new object that is equivalent to the receiver object. The new object created is not the "same as" the original object (the same_as operation is an identity test). Objects, once created, are explicitly deleted from the database using the delete operation. This operation will remove the object from memory and the database.

While the default locking policy of ODMG objects is implicit, all ODMG objects also support explicit locking operations. The lock operation explicitly obtains a specific lock on an object. If an attempt is made to acquire a lock on an object that conflicts with that object's existing locks, the lock operation will block until the specified lock can be acquired, some time-out threshold is exceeded, or a transaction deadlock is detected. If the time-out threshold is crossed, the LockNotGranted exception is raised. If a transaction deadlock is detected, the transaction deadlock exception is raised. The try_lock operation will attempt to acquire the specified lock and immediately return a boolean specifying whether the lock was obtained. The try_lock operation will return TRUE if the specified lock was obtained and FALSE if the lock to be obtained is in conflict with an existing lock on that object. See Section 2.9 for additional information on locking and concurrency.

2.3.2 Object Identifiers

Because all objects have identifiers, an object can always be distinguished from all other objects within its *storage domain*. In this release of the ODMG Object Model, a storage domain is a database. All identifiers of objects in a database are unique, relative to each other. The representation of the identity of an object is referred to as its *object identifier*. An object retains the same object identifier for its entire lifetime. Thus the value of an object's identifier will never change. The object remains the same object, even if its attribute values or relationships change. An object identifier is commonly used as a means for one object to reference another.

Note that the notion of object identifier is different from the notion of primary key in the relational model. A row in a relational table is uniquely identified by the value of the column(s) comprising the table's primary key. If the value in one of those columns changes, the row changes its identity and becomes a different row. Even traceability to the prior value of the primary key is lost.

Literals do not have their own identifiers and cannot stand alone as objects; they are embedded in objects and cannot be individually referenced. Literal values are sometimes described as being constant. An earlier release of the ODMG Object Model described literals as being immutable. The value of a literal cannot change. Examples of literal values are the numbers 7 and 3.141596, the characters A and B, and the strings Fred and April 1. By contrast, objects, which have identifiers, have been described as being *mutable*. Changing the values of the attributes of an object, or the relationships in which it participates, does not change the identity of the object.

Object identifiers are generated by the ODBMS, not by applications. There are many possible ways to implement object identifiers. The structure of the bit pattern representing an object identifier is not defined by the Object Model, as this is considered to be an implementation issue, inappropriate for incorporation in the Object Model.

Instead, the operation same_as() is supported, which allows the identity of any two objects to be compared.

2.3.3 Object Names

In addition to being assigned an object identifier by the ODBMS, an object may be given one or more names that are meaningful to the programmer or end user. The ODBMS provides a function that it uses to map from an object name to an object. The application can refer at its convenience to an object by name; the ODBMS applies the mapping function to determine the object identifier that locates the desired object. ODMG expects names to be commonly used by applications to refer to "root" objects, which provide entry points into databases.

Object names are like global variable names in programming languages. They are not the same as keys. A key is composed of properties specified in an object type's interface. An object name, by contrast, is not defined in a type interface and does not correspond to an object's property values.

The scope of uniqueness of names is a database. The Object Model does not include a notion of hierarchical name spaces within a database or of name spaces that span databases.

2.3.4 Object Lifetimes

The *lifetime* of an object determines how the memory and storage allocated to the object are managed. The lifetime of an object is specified at the time the object is created.

Two lifetimes are supported in the Object Model:

- **transient**
- **persistent**

An object whose lifetime is *transient* is allocated memory that is managed by the programming language run-time system. Sometimes a transient object is declared in the heading of a procedure and is allocated memory from the stack frame created by the programming language run-time system when the procedure is invoked. That memory is released when the procedure returns. Other transient objects are scoped by a process rather than a procedure activation and are typically allocated to either static memory or the heap by the programming language system. When the process terminates, the memory is deallocated. An object whose lifetime is *persistent* is allocated memory and storage managed by the ODBMS run-time system. These objects continue to exist after the procedure or process that creates them terminates. Persistent objects are sometimes referred to as *database objects*. Particular programming languages may refine the notion of transient lifetimes in manners consistent with their lifetime concepts.

An important aspect of object lifetimes is that they are independent of types. A type may have some instances that are persistent and others that are transient. This independence of type and lifetime is quite different from the relational model. In the relational model, any type known to the DBMS by definition has only persistent instances, and any type not known to the DBMS (i.e., any type not defined using SQL) by definition has only transient instances. Because the ODMG Object Model supports independence of type and lifetime, both persistent and transient objects can be manipulated using the same operations. In the relational model, SQL must be used for defining and using persistent data, while the programming language is used for defining and using transient data.

2.3.5 Atomic Objects

An atomic object type is user-defined. There are no built-in atomic object types included in the ODMG Object Model. See Section 2.6 for information about the properties and behavior that can be defined for atomic objects.

2.3.6 Collection Objects

In the ODMG Object Model, instances of *collection objects* are composed of distinct elements, each of which can be an instance of an atomic type, another collection, or a literal type. Literal types will be discussed in section 2.4 on page 31. An important distinguishing characteristic of a collection is that *all* the elements of the collection must be of the *same* type. They are either all the same atomic type, or all the same type of collection, or all the same type of literal.

The collections supported by the ODMG Object Model include:

- **Set<t>**
- **Bag<t>**
- **List<t>**
- **Array<t>**
- **Dictionary<t,v>**

Each of these is a type generator, parameterized by the type shown within the angle brackets. All the elements of a Set object are of the same type **t**. All the elements of a List object are of the same type **t**. In the following interfaces, we have chosen to use the ODL type any to represent these typed parameters, recognizing that this can imply a heterogeneity that is not the intent of this object model.

Collections are created by invoking the operations on the CollectionFactory interface defined below. The new operation, inherited from the ObjectFactory interface, creates a Collection with a system-dependent default amount of storage for its elements. The new_of_size operation creates a Collection with the given amount of initial storage allocated, where the given size is the number of elements for which storage is to be reserved.

```
interface CollectionFactory : ObjectFactory {
    Collection          new_of_size(in long size);
};
```

Collections all have the following operations:

```
interface Collection : Object {
    exception               InvalidCollectionType{};
    exception               ElementNotFound{any element; };
    unsigned long           cardinality();
    boolean                 is_empty();
    boolean                 is_ordered();
    boolean                 allows_duplicates();
    boolean                 contains_element(in any element);
    void                    insert_element(in any element);
    void                    remove_element(in any element)
                                raises(ElementNotFound);
    Iterator                create_iterator(in boolean stable);
    BidirectionalIterator   create_bidirectional_iterator(in boolean stable)
                                raises(InvalidCollectionType);
};
```

The number of elements contained in a collection is obtained using the cardinality operation. The operations is_empty, is_ordered, and allows_duplicates provide a means for dynamically querying a collection to obtain its characteristics. Element management within a collection is supported via the insert_element, remove_element, and contains_element operations. The create_iterator and create_bidirectional_iterator operations support the traversal of elements within a collection (see Iterator interface below).

In addition to the operations defined in the Collection interface, Collection objects also inherit operations defined in the Object interface. Identity comparisons are determined using the same_as operation. A copy of a collection returns a new Collection object whose elements are the same as the elements of the original Collection object (i.e., this is a shallow copy operation). The delete operation removes the collection from the database, and if the collection contains literals, also deletes the contents of the collection. However, if the collection contains objects, remain unchanged.

An Iterator, which is a mechanism for accessing the elements of a Collection object, can be created to traverse a collection. The following operations are defined in the Iterator interface:

```
interface Iterator {
      exception        NoMoreElements{};
      exception        InvalidCollectionType{};
      boolean          is_stable();
      boolean          at_end();
      void             reset();
      any              get_element() raises(NoMoreElements);
      void             next_position() raises(NoMoreElements);
      void             replace_element (in any element)
                           raises(InvalidCollectionType);
};
interface BidirectionalIterator : Iterator {
      boolean          at_beginning();
      void             previous_position() raises(NoMoreElements);
};
```

The create_iterator and create_bidirectional_iterator operations create iterators that support forward only traversals on all collections and bidirectional traversals of ordered collections. The stability of an iterator determines whether an iteration is safe from changes made to the collection during iteration. A stable iterator ensures that modifications made to a collection during iteration will not affect traversal. If an iterator is not stable, the iteration supports only retrieving elements from a collection during traversal, as changes made to the collection during iteration may result in missed elements or the double processing of an element. Creating an iterator automatically positions the iterator to the first element in the iteration. The get_element operation retrieves the element currently pointed to by the iterator. The next_position operation increments the iterator to the next element in the iteration. The previous_position operation decrements the iterator to the previous element in the iteration. The replace_element operation, valid when iterating over List and Array objects, replaces the element currently pointed to by the iterator with the argument passed to the operation. The reset operation repositions the iterator to the first element in the iteration.

2.3.6.1 Set Objects

A Set object is an unordered collection of elements, with no duplicates allowed. The following operations are defined in the Set interface:

```
interface Set : Collection {
      Set            create_union(in Set other_set);
      Set            create_intersection(in Set other_set);
      Set            create_difference(in Set other_set);
      boolean        is_subset_of(in Set other_set);
      boolean        is_proper_subset_of(in Set other_set);
      boolean        is_superset_of(in Set other_set);
      boolean        is_proper_superset_of(in Set other_set);
};
```

The Set type interface has the conventional mathematical set operations, as well as subsetting and supersetting boolean tests. The create_union, create_intersection, and create_difference operations each return a new result Set object.

Set refines the insert_element operation inherited from its Collection supertype. If the object passed as the argument to the insert_element operation is not already a member of the set, the object is added to the set. Otherwise, the set remains unchanged.

2.3.6.2 Bag Objects

A Bag object is an unordered collection of elements that may contain duplicates. The following interfaces are defined in the Bag interface:

```
interface Bag : Collection {
      unsigned long   occurrences_of(in any element);
      Bag             create_union(in Bag other_bag);
      Bag             create_intersection(in Bag other_bag);
      Bag             create_difference(in Bag other_bag);
};
```

The occurrences_of operation calculates the number of times a specific element occurs in the Bag. The create_union, create_intersection, and create_difference operations each return a new result Bag object.

Bag refines the insert_element and remove_element operations inherited from its Collection supertype. The insert_element operation inserts into the Bag object the element passed as an argument. If the element is already a member of the bag, it is inserted another time, increasing the multiplicity in the bag. The remove_element operation removes one occurrence of the specified element from the bag.

2.3.6.3 List Objects

A List object is an ordered collection of elements. The operations defined in the List interface are positional in nature, in reference either to a given index or to the beginning or end of a List object. Indexing of a List object starts at zero. The following operations are defined in the List interface:

```
interface List : Collection {
    exception   InvalidIndex{unsigned long index; };
    void        remove_element_at(in unsigned long index)
                    raises(InvalidIndex);
    any         retrieve_element_at(in unsigned long index)
                    raises(InvalidIndex);
    void        replace_element_at(in any element, in unsigned long index)
                    raises(InvalidIndex);
    void        insert_element_after(in any element, in unsigned long index)
                    raises(InvalidIndex);
    void        insert_element_before(in any element, in unsigned long index)
                    raises(InvalidIndex);
    void        insert_element_first (in any element);
    void        insert_element_last (in any element);
    void        remove_first_element()
                    raises(ElementNotFound);
    void        remove_last_element()
                    raises(ElementNotFound);
    any         retrieve_first_element()
                    raises(ElementNotFound);
    any         retrieve_last_element()
                    raises(ElementNotFound);
    List        concat(in List other_list);
    void        append(in List other_list);
};
```

The List interface defines operations for selecting, updating, and deleting elements from a list. In addition, operations that manipulate multiple lists are defined. The concat operation returns a new List object that contains the list passed as an argument appended to the receiver list. Both the receiver list and argument list remain unchanged. The append operation modifies the receiver list by appending the argument list.

List refines the insert_element and remove_element operations inherited from its Collection supertype. The insert_element operation inserts the specified object at the end of the list. The semantics of this operation are equivalent to the list operation insert_element_last. The remove_element operation removes the first occurrence of the specified object from the list.

2.3.6.4 Array Objects

An Array object is a dynamically sized ordered collection of elements that can be located by position. The following operations are defined in the Array interface:

```
interface Array : Collection {
    exception   InvalidIndex{unsigned long index; };
    void        replace_element_at(in unsigned long index, in any element)
                    raises(InvalidIndex);
    void        remove_element_at(in unsigned long index)
                    raises(InvalidIndex);
    any         retrieve_element_at(in unsigned long index)
                    raises(InvalidIndex);
    void        resize(in unsigned long new_size);
};
```

The remove_element_at operation replaces any current element contained in the cell of the array object identified by index with a null value. It does not remove the cell or change the size of the array. This is in contrast to the remove_element_at operation, defined on type List, which does change the number of elements in a List object. The resize operation enables an Array object to change the maximum number of elements it can contain.

Array refines the insert_element and remove_element operations inherited from its Collection supertype. The insert_element operation increases the size of the array by one and inserts the specified object in the new position. The remove_element operation replaces the first occurrence of the specified object in the list with a null value.

2.3.6.5 Dictionary Objects

A Dictionary object is an unordered sequence of key-value pairs with no duplicate keys. Each key-value pair is constructed as an instance of the following structure:

```
struct Association {any key; any value; };
```

Iterating over a Dictionary object will result in the iteration over a sequence of Associations. Each get_element operation, executed on an Iterator object, returns a structure of type Association.

The following operations are defined in the Dictionary interface:

```
interface Dictionary : Collection {
    exception       KeyNotFound{any key; };
    void            bind(in any key, in any value);
    void            unbind(in any key) raises(KeyNotFound);
    any             lookup(in any key) raises(KeyNotFound);
    boolean         contains_key(in any key);
};
```

Inserting, deleting, and selecting entries in a Dictionary object are achieved using the bind, unbind, and lookup operations, respectively. The contains_key operation tests for the existence of a specific key in the Dictionary object.

Dictionary refines the insert_element, remove_element, and contains_element operations inherited from its Collection supertype. All of these operations are valid for Dictionary types when an Association is specified as the argument. The insert_element operation inserts an entry into the Dictionary that reflects the key-value pair contained in the Association parameter. If the key already resides in the Dictionary, the existing entry is replaced. The remove_element operation removes the entry from the Dictionary that matches the key-value pair contained in the Association passed as an argument. If a matching key-value pair entry is not found in the Dictionary, the ElementNotFound exception is raised. Similarly, the contains_element operation also uses both the key and value contained in the Association argument to locate a particular entry in the Dictionary object. A boolean is returned specifying whether the key-value pair exists in the Dictionary.

2.3.7 Structured Objects

All *structured objects* support the Object ODL interface. The ODMG Object Model defines the following *structured objects*:

- **Date**
- **Interval**
- **Time**
- **Timestamp**

These types are defined as in the ANSI SQL specification by the following interfaces.

2.3.7.1 Date

The following interface defines the factory operations for creating Date objects:

```
interface DateFactory : ObjectFactory {
    exception InvalidDate{};
    Date              julian_date(in unsigned short year,
                                  in unsigned short julian_day)
                          raises(InvalidDate);
    Date              calendar_date(in unsigned short year,
                                  in unsigned short month,
                                  in unsigned short day)
                          raises(InvalidDate);
    boolean           is_leap_year(in unsigned short year);
    boolean           is_valid_date(in unsigned short year,
                                  in unsigned short month,
                                  in unsigned short day);
    unsigned short    days_in_year(in unsigned short year);
    unsigned short    days_in_month(in unsigned short year,
                                  in Date::Month month);
    Date              current();
};
```

The following interface defines the operations on Date objects:

```
interface Date : Object {
    typedef           unsigned shortushort;
    enum              Weekday {Sunday, Monday, Tuesday, Wednesday,
                                  Thursday, Friday, Saturday};
    enum              Month {January, February, March, April, May, June, July,
                                  August, September, October, November,
                                  December};

    // used to represent a Date object by a typed value
    struct asValue {ushort month, day, year; };

    ushort            year();
    ushort            month();
    ushort            day();
    ushort            day_of_year();
    Month             month_of_year();
    Weekday           day_of_week();
```

```
    boolean     is_leap_year();
    boolean     is_equal(in Date a_date);
    boolean     is_greater(in Date a_date);
    boolean     is_greater_or_equal(in Date a_date);
    boolean     is_less(in Date a_date);
    boolean     is_less_or_equal(in Date a_date);
    boolean     is_between(in Date a_date, in Date b_date);
    Date        next(in Weekday day);
    Date        previous(in Weekday day);
    Date        add_days(in long days);
    Date        subtract_days(in long days);
    long        subtract_date(in Date a_date);
};
```

2.3.7.2 Interval

Intervals represent a duration of time and are used to perform some operations on Time and Timestamp objects. Intervals are created using the subtract_time operation defined in the Time interface below. The following interface defines the operations on Interval objects:

```
interface Interval : Object {
    typedef     unsigned shortushort;
    ushort      day();
    ushort      hour();
    ushort      minute();
    ushort      second();
    ushort      millisecond();
    // used to represent an Interval object as a typed value
    struct      asValue {ushort day, hour, minute; float second; };
    boolean     is_zero();
    Interval    plus(in Interval an_interval);
    Interval    minus(in Interval an_interval);
    Interval    product(in long val);
    Interval    quotient(in long val);
    boolean     is_equal(in Interval an_interval);
    boolean     is_greater(in Interval an_interval);
    boolean     is_greater_or_equal(in Interval an_interval);
    boolean     is_less(in Interval an_interval);
    boolean     is_less_or_equal(in Interval an_interval);
};
```

2.3.7.3 Time

Times denote specific world times, which are internally stored in Greenwich Mean Time (GMT). Time zones are specified according to the number of hours that must be added or subtracted from local time in order to get the time in Greenwich, England.

The following interface defines the factory operations for creating Time objects:

```
interface TimeFactory : ObjectFactory {
    void            set_default_time_zone(in Time_Zone a_time_zone);
    Time_Zone       default_time_zone();
    Time_Zone       time_zone();
    Time            from_hms(in unsigned short hour,
                             in unsigned short minute,
                             in float second);
    Time            from_hmstz(in unsigned short hour,
                             in unsigned short minute,
                             in float second,
                             in short tzhour,
                             in short tzminute);
    Time            current();
};
```

The following interface defines the operations on Time objects:

```
interface Time : Object {
    typedef short      Time_Zone;
    const   Time_Zone  GMT = 0;
    const   Time_Zone  GMT1 = 1;
    const   Time_Zone  GMT2 = 2;
    const   Time_Zone  GMT3 = 3;
    const   Time_Zone  GMT4 = 4;
    const   Time_Zone  GMT5 = 5;
    const   Time_Zone  GMT6 = 6;
    const   Time_Zone  GMT7 = 7;
    const   Time_Zone  GMT8 = 8;
    const   Time_Zone  GMT9 = 9;
    const   Time_Zone  GMT10 = 10;
    const   Time_Zone  GMT11 = 11;
    const   Time_Zone  GMT12 = 12;
```

```
    const    Time_Zone    GMT_1 = -1;
    const    Time_Zone    GMT_2 = -2;
    const    Time_Zone    GMT_3 = -3;
    const    Time_Zone    GMT_4 = -4;
    const    Time_Zone    GMT_5 = -5;
    const    Time_Zone    GMT_6 = -6;
    const    Time_Zone    GMT_7 = -7;
    const    Time_Zone    GMT_8 = -8;
    const    Time_Zone    GMT_9 = -9;
    const    Time_Zone    GMT_10 = -10;
    const    Time_Zone    GMT_11 = -11;
    const    Time_Zone    GMT_12 = -12;
    const    Time_Zone    USeastern = -5;
    const    Time_Zone    UScentral = -6;
    const    Time_Zone    USmountain = -7;
    const    Time_Zone    USpacific = -8;
    ushort        hour();
    ushort        minute();
    ushort        second();
    ushort        millisecond();
    short         tz_hour();
    short         tz_minute();
    boolean       is_equal(in Time a_Time);
    boolean       is_greater(in Time a_Time);
    boolean       is_greater_or_equal(in Time a_Time);
    boolean       is_less(in Time a_Time);
    boolean       is_less_or_equal(in Time a_Time);
    boolean       is_between(in Time a_Time,
                        in Time b_Time);
    Time          add_interval(in Interval an_interval);
    Time          subtract_interval(in Interval an_interval);
    Interval      subtract_time(in Time a_time);
};
```

2.3.7.4 Timestamp

Timestamps consist of an encapsulated Date and Time. The following interface defines the factory operations for creating Timestamp objects:

```
interface TimestampFactory : ObjectFactory {
    exception       InvalidTimestamp{Date a_date, Time a_time; };
    Timestamp       current();
    Timestamp       create(in Date a_date, in Time a_time)
                        raises(InvalidTimestamp);
};
```

The following interface defines the operations on Timestamp objects:

```
interface Timestamp : Object {
    typedef      unsigned short    ushort;
    Date            get_date();
    Time            get_time();
    ushort          year();
    ushort          month();
    ushort          day();
    ushort          hour();
    ushort          minute();
    ushort          second();
    ushort          millisecond();
    short           tz_hour();
    short           tz_minute();
    Timestamp       plus(in Interval an_interval);
    Timestamp       minus(in Interval an_interval);
    boolean         is_equal(in Timestamp a_Stamp);
    boolean         is_greater(in Timestamp a_Stamp);
    boolean         is_greater_or_equal(in Timestamp a_Stamp);
    boolean         is_less(in Timestamp a_Stamp);
    boolean         is_less_or_equal(in Timestamp a_Stamp);
    boolean         is_between(in Timestamp a_Stamp,
                        in Timestamp b_Stamp);
};
```

2.4 Literals

Literals do not have object identifiers. The Object Model supports four literal types:

- **atomic literal**
- **collection literal**
- **structured literal**
- **null literal**

2.4.1 Atomic Literals

Numbers and characters are examples of atomic literal types. Instances of these types are not explicitly created by applications, but rather implicitly exist. The ODMG Object Model supports the following types of atomic literals:

- **long**
- **short**
- **unsigned long**
- **unsigned short**
- **float**
- **double**
- **boolean**
- **octet**
- **char (character)**
- **string**
- **enum (enumeration)**

These types are all also supported by the OMG Interface Definition Language (IDL). The intent of the Object Model is that a programming language binding should support the language-specific analog of these types, as well as any other atomic literal types defined by the programming language. If the programming language does not contain an analog for one of the Object Model types, then a class library defining the implementation of the type should be supplied as part of the programming language binding.

Enum is a type generator. An enum declaration defines a named literal type that can take on only the values listed in the declaration. For example, an attribute gender might be defined by

```
attribute enum gender {male, female};
```

An attribute state_code might be defined by

```
attribute enum state_code {AK,AL,AR,AZ,CA, ... WY};
```

2.4.2 Collection Literals

The ODMG Object Model supports collection literals of the following types:

- **set<t>**
- **bag<t>**
- **list<t>**
- **array<t>**
- **dictionary<t,v>**

These type generators are analogous to those of collection objects, but these collections do not have object identifiers. Their elements, however, can be of literal types or object types.

2.4.2.1 Table Type

The ODMG data model encompasses the relational data model by defining a Table type to express SQL tables. The ODMG Table type is semantically equivalent to a collection of structs.

2.4.3 Structured Literals

A structured literal, or simply *structure*, has a fixed number of elements, each of which has a variable name and can contain either a literal value or an object. An element of a structure is typically referred to by a variable name, e.g., address.zip_code = 12345; address.city = "San Francisco". Structure types supported by the ODMG Object Model include

- **date**
- **interval**
- **time**
- **timestamp**

2.4.3.1 User-Defined Structures

Because the Object Model is extensible, developers can define other structure types as needed. The Object Model includes a built-in type generator struct, to be used to define application structures. For example:

```
struct Address {
      string          dorm_name;
      string          room_no;
};
attribute Address dorm_address;
```

Structures may be freely composed. The Object Model supports sets of structures, structures of sets, arrays of structures, and so forth. This composability allows the definition of types like Degrees, as a list whose elements are structures containing three fields:

```
struct Degree {
      string              school_name;
      string              degree_type;
      unsigned short      degree_year;
};
typedef list<Degree>  Degrees;
```

Each Degrees instance could have its elements sorted by value of degree_year.

Each language binding will map the Object Model structures and collections to mechanisms that are provided by the programming language. For example, Smalltalk includes its own Collection, Date, Time, and Timestamp classes.

2.4.4 Null Literals

For every literal type (e.g., float or set<>) there exists another literal type supporting a null value (e.g., nullable_float or nullable_set<>). This nullable type is the same as the literal type augmented by the null value "*nil*". The semantics of null are the same as those defined by SQL-92.

2.5 The Full Built-in Type Hierarchy

Figure 2-2 shows the full set of built-in types of the Object Model type hierarchy. Concrete types are shown in nonitalic font and are directly instantiable. Abstract types are shown in italics. In the interests of simplifying matters, both types and type generators are included in the same hierarchy. Type generators are signified by angle brackets (e.g., Set<>).

The ODMG Object Model is strongly typed. Every object or literal has a type, and every operation requires typed operands. The rules for type identity and type compatibility are defined in this section.

Two objects or literals have the same type if and only if they have been declared to be instances of the same named type. Objects or literals that have been declared to be instances of two different types are not of the same type, even if the types in question define the same set of properties and operations. Type compatibility follows the subtyping relationships defined by the type hierarchy. If **TS** is a subtype of **T**, then an object of type **TS** can be assigned to a variable of type **T**, but the reverse is not possible. No implicit conversions between types are provided by the Object Model.

Two atomic literals have the same type if they belong to the same set of literals. Depending on programming language bindings, implicit conversions may be provided between the scalar literal types, i.e., long, short, unsigned long, unsigned short, float, double, boolean, octet, and char. No implicit conversions are provided for structured literals.

Literal_type
  Atomic_literal
    long
    short
    unsigned long
    unsigned short
    float

- - - **double**
      - **boolean**
      - **octet**
      - **char**
      - **string**
      - **enum<>**
    - *Collection_literal*
      - **set<>**
      - **bag<>**
      - **list<>**
      - **array<>**
      - **dictionary<>**
    - *Structured_literal*
      - **date**
      - **time**
      - **timestamp**
      - **interval**
      - **structure<>**
- *Object_type*
  - *Atomic_object*
  - *Collection_object*
    - **Set<>**
    - **Bag<>**
    - **List<>**
    - **Array<>**
    - **Dictionary<>**
  - *Structured_object*
    - **Date**
    - **Time**
    - **Timestamp**
    - **Interval**

Figure 2-2. Full Set of Built-in Types

2.6 Modeling State — Properties

A type defines a set of properties through which users can access, and in some cases directly manipulate, the state of instances of the type. Two kinds of properties are defined in the ODMG Object Model: *attribute* and *relationship*. An attribute is of one type. A relationship is defined between two types, each of which must have instances that are referenceable by object identifiers. Thus literal types, because they do not have object identifiers, cannot participate in relationships.

2.6.1 Attributes

The attribute declarations in an interface define the abstract state of a type. For example, the type Person might contain the following attribute declarations:

```
interface Person {
        attribute short age;
        attribute string name;
        attribute enum gender {male, female};
        attribute Address home_address;
        attribute set<Phone_no> phones;
        attribute Department dept;
};
```

A particular instance of Person would have a specific value for each of the defined attributes. The value for the dept attribute above is the object identifier of an instance of Department. An attribute's value is always either a literal or an object identifier.

It is important to note that an attribute is not the same as a data structure. An attribute is abstract, while a data structure is a physical representation. While it is common for attributes to be implemented as data structures, it is sometimes appropriate for an attribute to be implemented as a method. For example, the age attribute might very well be implemented as a method that calculates age from a stored value of the person's date_of_birth and the current date.

In this release of the ODMG Object Model, attributes are not "first class." This means that an attribute itself is not an object and therefore does not have an object identifier. It is not possible to define attributes of attributes or relationships between attributes or subtype-specific operations for attributes.

2.6.2 Relationships

Relationships are defined between types. The ODMG Object Model supports only binary relationships, i.e., relationships between two types. The model does not support n-ary relationships, which involve more than two types. A binary relationship may be one-to-one, one-to-many, or many-to-many, depending on how many instances of each type participate in the relationship. For example, *marriage* is a one-to-one relationship between two instances of type Person. A person can have a one-to-many *parent of* relationship with many children. Teachers and students typically participate in many-to-many relationships. Relationships in the Object Model are similar to relationships in entity-relationship data modeling.

Relationships in this release of the Object Model are not named and are not "first class." A relationship is not itself an object and does not have an object identifier. A relationship is defined implicitly by declaration of *traversal paths* that enable applications to use the logical connections between the objects participating in the relationship. Traversal paths are declared in pairs, one for each direction of traversal of the binary relationship. For example, a professor *teaches* courses and a course *is taught by* a professor. The teaches traversal path would be defined in the interface declaration for the Professor type. The is_taught_by traversal path would be defined in the interface declaration for the Course type. The fact that these traversal paths both apply to the same relationship is indicated by an inverse clause in both of the traversal path declarations. For example:

```
interface Professor {
    ...
    relationship set<Course> teaches
        inverse Course::is_taught_by;
    ...
}
```

and

```
interface Course {
    ...
    relationship Professor is_taught_by
        inverse Professor::teaches;
    ...
}
```

The relationship defined by the teaches and is_taught_by traversal paths is a one-to-many relationship between Professor and Course objects. This cardinality is shown in the traversal path declarations. A Professor instance is associated with a set of Course instances via the teaches traversal path. A Course instance is associated with a single Professor instance via the is_taught_by traversal path.

Traversal paths that lead to many objects can be unordered or ordered, as indicated by the type of collection specified in the traversal path declaration. If set is used, as in set<Course>, the objects at the end of the traversal path are unordered.

The ODBMS is responsible for maintaining the referential integrity of relationships. This means that if an object that participates in a relationship is deleted, then any traversal path to that object must also be deleted. For example, if a particular Course instance is deleted, then not only is that object's reference to a Professor instance via the is_taught_by traversal path deleted, but also any references in Professor objects to the Course instance via the teaches traversal path must also be deleted. Maintaining referential integrity ensures that applications cannot dereference traversal paths that lead to nonexistent objects.

```
attribute Student        top_of_class;
```

An attribute may be object-valued. This kind of attribute enables one object to reference another, without expectation of an inverse traversal path or referential integrity. While object-valued attributes may be used to implement so-called "unidirectional relationships," such constructions are not considered to be true relationships in this standard. Relationships always guarantee referential integrity.

It is important to note that a relationship traversal path is not equivalent to a pointer. A pointer in C++ or Smalltalk has no connotation of a corresponding inverse traversal path, which would form a relationship. The operations defined on relationship parties and their traversal paths vary according to the traversal path's cardinality.

The implementation of relationships is encapsulated by public operations that *form* and *drop* members from the relationship, plus public operations on the relationship target classes to provide access and to manage the required referential integrity constraints. When the traversal path has cardinality "one," operations are defined to form a relationship, to drop a relationship, and to traverse the relationship. When the traversal path has cardinality "many," the object will support methods to add and remove elements from its traversal path collection. Traversal paths support all of the behaviors defined above on the Collection class used to define the behavior of the relationship. Implementations of form and drop operations will guarantee referential integrity in all cases. In order to facilitate the use of ODL object models in situations where such models may cross distribution boundaries, we define the relationship interface in purely procedural terms by introducing a mapping rule from ODL relationships to equivalent IDL constructions. Then, each language binding will determine the exact manner in which these constructions are to be accessed.

2.6.2.1 Cardinality "One" Relationships

For relationships with cardinality "one" such as

```
relationship        X    inverse Z;
```

we expand the relationship to an equivalent IDL attribute and operations:

```
attribute           X    Y;
void                form_Y(in X target);
void                drop_Y(in X target);
```

For example, the relationship in the above example interface *Course* would result in the following definitions (on the class *Course*):

```
attribute           Professoris_taught_by;
void                        form_is_taught_by(in Professor aProfessor);
void                        drop_is_taught_by(in Professor aProfessor);
```

2.6.2.2 Cardinality "Many" Relationships

For ODL relationships with cardinality "many" such as

```
relationship            set<x>Y inverse Z;
```

we expand the relationship to an equivalent IDL attribute and operations. To convert these definitions into pure IDL, the ODL collection need only be replaced by the keyword *sequence*. Note that the add_Y operation may raise an IntegrityError exception in the event that the traversal is a set that already contains a reference to the given target X. This exception, if it occurs, will also be raised by the form_Y operation that invoked the add_Y. For example:

```
readonly attribute    set<X> Y;
void                  form_Y(in X target) raises(IntegrityError);
void                  drop_Y(in X target);
void                  add_Y(in X target) raises(IntegrityError);
void                  remove_Y(in X target);
```

The relationship in the above example interface Professor would result in the following definitions (on the class Professor):

```
readonly attribute    set<course> teaches;
void                  form_teaches(in Course aCourse)
                         raises(IntegrityError);
void                  drop_teaches(in Course aCourse);
void                  add_teaches(in Course aCourse)
                         raises(IntegrityError);
void                  remove_teaches(in Course aCourse);
```

2.7 Modeling Behavior — Operations

Besides the attribute and relationship properties, the other characteristic of a type is its behavior, which is specified as a set of *operation signatures*. Each signature defines the name of an operation, the name and type of each of its arguments, the types of value(s) returned, and the names of any *exceptions* (error conditions) the operation can raise. Our Object Model specification for operations is identical to the OMG CORBA specification for operations.

An operation is defined on only a single type. There is no notion in the Object Model of an operation that exists independent of a type, or of an operation defined on two or more types. An operation name need be unique only within a single type definition. Thus different types could have operations defined with the same name. The names of these operations are said to be *overloaded*. When an operation is invoked using an overloaded name, a specific operation must be selected for execution. This selection, sometimes called *operation name resolution* or *operation dispatching*, is based on the most specific type of the object supplied as the first argument of the actual call.

The ODMG had several reasons for choosing to adopt this single-dispatch model rather than a multiple-dispatch model. The major reason was for consistency with the C++ and Smalltalk programming languages. This consistency enables seamless integration of ODBMSs into the object programming environment. Another reason to adopt the classical object model was to avoid incompatibilities with the OMG CORBA object model, which is classical rather than general.

An operation may have side effects. Some operations may return no value. The ODMG Object Model does not include formal specification of the semantics of operations. It is good practice, however, to include comments in interface specifications, for example, remarking on the purpose of an operation, any side effects it might have, pre- and post-conditions, and any invariants it is intended to preserve.

The Object Model assumes sequential execution of operations. It does not require support for concurrent or parallel operations, but does not preclude an ODBMS from taking advantage of multiprocessor support.

2.7.1 Exception Model

The ODMG Object Model supports dynamically nested exception handlers, using a termination model of exception handling. Operations can raise exceptions, and exceptions can communicate exception results. Exceptions in the Object Model are themselves objects and have an interface that allows them to be related to other exceptions in a generalization-specialization hierarchy.

A root type Exception is provided by the ODBMS. This type includes an operation to issue a message noting that an unhandled exception of type Exception_type has occurred to terminate the process. Information on the cause of an exception or the context in which it occurred is passed back to the exception handler as properties of the Exception object.

Control is as follows:

1. The programmer declares an exception handler within scope **s** capable of handling exceptions of type **t**.
2. An operation within a contained scope **sn** may "raise" an exception of type **t**.
3. The exception is "caught" by the most immediately containing scope that has an exception handler. The call stack is automatically unwound by the run-time system out to the level of the handler. Memory is freed for all objects allocated in intervening stack frames. Any transactions begun within a nested scope, that is, unwound by the run-time system in the process of searching up the stack for an exception handler, are aborted.
4. When control reaches the handler, the handler may either decide that it can handle the exception or pass it on (reraise it) to a containing handler.

An exception handler that declares itself capable of handling exceptions of type **t** will also handle exceptions of any subtype of **t**. A programmer who requires more specific control over exceptions of a specific subtype of **t** may declare a handler for this more specific subtype within a contained scope.

The signature of an operation includes declaration of the exceptions that the operation can raise.

2.8 Metadata

Metadata is descriptive information about database objects that defines the *schema* of a database. It is used by the ODBMS to define the structure of the database and at runtime to guide its access to the database. Metadata is stored in an *ODL Schema Repository*, which is also accessible to tools and applications using the same operations that apply to user-defined types. In OMG CORBA environments, similar metadata is stored in an IDL Interface Repository.

The following interfaces define the internal structure of an ODL Schema Repository. These interfaces are defined in ODL using *relationships* that define the graph of interconnections between *meta objects*, which are produced, for example, during ODL source compilation. While these relationships guarantee the referential integrity of the meta object graph, they do not guarantee its semantic integrity or completeness. In order to provide operations that programmers can use to correctly construct valid schemas, several creation, addition, and removal operations are defined that provide automatic linking and unlinking of the required relationships and appropriate error recovery in the event of semantic errors.

All of the meta object definitions, defined below, are to be grouped into an enclosing module that defines a name scope for the elements of the model.

```
module ODLMetaObjects {
    // the following interfaces are defined here
};
```

2.8.1 Scopes

Scopes define a naming hierarchy for the meta objects in the repository. They support a bind operation for adding meta objects, a resolve operation for resolving path names within the repository, and an un_bind operation for removing bindings.

```
interface Scope {
    exception       DuplicateName{};
    void            bind(in string name, in MetaObject value)
                        raises(DuplicateName);
    MetaObject      resolve(in string name);
    MetaObject      un_bind(in string name);
};
```

2.8.2 Meta Objects

All objects in the repository are subclasses of three main interfaces: MetaObject, Specifier, and Operand. All MetaObjects, defined below, have name and comment attributes. They participate in a single definedIn relationship with other meta objects, which are their defining scopes. DefiningScopes are Scopes that contain other meta object definitions using their defines relationship and that have operations for creating, adding, and removing meta objects within themselves.

```
interface MetaObject {
    attribute        string   name;
    attribute        string   comment;
    relationship     DefiningScopedefinedIn
                         inverse DefiningScope::defines;
};

enum    PrimitiveKind {pk_boolean, pk_char, pk_short, pk_ushort, pk_long,
                     pk_ulong, pk_float, pk_double, pk_octet, pk_string,
                     pk_void, pk_any};

enum    CollectionKind {ck_list, ck_array, ck_bag, ck_set, ck_dictionary};

interface DefiningScope : Scope {
    relationship     list<MetaObject>defines
                         inverse MetaObject::definedIn;
    exception        InvalidType{string reason; };
    exception        InvalidExpression{string reason; };
    exception        CannotRemove{string reason; };

    PrimitiveType    create_primitive_type(in PrimitiveKind kind);
    Collection       create_collection_type(in CollectionKind kind,
                         in Operand maxSize, in Type subType);
    Operand          create_operand(in string expression)
                         raises(InvalidExpression);
    Member           create_member(in string memberName,
                         in Type memberType);
    UnionCase        create_case(in string caseName, in Type caseType,
                         in list<Operand> caseLabels)
                         raises(DuplicateName, InvalidType);
    Constant         add_constant(in string name, in Operand value)
                         raises(DuplicateName);
    TypeDefinition   add_typedef(in string name, in Type alias)
                         raises(DuplicateName);
```

```
    Enumeration     add_enumeration(in string name,
                        in list<string> elementNames)
                        raises(DuplicateName, InvalidType);
    Structure       add_structure(in string name, in list<Member> fields)
                        raises(DuplicateName, InvalidType);
    Union           add_union(in string name, In Type switchType,
                        in list<UnionCase> cases)
                        raises(DuplicateName, InvalidType);
    Exception       add_exception(in string name, in Structure result)
                        raises(DuplicateName);
    void            remove_constant(in Constant object)
                        raises(CannotRemove);
    void            remove_typedef(in TypeDefinition object)
                        raises(CannotRemove);
    void            remove_enumeration(in Enumeration object)
                        raises(CannotRemove);
    void            remove_structure(in Structure object)
                        raises(CannotRemove);
    void            remove_union(in Union object) raises(CannotRemove);
    void            remove_exception(in Exception object)
                        raises(CannotRemove);
};
```

2.8.2.1 Modules

Modules and the Schema Repository itself, which is a specialized module, are DefiningScopes that define operations for creating modules and interfaces within themselves.

```
interface Module : MetaObject, DefiningScope {
    Module      add_module(in string name) raises(DuplicateName);
    Interface   add_interface(in string name, in list<Interface> inherits)
                    raises(DuplicateName);
    void        remove_module(in Module object) raises(CannotRemove);
    void        remove_interface(in Interface object) raises(CannotRemove);
};
interface Repository : Module {};
```

2.8.2.2 Operations

Operations model the behavior that application objects support. They maintain a signature list of Parameters and refer to a result type. Operations may raise Exceptions. The

ScopedMetaObject interface consolidates Scope operations for its subclasses Operation and Exception.

```
interface ScopedMetaObject : MetaObject, Scope {};
interface Operation : ScopedMetaObject {
    relationship    list<Parameter>     signature
                        inverse Parameter::operation;
    relationship    Type                result
                        inverse Type::operations;
    relationship    list<Exception>     exceptions
                        inverse Exception::operations;
};
```

2.8.2.3 Exceptions

Operations may raise Exceptions and thereby return a different set of results. Exceptions refer to a Structure that defines their results and keep track of the Operations that may raise them.

```
interface Exception : MetaObject {
    relationship    Structure           result
                        inverse Structure::exceptionResult;
    relationship    set<Operation>      operations
                        inverse Operation::exceptions;
};
```

2.8.2.4 Constants

Constants provide a mechanism for statically associating values with names in the repository. The value is defined by an Operand subclass that is either a literal value (Literal), a reference to another Constant (ConstOperand), or the value of a constant expression (Expression). Each constant has an associated type and keeps track of the other ConstOperands that refer to it in the repository. The value operation allows the constant's actual value to be computed at any time.

```
interface Constant : MetaObject {
    relationship    Operand             hasValue
                        inverse Operand::valueOf;
    relationship    Type                type
                        inverse Type::constants;
    relationship    set<ConstOperand>   referencedBy
                        inverse ConstOperand::references;
    relationship    Enumeration         enumeration
                        inverse Enumeration::elements;
    any             value();
};
```

2.8.2.5 Properties

Properties form an abstract class over the Attribute and Relationship meta objects that define the abstract state of an application object. They have an associated type.

```
interface Property : MetaObject {
    relationship     Type          type
                        inverse Type::properties;
};
```

2.8.2.5.1 Attributes

Attributes are properties that maintain simple abstract state. They may be read-only, in which case there is no associated accessor for changing their values.

```
interface Attribute : Property {
    attribute        boolean       isReadOnly;
};
```

2.8.2.5.2 Relationships

Relationships model bilateral object references between participating objects. In use, two relationship meta objects are required to represent each traversal direction of the relationship. Operations are defined implicitly to form and drop the relationship, as well as accessor operations for manipulating its traversals.

```
enum Cardinality {c1_1, c1_N, cN_1, cN_M};

interface Relationship : Property {
    exception        integrityError{};
    relationship     Relationship  traversal
                        inverse Relationship::traversal;
    Cardinality      getCardinality();
};
```

2.8.2.6 Types

TypeDefinitions are meta objects that define new names, or aliases, for the types to which they refer. Much of the information in the repository consists of type definitions that define the data types used by the application.

```
interface TypeDefinition : Type {
    relationship     Type          alias
                        inverse Type::typeDefs;
};
```

Type meta objects are used to represent information about datatypes. They participate in a number of relationships with the other meta objects that use them. These relationships allow Types to be easily administered within the repository and help to ensure the referential integrity of the repository as a whole.

```
interface Type : MetaObject {
    relationship    set<Collection>      collections
                        inverse Collection::subtype;
    relationship    set<Specifier>       specifiers
                        inverse Specifier::type;
    relationship    set<Union>           unions
                        inverse Union::switchType;
    relationship    set<Operation>       operations
                        inverse Operation::result;
    relationship    set<Property>        properties
                        inverse Property::type;
    relationship    set<Constant>        constants
                        inverse Constant::type;
    relationship    set<TypeDefinition>  typeDefs
                        inverse TypeDefinition::alias;
};
interface PrimitiveType : Type {
    attribute       PrimitiveKind        kind;
};
```

2.8.2.6.1 Interfaces

Interfaces are the most important types in the repository. Interfaces define the abstract behavior of application objects and contain operations for creating and removing Attributes, Relationships, and Operations within themselves in addition to the operations inherited from DefiningScope. Interfaces are linked in a multiple-inheritance graph with other Inheritance objects by two relationships, inherits and derives. They may contain most kinds of MetaObjects, excepting Modules and Interfaces.

```
interface Interface : Type, DefiningScope {
    struct ParameterSpec {
        string          paramName;
        Direction       paramMode;
        Type            paramType; };
    relationship    set<Inheritance>     inherits
                        inverse Inheritance::derivesFrom;
    relationship    set<Inheritance>     derives
                        inverse Inheritance::inheritsTo;
    exception       BadParameter{string reason; };
    exception       BadRelationship{string reason; };
```

```
    Attribute         add_attribute(in string attrName, in Type attrType)
                          raises(DuplicateName);
    Relationship      add_relationship(in string relName,
                              in Type relType,
                              in Relationship relTraversal)
                          raises(DuplicateName, BadRelationship);
    Operation         add_operation(in string opName,
                              in Type opResult,
                              in list<ParameterSpec> opParams,
                          in list<Exception> opRaises)
                          raises(DuplicateName, BadParameter);
    void              remove_attribute(in Attribute object)
                          raises(CannotRemove);
    void              remove_relationship(in Relationship object)
                          raises(CannotRemove);
    void              remove_operation(in Operation object)
                          raises(CannotRemove);
};
interface Inheritance {
    relationship      Interface         derivesFrom
                          inverse Interface::inherits;
    relationship      Interface         inheritsTo
                          inverse Interface::derives;
};
```

2.8.2.6.2 Classes

Classes are a subtype of *Interface* whose properties define the abstract state of objects stored in an ODBMS. *Classes* are linked in a single inheritance hierarchy whereby state and behavior are inherited from an extender class. *Classes* may define keys and extents over their instances.

```
interface Class : Interface {
    attribute         list<string>      extents;
    attribute         list<string>      keys;
    relationship      Class             extender
                        inverse Class::extensions;
    relationship      set<Class>        extensions
                        inverse Class::extender;
};
```

2.8.2.6.3 Collections

Collections are types that aggregate variable numbers of elements of a single subtype and provide different ordering, accessing, and comparison behaviors. The maximum size of the collection may be specified by a constant or constant expression. If unspecified, this relationship will be bound to the literal 0.

```
interface Collection : Type {
    attribute       CollectionKind      kind;
    relationship    Operand             maxSize
                        inverse Operand::sizeOf;
    relationship    Type                subtype
                        inverse Type::collections;
    boolean         isOrdered();
    unsigned long   bound();
};
```

2.8.2.6.4 Constructed Types

Some types contain named elements that themselves refer to other types and are said to be *constructed* from those types. The ScopedType interface is an abstract class that consolidates these mechanisms for its sub-classes Enumeration, Structure, and Union. Enumerations contain Constants, Structures contain Members, and Unions contain UnionCases. Unions, in addition, have a relationship with a switchType that defines the discriminator of the union.

```
interface ScopedType : Scope, Type {};
interface Enumeration : ScopedType {
    relationship    list<Constant>      elements
                        inverse Constant::enumeration;
};
interface Structure : ScopedType {
    relationship    list<Member>        fields
                        inverse Member::structure_type;
    relationship    Exception           exceptionResult
                        inverse Exception::result;
};
interface Union : ScopedType {
    relationship    Type                switchType
                        inverse Type::unions;
    relationship    list<UnionCase>     cases
                        inverse UnionCase::union_type;
};
```

2.8.3 Specifiers

Specifiers are used to assign a name to a type in certain contexts. They consolidate these elements for their subclasses. Members, UnionCases, and Parameters are referenced by Structures, Unions, and Operations, respectively.

```
interface Specifier {
    attribute       string          name;
    relationship    Type            type
                        inverse Type::specifiers;
};

interface Member : Specifier {
    relationship    Structure       structure_type
                        inverse Structure::fields;
};
interface UnionCase : Specifier {
    relationship    Union           union_type
                        inverse Union::cases;
    relationship    list<Operand>   caseLabels
                        inverse Operand::caseIn;
};

enum Direction {mode_in, mode_out, mode_inout } ;
interface Parameter : Specifier {
    attribute       Direction       parameterMode;
    relationship    Operation       operation
                        inverse Operation::signature;
};
```

2.8.4 Operands

Operands form the base type for all constant values in the repository. They have a value operation and maintain relationships with the other Constants, Collections, UnionCases, and Expressions that refer to them. Literals contain a single literalValue attribute and produce their value directly. ConstOperands produce their value by delegating to their associated constant. Expressions compute their value by evaluating their operator on the values of their operands.

```
interface Operand {
    relationship    Expression      operandIn
                        inverse Expression::hasOperands;
    relationship    Constant        valueOf
                        inverse Constant::hasValue;
    relationship    Collection      sizeOf
                        inverse Collection::maxSize;
    relationship    UnionCase       caseIn
                        inverse UnionCase::caseLabels;
    any             value();
};
interface Literal : Operand {
    attribute   any     literalValue;
};
interface ConstOperand : Operand {
    relationship    Constant    references
                        inverse Constant::referencedBy;
};
```

Expressions are composed of one or more Operands and an associated operator. While unary and binary operators are the only operations allowed by ODL, this structure allows generalized n-ary operations to be defined in the future.

```
interface Expression : Operand {
    attribute       string          operator;
    relationship    list<Operand>   hasOperands
                        inverse Operand::operandIn;
};
```

2.9 Locking and Concurrency Control

The ODMG Object Model uses a conventional lock-based approach to concurrency control. This approach provides a mechanism for enforcing shared or exclusive access to objects. The ODBMS supports the property of serializability by monitoring requests for locks, and only granting a lock if no conflicting locks exist. As a result, access to the database is coordinated across multiple transactions and a consistent view of the database is maintained for each transaction.

The ODMG Object Model supports traditional pessimistic concurrency control as its default policy, but does not preclude an ODBMS from supporting a wider range of concurrency control policies.

2.9.1 Lock Types

The following locks are supported in the ODMG Object Model:

- read
- write
- upgrade

Read locks allow shared access to an object. *Write* locks indicate exclusive access to an object. Readers of a particular object do not conflict with other readers, but writers conflict with both readers and writers. *Upgrade* locks are used to prevent a form of deadlock that occurs when two processes both obtain *read* locks on an object and then attempt to obtain *write* locks on that same object. *Upgrade* locks are compatible with *read* locks, but conflict with *upgrade* and *write* locks. Deadlock is avoided by initially obtaining *upgrade* locks, instead of *read* locks, for all objects that intend to be modified. This avoids any potential conflicts when a *write* lock is later obtained to modify the object.

The locks described above follow the same semantics as those defined in the OMG Concurrency Control Service.

2.9.2 Implicit and Explicit Locking

The ODMG Object Model supports both implicit and explicit locking. Implicit locks are locks acquired during the course of the traversal of an object graph. For example, *read* locks are obtained each time an object is accessed and *write* locks are obtained each time an object is modified. In the case of implicit locks, no specific operation is executed in order to obtain a lock on an object. However, explicit locks are acquired by expressly requesting a specific lock on a particular object. These locks are obtained using the lock and try_lock operations defined in the Object interface. While *read* and *write* locks can be obtained implicitly or explicitly, *upgrade* locks can only be obtained explicitly via the lock and try_lock operations.

2.9.3 Lock Duration

By default, all locks (*read*, *write*, and *upgrade*) are held until the transaction is either committed or aborted. This type of lock retention is consistent with the SQL92 definition of transaction isolation level 3. This isolation level prevents dirty reads, nonrepeatable reads, and phantoms.

2.10 Transaction Model

Programs that use persistent objects are organized into transactions. Transaction management is an important ODBMS functionality, fundamental to database integrity, shareability, and recovery. Any access, creation, modification, and deletion of persistent objects must be done within a transaction.

A transaction is a unit of logic for which an ODBMS guarantees *atomicity*, *consistency*, *isolation*, and *durability*. *Atomicity* means that the transaction either finishes or has no effect at all. *Consistency* means that a transaction takes the database from one internally consistent state to another internally consistent state. There may be times during the transaction when the database is inconsistent. However, *isolation* guarantees that no other user of a database sees changes made by a transaction until that transaction commits. Concurrent users always see an internally consistent database. *Durability* means that the effects of committed transactions are preserved, even if there should be failures of storage media, loss of memory, or system crashes. Once a transaction has committed, the ODBMS guarantees that changes made by that transaction are never lost. When a transaction commits, all of the changes made by that transaction are permanently installed in the database and made visible to other users of the database. When a transaction aborts, none of the changes made by it are installed in the database, including any changes made prior to the time of abort. The execution of concurrent transactions must yield results that are indistinguishable from results that would have been obtained if the transactions had been executed serially. This property is sometimes called *serializability*.

2.10.1 Distributed Transactions

Distributed transactions are transactions that span multiple processes and/or that span more than one database, as described in ISO XA and the OMG Object Transaction Service. The ODMG does not define an interface for distributed transactions because this is already defined in the ISO XA standard and since it is not visible to the programmers, but only used by transaction monitors.Vendors are not required to support distributed transactions, but if they do, their implementations must be XA-compliant.

2.10.2 Transactions and Processes

The ODMG Object Model assumes a linear sequence of transactions executing within a thread of control; that is, there is exactly one current transaction for a thread, and that transaction is implicit in that thread's database operations. If an ODMG language binding supports multiple threads in one address space, then transaction *isolation* must be provided between the threads. Of course, transaction *isolation* is also provided between threads in different address spaces or threads running on different machines.

A transaction runs against a single logical database. Note that a single logical database may be implemented as one or more physical databases, possibly distributed on a network. The transaction model neither requires nor precludes support for transactions that span multiple threads, multiple address spaces, or more than one logical database.

In the current Object Model, transient objects in an address space are not subject to transaction semantics. This means that aborting a transaction does not restore the state of modified transient objects.

2.10.3 Transaction Operations

There are two types that are defined to support transaction activity within an ODBMS: TransactionFactory and Transaction.

The TransactionFactory type is used to create transactions. The following operations are defined in the TransactionFactory interface:

```
interface TransactionFactory {
    Transaction      new();
    Transaction      current();
};
```

The new operation creates Transaction objects. The current operation returns the Transaction that is associated with the current thread of control. If there is no such association, the current operation returns *nil.*

Once a Transaction object is created, it is manipulated using the Transaction interface. The following operations are defined in the Transaction interface:

```
interface Transaction {
    exception        TransactionInProgress{};
    exception        TransactionNotInProgress{};
    void             begin() raises(TransactionInProgress);
    void             commit() raises(TransactionNotInProgress);
    void             abort() raises(TransactionNotInProgress);
    void             checkpoint() raises(TransactionNotInProgress);
    void             join();
    void             leave();
    boolean          isOpen();
};
```

After a Transaction object is created, it is initially closed. An explicit begin operation is required to open a transaction. If a transaction is already open, additional begin operations raise the TransactionInProgress exception.

The commit operation causes all persistent objects created or modified during a transaction to be written to the database and become accessible to other Transaction objects running against that database. All locks held by the Transaction object are released. Finally, it also causes the Transaction object to complete and become closed. The TransactionNotInProgress exception is raised if a commit operation is executed on a closed Transaction object.

The abort operation causes the Transaction object to complete and become closed. The database is returned to the state it was in prior to the beginning of the transaction. All locks held by the Transaction object are released. The TransactionNotInProgress exception is raised if an abort operation is executed on a closed Transaction object.

A checkpoint operation is equivalent to a commit operation followed by a begin operation, except that locks held by the Transaction object are NOT released. Therefore, it causes all modified objects to be committed to the database and it retains all locks held by the Transaction object. The Transaction object remains open. The TransactionNotInProgress exception is raised if a checkpoint operation is executed on a closed Transaction object.

Database operations are always applied to the database during a transaction. Therefore, to execute any database operations, an active Transaction object must be associated with the current thread. The join operation associates the current thread with a Transaction object. If the Transaction object is open, database operations may be executed; otherwise a TransactionNotInProgress exception is raised.

If an implementation allows multiple active Transaction objects to exist, the join and leave operations allow a thread to alternate between them. To associate the current thread with another Transaction object, simply execute a join on the new Transaction object. If necessary, a leave operation is automatically executed to disassociate the current thread from its current Transaction object. Moving from one Transaction object to another does not commit or abort a Transaction object. When the current thread has no current Transaction object, the leave operation is ignored.

After a Transaction object is completed, to continue executing database operations, either another open Transaction object must be associated with the current thread, or a begin operation must be applied to the current Transaction object to make it open again.

Multiple threads of control in one address space can share the same transaction through multiple join operations on the same Transaction object. In this case, no locking is provided between these threads; concurrency control must be provided by the user. The transaction completes when any one of the threads executes a commit or abort operation against the Transaction object.

2.11 Database Operations

An ODBMS may manage one or more logical databases, each of which may be stored in one or more physical databases. Each logical database is an instance of the type Database, which is supplied by the ODBMS. Instances of type Database are created using the DatabaseFactory interface:

```
interface DatabaseFactory {
    Database        new();
};
```

Once a Database object is created by using the new operation, it is manipulated using the Database interface. The following operations are defined in the Database interface:

```
interface Database {
      void          open(in string database_name);
      void          close();
      void          bind(in any an_object, in string name);
      Object        unbind(in string name);
      Object        lookup(in string object_name);
      Module        schema();
};
```

The open operation must be invoked, with a database name as its argument, before any access can be made to the persistent objects in the database. The Object Model requires only a single database to be open at a time. Implementations may extend this capability, including transactions that span multiple databases. The close operation must be invoked when a program has completed all access to the database. When the ODBMS closes a database, it performs necessary cleanup operations.

The lookup operation finds the identifier of the object with the name supplied as the argument to the operation. This operation is defined on the Database type, because the scope of object names is the database. The names of objects in the database, the names of types in the database schema, and the extents of types instantiated in the database are global to the database. They become accessible to a program once it has opened the database. Named objects are convenient entry points to the database. A name is bound to an object using the bind operation. Named objects may be unnamed using the unbind operation.

The schema operation accesses the root meta object that defines the schema of the database. The schema of an ODBMS is contained within a single Module meta object. Meta objects contained within the schema may be located via navigation of the appropriate relationships or by using the resolve operation with a scoped name as the argument. A scoped name is defined by the syntax of ODL and uses double colon (::) delimiters to specify a search path composed of meta object names that uniquely identify each meta object by its location within the schema. For example, using examples defined in Chapter 3, the scoped name "Professor::name" resolves to the Attribute meta object that represents the name of class Professor.

The Database type may also support operations designed for database administration, e.g., create, delete, move, copy, reorganize, verify, backup, restore. These kinds of operations are not specified here, as they are considered an implementation consideration outside the scope of the Object Model.

Chapter 3

Object Specification Languages

3.1 Introduction

This chapter defines the specification languages used to represent ODMG-compliant object database management systems. These programming language–independent specification languages are used to define the schema, operations, and state of an object database. The primary objective of these languages is to facilitate the portability of databases across ODMG-compliant implementations. These languages also provide a step toward the interoperability of ODBMSs from multiple vendors.

Two specification languages are discussed in this chapter: Object Definition Language (ODL) and Object Interchange Format (OIF).

3.2 Object Definition Language

The Object Definition Language is a specification language used to define the specifications of object types that conform to the ODMG Object Model. ODL is used to support the portability of database schemas across conforming ODBMSs.

Several principles have guided the development of the ODL, including:

- ODL should support all semantic constructs of the ODMG Object Model.
- ODL should not be a full programming language, but rather a definition language for object specifications.
- ODL should be programming language independent.
- ODL should be compatible with the OMG's Interface Definition Language (IDL).
- ODL should be extensible, not only for future functionality, but also for physical optimizations.
- ODL should be practical, providing value to application developers, while being supportable by the ODBMS vendors within a relatively short time frame after publication of the specification.

ODL is not intended to be a full programming language. It is a definition language for object specifications. Database management systems (DBMSs) have traditionally provided facilities that support data definition (using a Data Definition Language —DDL) and data manipulation (using a Data Manipulation Language—DML). The DDL allows users to define their data types and interfaces. DML allows programs to create, delete, read, change, etc., instances of those data types. The ODL described in this chapter is a DDL for object types. It defines the characteristics of types, including their properties and operations. ODL defines only the signatures of operations and does not address definition of the methods that implement those operations. The ODMG standard does not provide an OML specification. Chapters 5, 6, and 7 define standard APIs to bind conformant ODBMSs to C++, Smalltalk, and Java, respectively.

ODL is intended to define object types that can be implemented in a variety of programming languages. Therefore, ODL is not tied to the syntax of a particular programming language. Users can use ODL to define schema semantics in a programming language–independent way. A schema specified in ODL can be supported by any ODMG-compliant ODBMS and by mixed-language implementations. This portability is necessary for an application to be able to run with minimal modification on a variety of ODBMSs. Some applications may in fact need simultaneous support from multiple ODBMSs. Others may need to access objects created and stored using different programming languages. ODL provides a degree of insulation for applications against the variations in both programming languages and underlying ODBMS products.

The C++, Smalltalk, and Java ODL bindings are designed to fit smoothly into the declarative syntax of their host programming language. Due to the differences inherent in the object models native to these programming languages, it is not always possible to achieve consistent semantics across the programming language–specific versions of ODL. Our goal has been to minimize these inconsistencies, and we have noted, in Chapters 5, 6, and 7, the restrictions applicable to each particular language binding.

The syntax of ODL extends IDL — the Interface Definition Language developed by the OMG as part of the Common Object Request Broker Architecture (CORBA). IDL was itself influenced by C++, giving ODL a C++ flavor. Appendix B, "ODBMS in the OMG ORB Environment," describes the relationship between ODL and IDL. ODL adds to IDL the constructs required to specify the complete semantics of the ODMG Object Model.

ODL also provides a context for integrating schemas from multiple sources and applications. These source schemas may have been defined with any number of object models and data definition languages; ODL is a sort of lingua franca for integration. For example, various standards organizations like STEP/PDES (EXPRESS), ANSI X3H2 (SQL), ANSI X3H7 (Object Information Management), CFI (CAD Framework Initiative), and others have developed a variety of object models and, in some cases, data definition languages. Any of these models can be translated to an ODL specification (Figure 3-1). This common basis then allows the various models to be integrated with common semantics. An ODL specification can be realized concretely in an object programming language like C++, Smalltalk, or Java.

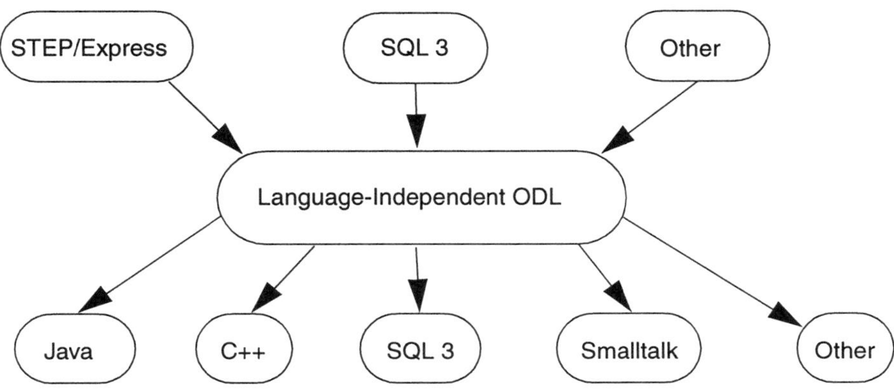

Figure 3-1. ODL Mapping to Other Languages

3.2.1 Specification

A type is defined by specifying its interface or by its class in ODL. The top-level BNF for ODL is as follows:

```
<interface>           ::=  <interface_dcl>
                           | <forward_dcl>
<interface_dcl>       ::=  <interface_header>
                           { [ <interface_body> ] }
<forward_dcl>         ::=  interface <identifier>
<interface_header>    ::=  interface <identifier>
                           [ <inheritance_spec> ]
<class>               ::=  <class_header> { <interface_body> }
<class_header>        ::=  class <identifier>
                           [ extends <scopedName> ]
                           [ <inheritance_spec> ]
                           [ <type_property_list> ]
```

The characteristics of the type itself appear first, followed by lists that define the properties and operations of its interface or class. Any list may be omitted if it is not applicable.

3.2.1.1 Type Characteristics

Supertype information, extent naming, and specification of keys (i.e., uniqueness constraints) are all characteristics of types, but do not apply directly to the types' instances. The BNF for type characteristics follows:

```
<inheritance_spec>     ::=  : <scoped_name> [ , <inheritance_spec> ]
<type_property_list>   ::=  ( [ <extent_spec> ] [ <key_spec> ] )
<extent_spec>          ::=  extent <string>
<key_spec>             ::=  key[s] <key_list>
<key_list>             ::=  <key> | <key> , <key_list>
<key>                  ::=  <property_name> | ( <property_list> )
<property_list>        ::=  <property_name>
                            | <property_name> , <property_list>
<property_name>        ::=  <identifier>
<scoped_name>          ::=  <identifier>
                            | :: <identifier>
                            | <scoped_name> :: <identifier>
```

Each supertype must be specified in its own type definition. Each attribute or relationship traversal path named as (part of) a type's key must be specified in the key_spec of the type definition. The extent and key definitions may be omitted if inapplicable to the type being defined. A type definition should include no more than one extent or key definition.

A simple example for the class definition of a Professor type is

```
class Professor
(       extent professors)
{
        properties
        operations
};
```

Keywords are highlighted.

3.2.1.2 Instance Properties

A type's instance properties are the attributes and relationships of its instances. These properties are specified in attribute and relationship specifications. The BNF is

```
<interface_body>    ::=  <export> | <export> <interface_body>
<export>            ::=  <type_dcl> ;
                         | <const_dcl> ;
                         | <except_dcl> ;
                         | <attr_dcl> ;
                         | <rel_dcl> ;
                         | <op_dcl> ;
```

3.2.1.3 Attributes

The BNF for specifying an attribute follows:

```
<attr_dcl>          ::=  [ readonly ] attribute
                         <domain_type> <attribute_name>
                          [ <fixed_array_size>]
<domain_type>       ::=  <simple_type_spec>
                         | <struct_type>
                         | <enum_type>
```

For example, adding attribute definitions to the Professor type's ODL specification:

```
class Professor
(           extent professors)
{
            attribute string name;
            attribute unsigned short faculty_id[6];
            attribute long soc_sec_no[10];
            attribute Address address;
            attribute set<string> degrees;
            relationships
            operations
};
```

Note that the keyword attribute is mandatory.

3.2.1.4 Relationships

A relationship specification names and defines a traversal path for a relationship. A traversal path definition includes designation of the target type and information about the inverse traversal path found in the target type. The BNF for relationship specification follows:

```
<rel_dcl>                   ::= relationship
                                <target_of_path> <identifier>
                                 inverse <inverse_traversal_path>
<target_of_path>            ::= <identifier>
                                | <rel_collection_type> < <identifier> >
<inverse_traversal_path>    ::= <identifier> :: <identifier>
```

Traversal path cardinality information is included in the specification of the target of a traversal path. The target type must be specified with its own type definition. Use of the collection_type option of the BNF indicates cardinality greater than one on the target side. If this option is omitted, the cardinality on the target side is one. The most commonly used collection types are expected to be Set, for unordered members on the target side of a traversal path, and List, for ordered members on the target side. Bags are supported as well. The inverse traversal path must be defined in the property list of the target type's definition. For example, adding relationships to the Professor type's interface specification:

```
class Professor
(           extent professors)
{
            attribute string name;
            attribute unsigned short faculty_id[6];
            attribute long soc_sec_no[10];
            attribute Address address;
            attribute set<string> degrees;
            relationship set<Student> advises
                 inverse Student::advisor;
            relationship set<TA> teaching_assistants
                 inverse TA::works_for;
            relationship Department department
                 inverse Department::faculty;
            operations
};
```

The keyword relationship is mandatory. Note that the attribute and relationship specifications can be mixed in the property list. It is not necessary to define all of one kind of property, then all of the other kind.

3.2.1.5 Operations

ODL is compatible with IDL for specification of operations:

```
<op_dcl>              ::=  [ <op_attribute>] <op_type_spec>
                           <identifier> <parameter_dcls>
                           [ <raises_expr> ] [ <context_expr> ]
<op_attribute>        ::=  oneway
<op_type_spec>        ::=  <simple_type_spec>
                           | void
<parameter_dcls>      ::=  ( [ <param_dcl_list> ] )
<param_dcl_list>      ::=  <param_dcl>
                           | <param_dcl> , <param_dcl_list>
<param_dcl>           ::=  <param_attribute> <simple_type_spec>
                           <declarator>
<param_attribute>     ::=  in | out| inout
<raises_expr>         ::=  raises ( <scoped_name_list>)
<context_expr>        ::=  context ( <string_literal_list> )
<scoped_name_list>    ::=  <scoped_name>
                           | <scoped_name> , <scoped_name_list>
<string_literal_list> ::=  <string_literal>
                           | <string_literal> , <string_literal_list>
```

See Section 3.2.4 for the full BNF for operation specification.

3.2.2 An Example in ODL

This section illustrates the use of ODL to declare the schema for a sample application based on a university database. The object types in the sample application are shown as rectangles in Figure 3-2. Relationship types are shown as lines. The cardinality permitted by the relationship type is indicated by the arrows on the ends of the lines:

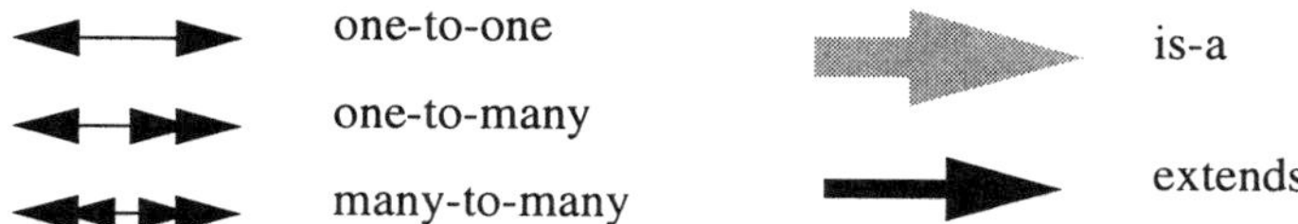

In the example, the type Professor is-a subtype of the type Employee, and the type TA (for Teaching Assistant) is-a subtype of both Employee and Student-IF. The large gray arrows run from subtype to supertype in the figure. Notice also that Student-IF is defined by an interface, whereas the other types are defined by classes. In the ODL that follows, the classes Student and TA that inherit from Student-IF have duplicated the attribute and relationship declarations from that interface. Class TA will have an extra instance variable to support its assists relationship.

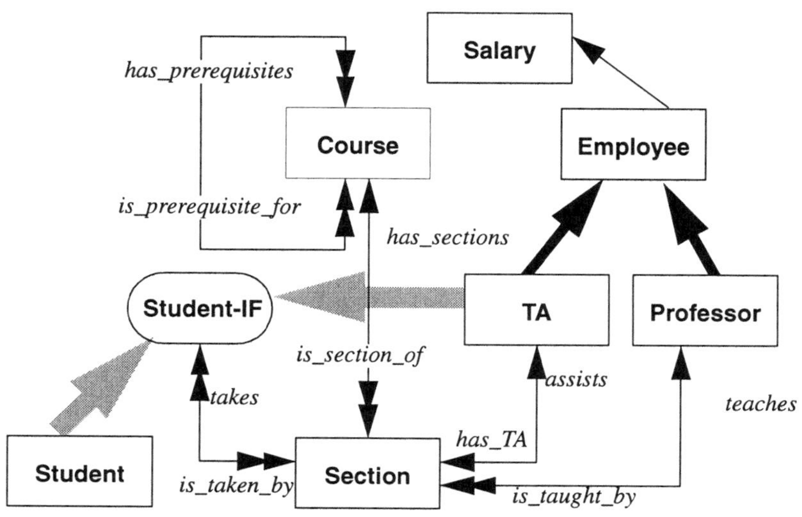

Figure 3-2. Graphical Representation of Schema

An ODL definition for the specifications of the schema's types follows:

```
class Course
(           extent courses)
{
            attribute string name;
            attribute string number;
            relationship list<Section> has_sections
                 inverse Section::is_section_of;
            relationship set<Course> has_prerequisites
                  inverse Course::is_prerequisite_for;
            relationship set<Course> is_prerequisite_for
                  inverse Course::has_prerequisites;

            boolean offer (in unsigned short semester)
raises (already_offered);
            boolean drop (in unsigned short semester) raises (not_offered);
};
class Section
(           extent sections)
{
            attribute string number;
            relationship Professor is_taught_by
                 inverse Professor::teaches;
            relationship TA has_TA
                 inverse TA::assists;
            relationship Course is_section_of
                 inverse Course::has_sections;
            relationship set<Student> is_taken_by
                 inverse Student::takes;
};
class Salary
{
     attribute     float     base;
     attribute     float     overtime;
     attribute     float     bonus;
};
```

```
class Employee
(       extent employees)
{
        attribute string name;
        attribute short id;
        attribute Salary  annual_salary;
        void hire();
        void fire() raises (no_such_employee);
};

class Professor extends Employee
(       extent professors)
{
        attribute enum Rank {full, associate, assistant} rank;
        relationship set<Section> teaches inverse Section::is_taught_by;
        short grant_tenure() raises (ineligible_for_tenure);
};

interface Student-IF
{
        struct Address {string college, string room_number}
        attribute string name;
        attribute string student_id;
        attribute Address dorm_address;
        relationship set<Section> takes
            inverse Section::is_taken_by;
        boolean register_for_course (in unsigned short course,
                    in unsigned short Section)
            raises (unsatisfied_prerequisites, section_full, course_full);
        void drop_course (in unsigned short Course)
            raises (not_registered_for_that_course);
        void assign_major (in unsigned short Department);
        short transfer (in unsigned short old_section,
                    in unsigned short new_section)
            raises (section_full, not_registered_in_section);
};
```

```
classTA extends Employee : Student-IF
{
        relationship Section assists
            inverse Section::has_TA;
        attribute string name;
        attribute string student_id;
        attribute struct Address dorm_address;
        relationship set<Section> takes
            inverse Section::is_taken_by;
};

class Student : Student-IF
(       extent students)
{
        attribute string name;
        attribute string student_id;
        attribute struct Address dorm_address;
        relationship set<Section> takes
            inverse Section::is_taken_by;
};
```

3.2.3 Another Example

Following is another example that will be used as an illustration of ODL. The same example will be used in Chapter 5 to illustrate the binding of ODL to C++. The application manages personnel records. The database manages information about people, their marriages, children, and history of residences. Person has an extent named people. A Person has name, address, spouse, children, and parents properties. The operations birth, marriage, ancestors, and move are also characteristics of Person: birth adds a new child to the children list of a Person instance, marriage defines a spouse for a Person instance, ancestors computes the set of Person instances who are the ancestors of a particular Person instance, and move changes a Person instance's address. An Address is a structure whose properties are number, street, and city_name; number is of type unsigned short, street and city are of type string. City has properties city_code, name, and population. City_code is of type unsigned short; name is of type string; population is a set of references to Person objects. Spouse is a traversal path to a spouse:spouse 1:1 recursive relationship; children is one of the traversal paths of a children:parents m:n recursive relationship. Parents is the other traversal path of the children:parents relationship.

The ODL specifications for this schema follows:

```
class Person
(       extent people)
{
        attribute string name;
        attribute struct Address {unsigned short number, string street,
            string city_name} address;
        relationship Person spouse
            inverse Person::spouse;
        relationship set<Person> children
            inverse Person::parents;
        relationship list<Person> parents
            inverse Person::children;
        void birth (in string name);
        boolean marriage (in string person_name)
            raises (no_such_person);
        unsigned short ancestors (out set<Person> all_ancestors)
            raises (no_such_person);
        void move (in string new_address);
};

class City
(       extent cities)
{
        attribute unsigned short city_code;
        attribute string name;
        attribute set<Person> population;
};
```

3.2.4 ODL Grammar

Following is the complete BNF for the ODL, which includes the IDL. The numbers on the production rules match their numbers in the OMG CORBA specification. Modified production rules have numbers suffixed by an asterisk, e.g., (2*). New production rules have alpha extensions, e.g., (2a).

```
(1)         <specification>::= <definition>
                | <definition> <specification>
(2*)        <definition>::= <type_dcl> ;
                | <const_dcl> ;
                | <except_dcl> ;
                | <interface> ;
                | <module> ;
                | <class> ;
```

```
(2a)   <class>::= <class_header> { <interface_body> }
(2b)   <class_header>::= class <identifier>
           [ extends <scopedName> ]
           [ <inheritance_spec> ]
           [ <type_property_list> ]
(2c)   <type_property_list>
           ::= ( [ <extent_spec> ] [ <key_spec> ] )
(2d)   <extent_spec>::= extent <string>
(2e)   <key_spec>::= key[s] <key_list>
(2f)   <key_list>::= <key> | <key> , <key_list>
(2g)   <key>::= <property_name> | ( <property_list> )
(2h)   <property_list>::= <property_name>
           | <property_name> , <property_list>
(2i)   <property_name>::= <identifier>
(3)    <module>::= module <identifier> { <specification> }
(4)    <interface>::= <interface_dcl>
           | <forward_dcl>
(5)    <interface_dcl>::= <interface_header>
           { [ <interface_body> ] }
(6)    <forward_dcl>::= interface <identifier>
(7)    <interface_header>::= interface <identifier>
           [ <inheritance_spec> ]
(8)    <interface_body>::=
           <export> | <export> <interface_body>
(9*)   <export>::= <type_dcl>;
           | <const_dcl>;
           | <except_dcl>;
           | <attr_dcl>;
           | <rel_dcl>;
           | <op_dcl>;
(10)   <inheritance_spec>::=
           : <scoped_name> [ , <inheritance_spec> ]
(11)   <scoped_name>::= <identifier>
           | :: <identifier>
           | <scoped_name> :: <identifier>
(12)   <const_dcl>::= const <const_type> <identifier> =
           <const_exp>
(13)   <const_type>::= <integer_type>
           | <char_type>
           | <boolean_type>
           | <floating_pt_type>
           | <string_type>
           | <scoped_name>
```

(14) <const_exp>::= <or_expr>

(15) <or_expr>::= <xor_expr>

| <or_expr> | <xor_expr>

(16) <xor_expr>::= <and_expr>

| <xor_expr> **^** <and_expr>

(17) <and_expr>::= <shift_expr>

| <and_expr> **&** <shift_expr>

(18) <shift_expr>::= <add_expr>

| <shift_expr> **>>** <add_exp>

| <shift_expr> **<<** <add_expr>

(19) <add_expr>::= <mult_expr>

| <add_expr> **+** <mult_expr>

| <add_expr> **-** <mult_expr>

(20) <mult_expr>::= <unary_expr>

| <mult_expr> ***** <unary_expr>

| <mult_expr> **/** <unary_expr>

| <mult_expr> **%** <unary_expr>

(21) <unary_expr>::= <unary_operator> <primary_expr>

| <primary_expr>

(22) <unary_operator>::= **-**

| **+**

| **~**

(23) <primary_expr>::= <scoped_name>

| <literal>

| **(** <const_exp> **)**

(24) <literal>::= <integer_literal>

| <string_literal>

| <character_literal>

| <floating_pt_literal>

| <boolean_literal>

(25) <boolean_literal>::= **TRUE**

| **FALSE**

(26) <positive_int_const>::= <const_exp>

(27) <type_dcl>::= **typedef** <type_declarator>

| <struct_type>

| <union_type>

| <enum_type>

(28) <type_declarator>::= <type_spec> <declarators>

(29) <type_spec>::= <simple_type_spec>

| <constr_type_spec>

(30) <simple_type_spec>::= <base_type_spec>

| <template_type_spec>

| <scoped_name>

(31*) <base_type_spec>::= <floating_pt_type>
| <integer_type>
| <char_type>
| <boolean_type>
| <octet_type>
| <any_type>
| <date_type>
| <time_type>
| <interval_type>
| <timestamp_type>

(31a) <date_type> ::= **date**

(31b) <time_type> ::= **time**

(31c) <iterval_type> ::= **interval**

(31d) <timestamp_type> ::= **timestamp**

(32*) <template_type_spec>::= <array_type>
| <string_type>
| <coll_type>

(32a) <coll_type> ::= <coll_spec> **<** <simple_type_spec> **>**
| dictionary < <simple_type_spec> ,
<simple_type_spec> **>**

(32b) <coll_spec> ::= **set** | **list** | **bag**

(33) <constr_type_spec>::= <struct_type>
| <union_type>
| <enum_type>

(34) <declarators>::= <declarator>
| <declarator> **,** <declarators>

(35) <declarator>::= <simple_declarator>
| <complex_declarator>

(36) <simple_declarator>::= <identifier>

(37) <complex_declarator>::= <array_declarator>

(38) <floating_pt_type>::= **float**
| **double**

(39) <integer_type>::= <signed_int>
| <unsigned_int>

(40) <signed_int>::= <signed_long_int>
| <signed_short_int>

(41) <signed_long_int>::= **long**

(42) <signed_short_int>::= **short**

(43) <unsigned_int>::= <unsigned_long_int>
| <unsigned_short_int>

(44) <unsigned_long_int>::= **unsigned long**

(45) <unsigned_short_int>::= **unsigned short**

(46) <char_type>::= **char**

(47) <boolean_type>::= **boolean**

(48) <octet_type>::= **octet**

(49) <any_type>::= **any**

(50) <struct_type>::= **struct** <identifier> **{** <member_list> **}**

(51) <member_list>::= <member> | <member>
<member_list>

(52) <member>::= <type_spec> <declarators> **;**

(53) <union_type>::= **union** <identifier> **switch**
(<switch_type_spec> **)** **{** <switch_body> **}**

(54) <switch_type_spec>::= <integer_type>
| <char_type>
| <boolean_type>
| <enum_type>
| <scoped_name>

(55) <switch_body>::= <case> | <case> <switch_body>

(56) <case>::= <case_label_list> <element_spec> **;**

(56a) <case_label_list>::= <case_label>
| <case_label> <case_label_list>

(57) <case_label>::= **case** <const_exp> **:**
| **default :**

(58) <element_spec>::= <type_spec> <declarator>

(59) <enum_type>::= **enum** <identifier> **{** <enumerator_list> **}**

(59a) <enumerator_list>::= <enumerator>
| <enumerator> **,** <enumerator_list>

(60) <enumerator>::= <identifier>

(61*) <array_type>::= <array_spec> **<** <simple_type_spec> **,**
<positive_int_const> **>**
| <array_spec> **<** <simple_type_spec> **>**

(61a*) <array_spec>::= **array** | **sequence**

(62) <string_type>::=**string** **<** <positive_int_const> **>**
| **string**

(63) <array_declarator>::= <identifier> <array_size_list>

(63a) <array_size_list>::= <fixed_array_size>
| <fixed_array_size> <array_size_list>

(64) <fixed_array_size>::= **[** <positive_int_const> **]**

(65*) <attr_dcl> ::= [**readonly**] **attribute**
<domain_type> <attribute_name>
[<fixed_array_size>]

(65a) <domain_type>::= <simple_type_spec>
| <struct_type>
| <enum_type>

(65b) <rel_dcl> ::= **relationship**
<target_of_path>
<identifier>
inverse <inverse_traversal_path>

(65c) <target_of_path>::= <identifier>
| <rel_collection_type> **<** <identifier> **>**

(65d) <inverse_traversal_path>::=
<identifier> **::** <identifier>

(65e) <rel_collection_type>::= **set** | **list** | **bag**

(66) <except_dcl>::= **exception** <identifier>
{ [<member_list>] **}**

(67) <op_dcl>::= [<op_attribute>] <op_type_spec>
<identifier> <parameter_dcls>
[<raises_expr>] [<context_expr>]

(68) <op_attribute>::= **oneway**

(69) <op_type_spec>::= <simple_type_spec>
| **void**

(70) <parameter_dcls>::= **(** [<param_dcl_list>] **)**

(70a) <param_dcl_list>::= <param_dcl>
| <param_dcl> **,** <param_dcl_list>

(71) <param_dcl>::= <param_attribute> <simple_type_spec>
<declarator>

(72) <param_attribute>::= **in**
| **out**
| **inout**

(73) <raises_expr>::= **raises (** <scoped_name_list> **)**

(73a) <scoped_name_list>::= <scoped_name>
| <scoped_name> **,**
<scoped_name_list>

(74) <context_expr>::= **context (** <string_literal_list> **)**

(74a) <string_literal_list>::= <string_literal>
| <string_literal> **,** <string_literal_list>

3.3 Object Interchange Format

The Object Interchange Format (OIF) is a specification language used to dump and load the current state of an object database to or from a file or set of files. OIF can be used to exchange objects between databases, seed databases, provide database documentation, and drive database test suites.

Several principles have guided the development of OIF:

- OIF should support all object database states compliant to the ODMG Object Model and ODL schema definitions.
- OIF should not be a full programming language, but rather a specification language for persistent objects and their states.
- OIF should be designed according to related standards as STEP or ANSI, wherever possible.
- OIF needs no keywords other than the type, attribute, and relationship identifiers provided with the ODL definition of a database schema.

3.3.1 Object Database States

The following are used to characterize the state of all objects contained in a database:

- object identifiers
- type bindings
- attribute values
- links to other objects

Each of these items are specified within OIF.

3.3.2 Basic Structure

An OIF file contains object definitions. Each object definition specifies the type, attribute values, and relationships to other objects for the defined object.

3.3.2.1 Object Tag Names

Object identifiers are specified with object tag names unique to the OIF file(s). A tag name is visible within the entire set of OIF files. Forward declarations for an object definition are not needed. Cyclic usage of tag names is supported.

3.3.3 Object Definitions

The following is a simple example of an object definition:

Jack **Person{}**

With this definition, an instance of the class Person is created. The attribute values of this object are not initialized. The object tag Jack is used to reference the defined object within the entire set of OIF files.

3.3.3.1 Physical Clustering

The definition

Paul (Jack) **Engineer{}**

instructs the load utility to create a new persistent instance of the class Engineer "physically near" the persistent object referenced by the identifier Jack. The semantics of the term "physically near" are implementation dependent. If no such "clustering directive" is provided, the order of object definitions in the OIF file is used to determine the clustering order.

The identifier Engineer is a global keyword within the entire set of OIF files and, therefore, cannot be used as an object tag name.

3.3.4 Attribute Value Initialization

An arbitrary subset of the attributes of an object can be initialized explicitly. Assume that an ODL definition is given as follows:

```
interface Person {
    attribute string Name;
    attribute unsigned short Age;
};
```

The code fragment

```
Sally Person{Name "Sally", Age 11}
```

defines an instance of the class Person and initializes the attribute Name with the value "Sally" and the attribute Age with the value 11. The assignment statements for the attributes of an object may appear in an arbitrary order. For example, the object definition

```
Sally Person{Age 11, Name "Sally"}
```

is equivalent to the object definition above.

The identifiers Name and Age are keywords within the scope of an object definition for instances of Person and its subclasses.

3.3.4.1 Short Initialization Format

If all attributes are initialized using the order specified in the ODL definition, the attribute names and commas can be omitted. For example, the object definition

```
Sally Person{"Sally" 11}
```

would be sufficient for initializing an object with the above ODL definition. If commas are omitted, white space is required to separate the attributes.

3.3.4.2 Copy Initialization

Often a large number of basic objects have to be initialized with the same set of attribute values. For this purpose, an alternative form of the object definition can be used. The object definition

McBain(McPerth) **Company**{McPerth}

creates a new instance of the class Company "physically near" the basic object referenced by the tag McPerth. The new object is initialized with the attribute values of the company object McPerth. Using this notation, the object tag name, McPerth, must be unique across all attribute names.

3.3.4.3 Boolean Literals

An attribute of type boolean can be initialized with the boolean literals TRUE or FALSE.

3.3.4.4 Character Literals

An attribute of type char can be initialized with a character literal. A character literal is one or more characters enclosed in single quotes. These characters are interpreted using MIME format.

3.3.4.5 Integer Literals

An attribute of type short or long can be initialized with an integer literal. An integer literal consists of an optional minus sign followed by a sequence of digits. If the sequence starts with a '0', the sequence is interpreted as an octal integer. If the sequence begins with '0x' or '0X', the sequence is interpreted as a hexadecimal integer. Otherwise, the sequence is interpreted as a decimal integer. Octal digits include 0 through 7, and hexadecimal digits include 'a' through 'f' and 'A' through 'F'.

An attribute of type unsigned short or unsigned long can be initialized with an unsigned integer literal. This is accomplished by specifying an integer literal without a minus sign.

3.3.4.6 Float Literals

Attributes of type float or double can be initialized with a float literal. A float literal consists of an optional minus sign, an integer part, a decimal point, a fraction part, an e or E, and an optional negatively signed exponent. The integer, fraction, and exponent parts of a float literal consist of a sequence of decimal digits. The specification of the integer part or the fraction part (not both) is optional. The specification of the decimal point or the letter e (or E) and the exponent (not both) is also optional.

3.3.4.7 String Literals

An attribute of type string can be initialized with a string literal. String constants are specified as a sequence of characters enclosed in double quotes. These characters are interpreted using MIME format.

3.3.4.8 Range Overflow

If an integer value or float value exceeds the range of an attribute type, a runtime error is generated.

3.3.4.9 Initializing Attributes of Structured Type

Attributes of structured types can be initialized similar to the initialization of persistent objects. For example, consider the following ODL definition of a Person object:

```
struct PhoneNumber {
    unsigned short    CountryCode;
    unsigned short    AreaCode;
    unsigned short    PersonCode;
};

struct Address {
    string            Street;
    string            City;
    PhoneNumber       Phone;
};

interface Person
    attribute string    Name;
    attribute Address   PersonAddress;
};
```

This example is initialized in OIF as follows:

```
Sarah Person{Name "Sarah",
    PersonAdress {Street "Willow Road",
        City "Palo Alto",
        Phone {CountryCode 1,
            AreaCode 415,
            PersonCode 1234}}}
```

3.3.4.10 Initializing Multidimensional Attributes

An attribute of a class may have a dimension greater than one. For example:

```
interface Engineer {
    attribute unsigned short    PersonID[3];
};
```

The OIF syntax to initialize such attributes is as follows:

```
Jane Engineer{PersonID{[0] 450,
    [2] 270}}
```

The fields of the array are indexed starting from zero. Any attributes not specified remain uninitialized.

If a subset of values for a continuous sequence of field indices starting with zero is provided, the index specifier can be omitted. For example, the ODL definition

```
interface Sample {
    attribute unsigned short    Values[1000];
};
```

could be defined in OIF as

```
T1 Sample{Values{450,
    23,
    270,
    22}}
```

or

```
T1 Sample{Values{[0] 450,
    [1] 23,
    [2] 270,
    [3] 22}}
```

The commas are optional in all of the above examples.

3.3.4.11 Initializing Collections

Persistent instances of classes containing collections like

```
interface Professor: Person {
    attribute set<string>    Degrees;
};
```

are initialized in OIF as follows:

```
Feynman Professor{Degrees {"Masters", "PhD"}}
```

If the collection is a dynamic array, for example:

```
struct Point {
    float    X;
    float    Y;
};

interface Polygon {
    attribute array<Point> RefPoints;
};
```

The following OIF code fragment initializes the fields with indices 5 and 11 with the specified values:

```
P1 Polygon{RefPoints{[5]{X 7.5, Y 12.0},
    [11]{X 22.5, Y 23.0}}}
```

The unspecified fields remain uninitialized. If one of the indices used in the object definition exceeds the current size of the variable size array, the array will be resized in order to handle the desired range.

Multidimensional attributes that contain variable size array types like

```
interface PolygonSet {
    attribute array<float>        PolygonRefPoints[10];
};
```

are initialized in OIF as

```
P2 PolygonSet{PolygonRefPoints{[0]{[0] 9.7, [1] 8.98, ...},
    ...,
    [10]{[0] 22.0, [1] 60.1, ...}}}
```

3.3.5 Link Definitions

The following sections describe the OIF syntax for specifying relationships.

3.3.5.1 Cardinality "One" Relationships

Links for relationships with cardinality "one" are treated as attributes. They are initialized using the tag name of the object. For example, the ODL definition

```
interface Person{
    relationship  Company    Employer
        inverse Company::Employees;
};
```

is specified in OIF as

```
Jack Person{Employer McPerth}
```

This object definition results in a link typed Employer between the object tagged Jack and the object tagged McPerth.

3.3.5.2 Cardinality "Many" Relationships

Links for relationships with cardinality "many" are treated as collections. They are initialized using the tag names of all the linked objects. For example, the ODL definition

```
interface Company {
    relationship  set<Person> Employees
        inverse Person::Employer;
};
```

is specified in OIF as

```
McPerth Company{Employees {Jack, Joe, Jim}}
```

This object definition establishes links typed Employees between instances of the object tagged McPerth and the objects Jack, Joe, and Jim.

3.3.5.3 Type Safety

The definition of a link within an object definition is type safe. That is, an object tag must be used whose type or subtype is the type of the relationship. If an object tag is specified whose type or subtype is not the same type as the relationship, a runtime error is generated.

3.3.5.4 Cycles

Cyclic links may be established as the result of object name tags being visible across the entire set of OIF files. For example, the following ODL definition

```
interface Person {
    relationship        Employer
        inverse Company::Employees;
    relationship        Property
        inverse Company::Owner;
};

interface Company {

    relationship        set<Person>  Employees
        inverse Person::Employer;
    relationship        Person       Owner
        inverse Person::Property;
};
```

is handled in OIF as

```
Jack Person{Employer McPerth}
McPerth Company{Owner Jack}
```

3.3.6 Data Migration

Objects named for a particular database can be used in OIF files using a forward declaration mechanism. In this case, a search for an object with an object name, and matching type, equivalent to the declared tag is performed in the existing database. If the declared object is not found, a runtime error is generated. For example, the ODL definition

```
interface Node {
    relationship      set<Node>   Pred
        inverse Node::Succ;
    relationship      set<Node>   Succ
        inverse Node::Pred;
};
```

is declared in OIF as

```
A Node{Pred {B}}
E Node
B Node{Pred {E}, Succ {C}}
C Node{Pred {A}, Succ{F}}
F Node
```

In this example, a lookup of the E and F objects, and their types, is performed in the existing database. If found, they are linked with the newly created objects B and C. Note, similar to object definitions, forward declarations are visible within the entire set of OIF files, and therefore, may appear at arbitrary locations within the files.

3.3.7 Command Line Utilities

Each compliant ODBMS supporting the OIF provides the utilities odbdump and odbload.

3.3.7.1 Dump Database

The following command line utility is used to dump a database. For example, the command

```
odbdump <database name>
```

will create an OIF representation of the specified database. Object tag names are created automatically using implementation-dependent name generation algorithms.

3.3.7.2 Load Database

The following command line utility is used to load a database. For example, the command

```
odbload <database name> <file 1> ... <file n>
```

populates the database with the objects defined in the specified files.

Chapter 4

Object Query Language

4.1 Introduction

In this chapter, we describe an object query language named OQL, which supports the ODMG data model. It is complete and simple. It deals with complex objects without privileging the set construct and the select-from-where clause.

We first describe the design principles of the language in Section 4.2, then we introduce in the next sections the main features of OQL. We explain the input and result of a query in Section 4.3. Section 4.4 deals with object identity. Section 4.5 presents the path expressions. In Section 4.7, we show how OQL can invoke operations, and Section 4.8 describes how polymorphism is managed by OQL. Section 4.9 concludes this part of the presentation of the main concepts by exemplifying the property of operators composition.

Finally, a formal and complete definition of the language is given in Section 4.10. For each feature of the language, we give the syntax, its semantics, and an example. Alternate syntax for some features are described in Section 4.11, which completes OQL in order to accept any syntactical form of SQL. The chapter ends with the formal syntax, which is given in Section 4.12.

4.2 Principles

Our design is based on the following principles and assumptions:

- OQL relies on the ODMG Object Model.
- OQL is very close to SQL 92. Extensions concern object-oriented notions, like complex objects, object identity, path expressions, polymorphism, operation invocation, and late binding.
- OQL provides high-level primitives to deal with sets of objects but is not restricted to this collection construct. It also provides primitives to deal with structures, lists, and arrays and treats such constructs with the same efficiency.
- OQL is a functional language where operators can freely be composed, as long as the operands respect the type system. This is a consequence of the fact that the result of any query has a type that belongs to the ODMG type model and thus can be queried again.
- OQL is not computationally complete. It is a simple-to-use query language that provides easy access to an ODBMS.

- Based on the same type system, OQL can be invoked from within programming languages for which an ODMG binding is defined. Conversely, OQL can invoke operations programmed in these languages.
- OQL does not provide explicit update operators but rather invokes operations defined on objects for that purpose, and thus does not breach the semantics of an ODBMS, which, by definition, is managed by the "methods" defined on the objects.
- OQL provides declarative access to objects. Thus OQL queries can be easily optimized by virtue of this declarative nature.
- The formal semantics of OQL can easily be defined.

4.3 Query Input and Result

As a stand-alone language, OQL allows querying denotable objects starting from their names, which act as entry points into a database. A name may denote any kind of object, i.e., atomic, structure, collection, or literal.

As an embedded language, OQL allows querying denotable objects that are supported by the native language through expressions yielding atoms, structures, collections, and literals. An OQL query is a function that delivers an object whose type may be inferred from the operator contributing to the query expression. This point is illustrated with two short examples.

The schema defines the types Person and Employee. These types have the extents Persons and Employees, respectively. One of these persons is the chairman (and there is an entry-point Chairman to that person). The type Person defines the name, birthdate, and salary as attributes and the operation age. The type Employee, a subtype of Person, defines the relationship subordinates and the operation seniority.

```
select distinct x.age
from Persons x
where x.name = "Pat"
```

This selects the set of ages of all persons named Pat, returning a literal of type set<integer>.

```
select distinct struct(a: x.age, s: x.sex)
from Persons x
where x.name = "Pat"
```

This does about the same, but for each person, it builds a structure containing age and sex. It returns a literal of type set<struct>.

```
select distinct struct(name: x.name, hps: (select y
                                            from x.subordinates as y
                                            where y.salary >100000))
from Employees x
```

This is the same type of example, but now we use a more complex function. For each employee we build a structure with the name of the employee and the set of the employee's highly paid subordinates. Notice we have used a select-from-where clause in the select part. For each employee x, to compute hps, we traverse the relationship subordinates and select among this set the employees with a salary superior to $100,000. The result of this query is therefore a literal of the type set<struct>, namely:

```
set<struct (name: string, hps: bag<Employee>)>
```

We could also use a select operator in the from part:

```
select struct (a: x.age, s: x.sex)
from (select y from Employees y where y.seniority = "10") as x
where x.name = "Pat"
```

Of course, you do not always have to use a select-from-where clause:

```
Chairman
```

retrieves the Chairman object.

```
Chairman.subordinates
```

retrieves the set of subordinates of the Chairman.

```
Persons
```

gives the set of all persons.

4.4 Dealing with Object Identity

The query language supports both objects (i.e., having an OID) and literals (identity equals their value), depending on the way these objects are constructed or selected.

4.4.1 Creating Objects

To create an object with identity a type name constructor is used. For instance, to create a Person defined in the previous example, simply write

```
Person(name: "Pat", birthdate: "3/28/56" , salary: 100,000)
```

The parameters in parentheses allow you to initialize certain properties of the object. Those that are not explicitly initialized are given a default value.

You distinguish such a construction from the construction expressions that yield objects without identity. For instance,

```
struct (a: 10, b: "Pat")
```

creates a structure with two fields.

If you now return to the example in Section 4.3, instead of computing literals, you can build objects. For example, assuming that these object types are defined:

```
typedef set<integer> vectint;
interface stat{
attributes
   attribute Short a;
   attribute Char c;
};
typedef  bag<stat> stats;
```

you can carry out the following queries:

```
vectint(select distinct age
        from Persons
        where name = "Pat")
```

which returns an object of type vectint and

```
stats(select stat (a: age, s: sex)
      from Persons
      where name = "Pat")
```

which returns an object of type stats.

4.4.2 Selecting Existing Objects

The extraction expressions may return:

- A collection of objects with identity, e.g., select x from Persons x where x.name ="Pat" returns a collection of persons whose name is Pat.
- An object with identity, e.g., element (select x from Persons x where x.passport_number=1234567) returns the person whose passport number is 1234567.
- A collection of literals, e.g., select x.passport_number from Persons x where x.name="Pat" returns a collection of integers giving the passport numbers of people named Pat.
- A literal, e.g., Chairman.salary.

Therefore the result of a query is an object with or without object identity: some objects are generated by the query language interpreter, and others produced from the current database.

4.5 Path Expressions

As explained above, one can enter a database through a named object, but more generally as long as one gets an object, one needs a way to *navigate* from it and reach the right data one needs. To do this in OQL, we use the "." (or indifferently "->") notation, which enables us to go inside complex objects, as well as to follow simple relationships. For example, we have a Person p and we want to know the name of the city where this person's spouse lives.

Example:

```
p.spouse.address.city.name
```

This query starts from a Person, gets his/her spouse, a Person again, goes inside the complex attribute of type Address to get the City object, whose name is then accessed.

This example treated a 1-1 relationship; let us now look at n-p relationships. Assume we want the names of the children of the person p. We cannot write p.children.name because children is a list of references, so the interpretation of the result of this query would be undefined. Intuitively, the result should be a collection of names, but we need an unambiguous notation to traverse such a multiple relationship, and we use the select-from-where clause to handle collections just as in SQL.

Example:

```
select c.name
from p.children c
```

The result of this query is a value of type Bag<String>. If we want to get a Set, we simply drop duplicates, like in SQL by using the distinct keyword.

Example:

```
select distinct c.name
from p.children c
```

Now we have a means to navigate from an object to any object following any relationship and entering any complex subvalues of an object. For instance, we want the set of addresses of the children of each Person of the database. We know the collection named Persons contains all the persons of the database. We have now to traverse two collections: Persons and Person.children. Like in SQL, the select-from operator allows us to query more than one collection. These collections then appear in the from part. In OQL, a collection in the from part can be derived from a previous one by following a path that starts from it.

Example:

```
select c.address
from Persons p,
   p.children c
```

This query inspects all children of all persons. Its result is a value whose type is Bag<Address>.

4.5.1 Predicate

Of course, the where clause can be used to define any predicate, which then serves to select only the data matching the predicate. For example, we want to restrict the previous result to the people living on Main Street and having at least two children. Moreover, we are only interested in the addresses of the children who do not live in the same city as their parents.

Example:

```
select c.address
from Persons p,
   p.children c
where p.address.street = "Main Street" and
    count(p.children) >= 2 and
    c.address.city != p.address.city
```

4.5.2 Join

In the from clause, collections that are not directly related can also be declared. As in SQL, this allows computation of *joins* between these collections. This example selects the people who bear the name of a flower, assuming there exists a set of all flowers called Flowers.

Example:

```
select p
from Persons p,
   Flowers f
where p.name = f.name
```

4.6 Null Values

The result of accessing a property of the nil object is UNDEFINED. The rules for managing UNDEFINED are:

- The . and -> operations (access to properties) applied to an UNDEFINED left operand produce UNDEFINED as their result.
- Comparison operations (=, !=, <, >, <=, >=) with either or both operands being UNDEFINED produce False as their result.
- is_undefined(UNDEFINED) returns True; is_defined(UNDEFINED) returns False.
- Any other operation with any UNDEFINED operands results in a run-time error.

Examples:

Let us suppose that we have three employees in the database. One lives in Paris, another lives in Palo Alto and the third has a nil address.

```
select e
from Employees e
where e.address.city = Paris
```

returns a bag containing the employee living in Paris.

```
select e.address.city
from Employees e
```

generates a run-time error.

```
select e.address.city
from Employees e
where is_defined(e.address.city)
```

returns a bag containing the two city names Paris and Palo Alto.

```
select e
from Employees e
where is_undefined(e.address.city)
```

returns a bag containing the employee who does not have an address.

```
select e
from Employees e
where not(e.address.city = Paris)
```

returns a bag containing two employees: the one living in Palo Alto and the one who does not have an address.

4.7 Method Invoking

OQL allows us to call a method with or without parameters anywhere the result type of the method matches the expected type in the query. The notation for calling a method is exactly the same as for accessing an attribute or traversing a relationship, in the case where the method has no parameter. If it has parameters, these are given between parentheses. This flexible syntax frees the user from knowing whether the property is stored (an attribute) or computed (a method, such as age in the following example). This example returns a bag containing the age of the oldest child of all persons with name "Paul".

Example:

```
select max(select c.age from p.children c)
from Persons p
where p.name = "Paul"
```

Of course, a method can return a complex object or a collection, and then its call can be embedded in a complex path expression. For instance, if oldest_child is a method defined on the class Person that returns an object of class Person, the following example computes the set of street names where the oldest children of Parisian people are living.

Example:

```
select p.oldest_child.address.street
from Persons p
where p.lives_in("Paris")
```

Although oldest_child is a method, we *traverse* it as if it were a relationship. Moreover, lives_in is a method with one parameter.

4.8 Polymorphism

A major contribution of object orientation is the possibility of manipulating polymorphic collections and, thanks to the *late binding* mechanism, to carry out generic actions on the elements of these collections. For instance, the set Persons contains objects of classes Person, Employee, and Student. So far, all the queries against the Persons extent dealt with the three possible classes of the elements of the collection.

A query is an expression whose operators operate on typed operands. A query is correct if the types of operands match those required by the operators. In this sense, OQL is a typed query language. This is a necessary condition for an efficient query optimizer. When a polymorphic collection is filtered (for instance, Persons), its elements are statically known to be of that class (for instance, Person). This means that a property of a subclass (attribute or method) cannot be applied to such an element, except in two important cases: late binding to a method or explicit class indication.

4.8.1 Late Binding

Give the activities of each person.

Example:

```
select p.activities
from Persons p
```

where activities is a method that has three incarnations. Depending on the kind of person of the current p, the right incarnation is called. If p is an Employee, OQL calls the operation activities defined on this object, or else if p is a Student, OQL calls the operation activities defined for Students, or else p is a Person and OQL calls the method activities of the type Person.

4.8.2 Class Indicator

To go down the class hierarchy, a user may explicitly declare the class of an object that cannot be inferred statically. The evaluator then has to check at runtime that this object actually belongs to the indicated class (or one of its subclasses). For example, assuming we know that only students spend their time in following a course of study, we can select those Persons and get their grade. We explicitly indicate in the query that these Persons are of class Student:

Example:

```
select ((Student)p). grade
from Persons p
where  "course of study" in p.activities
```

4.9 Operator Composition

OQL is a purely functional language. All operators can be composed freely as long as the type system is respected. This is why the language is so simple and its manual so short. This philosophy is different from SQL, which is an ad-hoc language whose composition rules are not orthogonal. Adopting a complete orthogonality allows OQL to not restrict the power of expression and makes the language easier to learn without losing the SQL syntax for the simplest queries. However, when very specific SQL syntax does not enter in a pure functional category, OQL accepts these SQL peculiarities as possible syntactical variations. This is explained more specifically in Section 4.11.

Among the operators offered by OQL but not yet introduced, we can mention the set operators (union, intersect, except), the universal (for all) and existential quantifiers (exists), the sort and group by operators, and the aggregation operators (count, sum, min, max, and avg).

To illustrate this free composition of operators, let us write a rather complex query. We want to know the name of the street where employees live and have the smallest salary on average, compared to employees living in other streets. We proceed by steps and then do it as one query. We use the OQL define instruction to evaluate temporary results.

Example:

1. Build the extent of class Employee (assuming that it is not supported directly by the schema and that in this database only objects of class Employee have "has a job" in their activities field):

   ```
   define Employees() as
       select (Employee) p from Persons p
       where "has a job" in p.activities
   ```

2. Group the employees by street and compute the average salary in each street:

   ```
   define salary_map() as
       select street, average_salary:avg(select x.e.salary from partition x)
       from Employees() e
       group by street: e.address.street
   ```

   The result is of type Bag<struct(street: string, average_salary:float)>. The group by operator splits the employees into partitions, according to the criterion (the name of the street where this person lives). The select clause computes, in each partition, the average of the salaries of the employees belonging to the partition.

3. Sort this set by salary:

   ```
   define sorted_salary_map() as
       select s from salary_map() s order by s.average_salary
   ```

   The result is now of type List<struct(street: string, average_salary:float)>.

4. Now get the smallest salary (the first in the list) and take the corresponding street name. This is the final result.

   ```
   first(sorted_salary_map()).street
   ```

Example as a single query:

```
first( select street, average_salary: avg(select e.salary from partition)
       from (select (Employee) p from Persons p
             where "has a job" in p.activities ) as e
       group by street : e.address.street
       order by average_salary).street
```

4.10 Language Definition

OQL is an expression language. A query expression is built from typed operands composed recursively by operators. We will use the term *expression* to designate a valid query in this section. An expression returns a result that can be an object or a literal.

OQL is a typed language. This means that each query expression has a type. This type can be derived from the structure of the query expression, the schema type declarations, and the type of the named objects and literals. Thus queries can be parsed at compile time and type checked against the schema for correctness.

For each query expression, we give the rules that allow to (1) check for type correctness and (2) deduct the type of the expression from the type of the subexpressions.

For collections, we need the following definition: Types t_1, t_2,..., t_n are compatible if elements of these types can be put in the same collection as defined in the object model section.

Compatibility is recursively defined as follows:

(1) t is compatible with t.

(2) If t is compatible with t', then
set(t) is compatible with set(t')
bag(t) is compatible with bag(t')
list(t) is compatible with list(t')
array(t) is compatible with array(t')

(3) If there exist t such that t is a supertype of t_1 and t_2, then t_1 and t_2 are compatible.

This means in particular that:

- Literal types are not compatible with object types.
- Atomic literal types are compatible only if they are the same.
- Structured literal types are compatible only if they have a common ancestor.
- Collections literal types are compatible if they are of the same collection and the types of their members are compatible.
- Atomic object types are compatible only if they have a common ancestor.
- Collections object types are compatible if they are of the same collection and the types of their members are compatible.

Note that if t_1, t_2,..., t_n are compatible, then there exists a unique t such that:

(1) $t > t_i$ for all i's

(2) For all t' such that t'!=t and $t' > t_i$ for all i's, $t' > t$

This t is denoted lub(t_1, t_2,..., t_n).

The examples are based on the schema described in Chapter 3.

4.10.1 Queries

A query is a query expression with no bound variables.

4.10.2 Named Query Definition

```
define [query] id(x1, x2,..., xn) as e(x1, x2,..., xn)
```

where id is an identifier, e is an OQL expression, and x_1, x_2,..., x_n are free variables in the expression e, has the following semantics: this records the definition of the function with name id in the database schema.

id cannot be a named object, a method name, a function name, or a class name in that schema; otherwise there is an error.

Once the definition has been made, each time we compile or evaluate a query and encounter a function expression, if it cannot be directly evaluated or bound to a function or method, the compiler/interpreter replaces id by the expression e. Thus this acts as a view mechanism.

Query definitions are persistent, i.e., they remain active until overridden (by a new definition with the same name) or deleted, by a command of the form:

```
delete definition id
```

Query definitions cannot be overloaded, i.e., if there is a definition of id with n parameters and we redefined id with p parameters, p different from n, this is still interpreted as a new definition of id and overrides the previous definition.

If the definition of a named query does not have parameters, the parentheses are optional when it is used.

Example

```
define age(x) as
    select p.age
    from Persons p
    where p.name=x
define smiths() as
    select p
    from Persons p
    where p.name = "Smith"
```

4.10.3 Elementary Expressions

4.10.3.1 Atomic Literals

If l is an atomic literal, then l is an expression whose value is the literal itself. Literals have the usual syntax:

- Object literal: nil
- Boolean literal: false, true
- Integer literal: sequence of digits, e.g., 27
- Float literal: mantissa/exponent. The exponent is optional, e.g., 3.14 or 314.16e-2
- Character literal: character between single quotes, e.g., 'z'
- String literal: character string between double quotes, e.g., "a string"

4.10.3.2 Named Objects

If e is an object name, then e is an expression. It returns the entity attached to the name. The type of e is the type of the named object as declared in the database schema.

Example:

```
Students
```

This query returns the set of students. We have assumed here that there exists a name Students corresponding to the extent of objects of the class Student.

4.10.3.3 Iterator Variable

If x is a variable declared in a from part of a select-from-where, then x is an expression whose value is the current element of the iteration over the corresponding collection.

If x is declared in the *from* part of a select-from-where expression by a statement of the form

```
e as x
```

or

```
e x
```

or

```
x in e,
```

where e is of type collection(t), then x is of type t.

4.10.3.4 Named Query

If define $q(x_1, x_2,..., x_n)$ as $e(x_1, x_2,..., x_n)$ is a query definition expression where e is an expression of type t with free variables $x_1, x_2,..., x_n$, then $q(x_1, x_2,..., x_n)$ is an expression of type t.

Example:

```
smiths()
```

This query returns the set of persons with name "Smith". It refers to the query definition expression declared in Section 4.10.2.

4.10.4 Construction Expressions

4.10.4.1 Constructing Objects

If t is a type name, $p_1, p_2,...p_n$ are properties of this type with respective types $t_1, t_2,..., t_n$, if $e_1, e_2,..., e_n$ are expressions of type $t_1, t_2,..., t_n$, then $t(p_1\text{: } e_1, p_2\text{: } e_2,..., p_n\text{: } e_n)$ is an expression of type t.

This returns a new object of type t whose properties $p_1, p_2,...,p_n$ are initialized with the expression $e_1, e_2,...,e_n$. The type of e_i must be the type of p_i or a subtype.

If t is a type name of a collection and e is a collection literal, then t(e) is a collection object. The type of e must be t.

Examples:

```
Employee (name: "Peter", boss: Chairman)
```

This creates an Employee object.

```
vectint (set(1,3,10))
```

This creates a set object (see the definition of vectint in Section 4.4.1).

4.10.4.2 Constructing Structures

If $p_1, p_2,...,p_n$ are property names, if $e_1, e_2,...,e_n$ are expressions with respective types $t_1, t_2,..., t_n$, then $\text{struct}(p_1\text{: } e_1, p_2\text{: } e_2,..., p_n\text{: } e_n)$ is an expression of type $\text{struct}(p_1\text{: } t_1, p_2\text{:}t_2,..., p_n\text{: } t_n)$. It returns the structure taking values $e_1, e_2,...,e_n$ on the properties $p_1, p_2,...,p_n$.

Note that this dynamically creates an instance of the type $\text{struct}(p_1\text{: } t_1, p_2\text{: } t_2, ..., p_n\text{: } t_n)$ if t_i is the type of e_i.

Example:

```
struct(name: "Peter", age: 25);
```

This returns a structure with two attributes, name and age, taking respective values Peter and 25.

See also abbreviated syntax for some contexts in Section 4.11.1.

4.10.4.3 Constructing Sets

If e_1, e_2,..., e_n are expressions of compatible types t_1, t_2,..., t_n, then set(e_1, e_2,..., e_n) is an expression of type set(t), where t = lub(t_1, t_2,..., t_n). It returns the set containing the elements e_1, e_2,..., e_n. It creates a set instance.

Example:

```
set(1,2,3)
```

This returns a set consisting of the three elements 1, 2, and 3.

4.10.4.4 Constructing Lists

If e_1, e_2,..., e_n are expressions of compatible types t_1, t_2,..., t_n, then list(e_1, e_2,..., e_n) or simply (e_1, e_2,..., e_n) are expressions of type list(t), where t = lub(t_1, t_2,..., t_n). They return the list having elements e_1, e_2,..., e_n. They create a list instance.

If min, max are two expressions of integer or character types, such that min < max, then list(min. max) or simply (min. max) is an expression of value: list(min, min+1,... max-1, max).

The type of list(min. max) is list(int) or list (char), depending of the type of min.

Example:

```
list(1,2,2,3)
```

This returns a list of four elements.

Example:

```
list(3 .. 5)
```

This returns the list (3,4,5)

4.10.4.5 Constructing Bags

If e_1, e_2,..., e_n are expressions of compatible types t_1, t_2,..., t_n, then bag(e_1, e_2,..., e_n) is an expression of type bag(t), where t = lub(t_1, t_2,..., t_n). It returns the bag having elements e_1, e_2,..., e_n. It creates a bag instance.

Example:

```
bag(1,1,2,3,3)
```

This returns a bag of five elements.

4.10.4.6 Constructing Arrays

If $e_1, e_2, \ldots, e_n$ are expressions of compatible types $t_1, t_2, \ldots, t_n$, then array($e_1, e_2, \ldots, e_n$) is an expression of type array(t), where t = lub($t_1, t_2, \ldots, t_n$). It returns an array having elements $e_1, e_2, \ldots, e_n$. It creates an array instance.

Example:

```
array(3,4,2,1,1)
```

This returns an array of five elements.

4.10.5 Atomic Type Expressions

4.10.5.1 Unary Expressions

If e is an expression and <op> is a unary operation valid for the type of e, then <op> e is an expression. It returns the result of applying <op> to e.

Arithmetic unary operators: +, -, abs

Boolean unary operator: not

Example:

```
not true
```

This returns false.

If <op> is +, -, or abs, and if e is of type integer or float, then <op>e is of type e.

If e is of type boolean, then not e is of type boolean.

4.10.5.2 Binary Expressions

If e_1 and e_2 are expressions and <op> is a binary operation, then e_1<op>e_2 is an expression. It returns the result of applying <op> to e_1 and e_2.

Arithmetic integer binary operators: +, -, *, /, mod (modulo)
Floating point binary operators: +, -, *, /
Relational binary operators: =, !=, <, <=, >, >=
These operators are defined on all atomic types.
Boolean binary operators: and, or

Example:

```
count(Students) - count(TA)
```

This returns the difference between the number of students and the number of TAs.

if <op> is +, -, * or / and e_1 and e_2 are of type integer or float, then e_1 <op> e_2 is of type float if e_1 or e_2 is of type float and integer otherwise.

If <op> is =, !=, <, <=, >, or >=, and e_1 and e_2 are of compatible types (here types integer and float are considered as compatible), then e_1 <op> e_2 is of type boolean.

If <op> is and or or, and e_1 and e_2 are of type boolean, then e_1 <op> e_2 is of type boolean.

Because OQL is a declarative query language, its semantics allows for a reordering of expression for the purpose of optimization. Boolean expressions are evaluated in an order that was not necessarily the one specified by the user but the one chosen by the query optimizer. This introduces some degree of nondeterminism in the semantics of a boolean expression:

(1) The evaluation of a boolean expressions stops as soon as we know the result (i.e., when evaluating an and clause, we stop as soon as the result is false, and when evaluating an or clause, we stop as soon as the result is true).

(2) Some clauses can generate a run-time error and depending in their order in evaluation, they will or will not be evaluated.

4.10.5.3 String Expressions

If s_1 and s_2 are expressions of type string, then s_1 || s_2 and s_1 + s_2 are equivalent expressions of type string whose value is the concatenation of the two strings.

If c is an expression of type character, and s an expression of type string, then c in s is an expression of type boolean whose value is true if the character belongs to the string, else false.

If s is an expression of type string, and i is an expression of type integer, then Si is an expression of type character whose value is the $i+1^{th}$ character of the string.

If s is an expression of type string, and low and up are expressions of type integer, then s[low:up] is an expression of type string whose value is the substring of s from the $low+1^{th}$ character up to the $up+1^{th}$ character.

If s is an expression of type string, and pattern is a string literal that may include the wildcard characters: "?" or "_", meaning any character, and "*" or "%", meaning any substring including an empty substring, then s like pattern is an expression of type boolean whose value is true if s matches the pattern, else false.

Example:

'a nice string' like '%nice%str_ng'   is true

The backslash character '\' can be used to escape the wildcard characters, so that they can be treated as normal characters in a string.

4.10.6 Object Expressions

4.10.6.1 Comparison of Objects

If e_1 and e_2 are expressions that denote objects of compatible object types (objects with identity), then $e_1 = e_2$ and $e_1 != e_2$ are expressions that return a boolean. The second expression is equivalent to not($e_1 = e_2$). Likewise $e_1 = e_2$ is true if they designate the same object.

Example:

If Doe is a named object that is the only element of the named set Students with the attribute name equals to "Doe" then

```
Doe = element(select s from Students s where s.name = "Doe")
```

is true.

4.10.6.2 Comparison of Literals

If e_1 and e_2 are expressions that denote literals of the compatible literal types (objects without identity), then $e_1 = e_2$ and $e_1 != e_2$ are expressions that return a boolean. The second expression is equivalent to not($e_1 = e_2$). Likewise, $e_1 = e_2$ is true if the value e_1 is equal to the value e_2.

The equality of literals is computed in the following way:

- If they are struct, they must have the same structure and each of the attributes must be equal.
- If they are sets, they must contain the same set of elements.
- If they are bags, they must contain the same set of elements and each element must have the same number of occurrences.
- If they are list or array, they must contain the same set of elements in the same order.

4.10.6.3 Extracting an Attribute or Traversing a Relationship from an Object

If e is an expression of a type (literal or object) having an attribute or a relationship p of type t, then e.p and e->p are expressions of type t. These are alternate syntax to extract property p of an object e.

If e happens to designate a deleted or a nonexisting object, i.e., nil, the access to an attribute or to a relationship will return UNDEFINED as described in Section 4.6.

4.10.6.4 Applying an Operation to an Object

If e is an expression of a type having a method f without parameters and returning a result of type t, then e->f and e.f are expressions of type t. These are alternate syntax to apply an operation on an object. The value of the expression is the one returned by the operation or else the object nil, if the operation returns nothing.

Example:

```
jones->number_of_students
```

This applies the operation number_of_students to jones.

If e happens to designate a deleted or a nonexisting object, i.e., nil, the use of a method on it will return UNDEFINED as described in Section 4.6.

4.10.6.5 Applying an Operation with Parameters to an Object

If e is an expression of an object type having a method f with parameters of type t_1, t_2,..., t_n and returning a result of type t, if e_1, e_2,..., e_n are expressions of type t_1, t_2,..., t_n, then e->f(e_1, e_2,..., e_n) and e.f(e_1, e_2,..., e_n) are expressions of type t that apply operation f with parameters e_1, e_2,..., e_n to object e. The value of the expression is the one returned by the operation or else the object nil, if the operation returns nothing.

If e happens to designate a deleted or a nonexisting object, i.e., nil, an attempt to apply an operation will return UNDEFINED as described in Section 4.6.

Example:

```
Doe->apply_course("Math", Turing)->number
```

This query calls the operation apply_course on class Student for the object Doe. It passes two parameters, a string and an object of class Professor. The operation returns an object of type Course, and the query returns the number of this course.

4.10.7 Collection Expressions

4.10.7.1 Universal Quantification

If x is a variable name, e_1 and e_2 are expressions, e_1 denotes a collection, and e_2 is an expression of type boolean, then for all x in e_1: e_2 is an expression of type boolean. It returns true if all the elements of collection e_1 satisfy e_2 and false otherwise.

Example:

```
for all x in Students: x.student_id > 0
```

This returns true if all the objects in the Students set have a positive value for their student_id attribute. Otherwise it returns false.

4.10.7.2 Existential Quantification

If x is a variable name, if e_1 and e_2 are expressions, e_1 denotes a collection, and e_2 is an expression of type boolean, then exists x in e_1: e_2 is an expression of type boolean. It returns true if there is at least one element of collection e_1 that satisfies e_2 and false otherwise.

Example:

```
exists x in Doe.takes: x.taught_by.name = "Turing"
```

This returns true if at least one course Doe takes is taught by someone named Turing.

If e is a collection expression, then exists(e) and unique(e) are expressions that return a boolean value. The first one returns true if there exists at least one element in the collection, while the second one returns true if there exists only one element in the collection.

Note that these operators accept the SQL syntax for nested queries like

```
select ... from col where exists ( select ... from col1 where predicate)
```

The nested query returns a bag to which the operator exists is applied. This is of course the task of an optimizer to recognize that it is useless to compute effectively the intermediate bag result.

4.10.7.3 Membership Testing

If e_1 and e_2 are expressions, e_2 is a collection, and e_1 is an object or a literal having the same type or a subtype as the elements of e_2, then e_1 in e_2 is an expression of type boolean. It returns true if element e_1 belongs to collection e_2.

Example:

```
Doe in Students
```

This returns true.

```
Doe in TA
```

This returns true if Doe is a teaching assistant.

4.10.7.4 Aggregate Operators

If e is an expression that denotes a collection, if <op> is an operator from {min, max, count, sum, avg}, then <op>(e) is an expression.

Example:

```
max (select salary from Professors)
```

This returns the maximum salary of the professors.

If e is of type collection(t), where t is integer or float, then <op>(e) where <op> is an aggregate operator different from "count" is an expression of type t.

If e is of type collection(t), then count(e) is an expression of type integer.

4.10.8 Select From Where

The general form of a select statement is as follows:

select [distinct] $f(x_1, x_2,\ldots, x_n, x_{n+1}, x_{n+2},\ldots, x_{n+p})$
from x_1 in $e_1(x_{n+1}, x_{n+2},\ldots, x_{n+p})$
x_2 in $e_2(x_1, x_{n+1}, x_{n+2},\ldots, x_{n+p})$
x_3 in $e_3(x_1, x_2, x_{n+1}, x_{n+2},\ldots, x_{n+p})$
...
x_n in $e_n(x_1, x_2,\ldots, x_{n-1}, x_{n+1}, x_{n+2},\ldots, x_{n+p})$
[where $p(x_1, x_2,.., x_n, x_{n+1}, x_{n+2},\ldots, x_{n+p})$]
[order by $f_1(x_1, x_2,.., x_{n+p}), f_2(x_1, x_2,.., x_{n+p}),\ldots, f_q(x_1, x_2,.., x_{n+p})$]

Or

select [distinct] $f(x_1, x_2,\ldots, x_n, x_{n+1}, x_{n+2},\ldots, x_{n+p})$
from $e_1(x_{n+1}, x_{n+2},\ldots, x_{n+p})$ as x_1
$e_2(x_1, x_{n+1}, x_{n+2},\ldots, x_{n+p})$ as x_2
$e_3(x_1, x_2, x_{n+1}, x_{n+2},\ldots, x_{n+p})$ as x_3
...
$e_n(x_1, x_2,\ldots, x_{n-1}, x_{n+1}, x_{n+2},\ldots, x_{n+p})$ as x_n
[where $p(x_1, x_2,\ldots, x_n, x_{n+1}, x_{n+2},\ldots, x_{n+p})$]
[order by $f_1(x_1, x_2,\ldots, x_{n+p}), f_2(x_1, x_2,\ldots, x_{n+p}),\ldots, f_q(x_1, x_2,\ldots, x_{n+p})$]

$x_{n+1}, x_{n+2},\ldots, x_{n+p}$ are free variables that have to be bound to evaluate the query.

The e_i's have to be of type collection, p has to be of type boolean, and the f_i's have to be of a sortable type, i.e., an atomic type.

The result of the query will be a collection of t, where t is the type of the result of f.

The semantics of the query are as follows:
Assuming $x_{n+1}, x_{n+2},\ldots, x_{n+p}$ are bound to $X_{n+1}, X_{n+2},\ldots, X_{n+p}$, the query is evaluated as follows:

(1) The result of the from clause is a bag of elements of the type struct(x_1: X_1, x_2: X_2,..., x_n:X_n), where
X_1 ranges over the collection bagof($e_1(X_{n+1}, X_{n+2},\ldots, X_{n+p})$)
X_2 ranges over the collection bagof($e_2(X_1, X_{n+1}, X_{n+2},\ldots, X_{n+p})$)
X_3 ranges over the collection bagof($e_3(X_1, X_2, X_{n+1}, X_{n+2},\ldots, X_{n+p})$)
...
X_n ranges over the collection bagof($e_n(X_1, X_2,\ldots, X_{n-1}, X_{n+1}, X_{n+2},\ldots, X_{n+p})$)

where bagof(C) is defined as follows, for a collection C:
if C is a bag: C
if C is a list: the bag consisting of all the elements of C
if C is a set: the bag consisting of all the elements of C

(2) Filter the result of the from clause by retaining only those tuples $(X_1, X_2,..., X_n)$ that satisfy the predicate $p(X_1, X_2,..., X_{n-1}, X_n, X_{n+1}, X_{n+2},..., X_{n+p})$.

(3) If the key word "order by" is there, sort this collection lexicographically using the functions $f_1, f_2,..., f_q$ and transform it into a list. Lexicographic order by a set of functions is performed as follows: first sort according to function f_1, then for all the elements having the same f_1 value sort them according to f_2, etc.

(4) Apply to each one of these tuples the function

$f(X_1, X_2,..., X_{n-1}, X_n, X_{n+1}, X_{n+2},..., X_{n+p})$.

If f is just "*", then keep the result of step (3) as such.

(5) If the key word "distinct" is there, then eliminate the eventual duplicates and obtain a set or a list without duplicates.
Note: to summarize, the type of the result of a "select from where" is as follows:

- It is always a collection.
- The collection type does not depend on the types of the collections specified in the from clause.
- The collection type depends only on the form of the query: if we use "order by" we get a list; if we use the "distinct" key word without "order by", we get a set; and if neither "order by" nor "distinct" are used, we get a bag.

Example:

```
select couple(student: x.name, professor: z.name)
   from Students as x,
       x.takes as y,
       y.taught_by as z
where z.rank = "full professor"
```

This returns a bag of objects of type couple giving student names and the names of the full professors from which they take classes.

Example:

```
select *
from Students as x,
   x.takes as y,
   y.taught_by as z
where z.rank = "full professor"
```

This returns a bag of structures, giving for each student "object" the section object followed by the student and the full professor "object" teaching in this section:

```
bag< struct(x: Student, y: Section, z: Professor) >
```

Syntactical variations are accepted for declaring the variables in the *from* part, exactly as with SQL. The *as* keyword may be omitted. Moreover, the variable itself can be omitted too, and in this case, the name of the collection itself serves as a variable name to range over it.

Example:

```
select couple(student: Students.name, professor: z.name)
from Students,
   Students.takes y,
   y.taught_by z
where z.rank = "full professor"
```

In a select-from-where query, the *where* clause can be omitted, with the meaning of a true predicate.

4.10.9 Group-by Operator

If *select_query* is a select-from-where query, *partition_attributes* is a structure expression, and *predicate* a boolean expression, then

select_query group by *partition_attributes*

is an expression and

select_query group by *partition_attributes* having *predicate*

is an expression.

The Cartesian product visited by the select operator is split into partitions. For each element of the Cartesian product, the partition attributes are evaluated. All elements that match the same values according to the given partition attributes belong to the same partition. Thus the partitioned set, after the grouping operation, is a set of structures: each structure has the valued properties for this partition (the valued *partition_attributes)*, completed by a property that is conventionally called *partition* and that is the bag of all elements of the Cartesian product matching this particular valued partition.

If the partition attributes are att_1: e_1, att_2: e_2,..., att_n: e_n, then the result of the grouping is of type

```
set< struct(att1: type_of(e1), att2: type_of(e2), ..., attn: type_of(en),
            partition: bag< type_of(grouped elements) >)>
```

The type of grouped elements is defined as follows:

If the *from* clause declares the variables v_1 on collection col_1, v_2 on col_2, ..., v_n on col_n, the grouped elements is a structure with one attribute, v_k, for each collection having the type of the elements of the corresponding collection partition:

```
bag< struct(v1: type_of(col1 elements),..., vn: type_of(coln elements))>
```

If a collection col_k has no variable declared, the corresponding attribute has an internal system name.

This partitioned set may then be filtered by the predicate of a *having* clause. Finally, the result is computed by evaluating the *select* clause for this partitioned and filtered set.

The having clause can thus apply aggregate functions on *partition*; likewise the select clause can refer to *partition* to compute the final result. Both clauses can refer also to the partition attributes.

Example:

```
select *
from Employees e
group by low:     salary < 1000,
         medium:  salary >= 1000 and salary < 10000,
         high:    salary >= 10000
```

This gives a set of three elements, each of which has a property called partition that contains the bag of employees that enter in this category. So the type of the result is

```
set<struct(low: boolean, medium: boolean, high: boolean,
           partition: bag<struct(e: Employee)>)>
```

The second form enhances the first one with a *having* clause that enables you to filter the result using aggregative functions that operate on each partition.

Example:

```
select department,
   avg_salary: avg(select x.e.salary from partition x)
from Employees e
group by department: e.deptno
having avg(select x.e.salary from partition x) > 30000
```

This gives a set of couples: department and average of the salaries of the employees working in this department, when this average is more than 30000. So the type of the result is

```
bag<struct(department: integer, avg_salary: float)>
```

To compute the average salary, we could have used a shortcut notation allowed by the Scope Rules defined in Section 4.10.15. The notation would be

```
avg_salary: avg(select e.salary from partition)
```

4.10.10 Order-by Operator

If *select_query* is a select-from-where or a select-from-where-group_by query, and if $e_1, e_2, ..., e_n$ are expressions, then select_query order by $e_1, e_2, ..., e_n$ is an expression. It returns a list of the selected elements sorted by the function e_1, and inside each subset yielding the same e_1, sorted by $e_2, ...$, and the final subsub...set, sorted by e_n.

Example:

```
select p from Persons p order by p.age, p.name
```

This sorts the set of persons on their age, then on their name, and puts the sorted objects into the result as a list.

Each sort expression criterion can be followed by the keyword asc or desc, specifying respectively an ascending or descending order. The default order is that of the previous declaration. For the first expression, the default is ascending.

Example:

```
select * from Persons order by age desc, name asc, department
```

4.10.11 Indexed Collection Expressions

4.10.11.1 Getting the ith Element of an Indexed Collection

If e_1 is an expression of type list(t) or array(t) and e_2 is an expression of type integer, then $e_1[e_2]$ is an expression of type t. This extracts the e_2+1 element of the indexed collection e_1. Notice that the first element has the rank 0.

Example:

```
list (a,b,c,d) [1]
```

This returns b.

Example:

```
element (select x
          from Courses x
          where x.name = "Math" and x.number ="101").requires[2]
```

This returns the third prerequisite of Math 101.

4.10.11.2 Extracting a Subcollection of an Indexed Collection

If e_1 is an expression of type list(t) (resp. array(t)), and e_2 and e_3 are expressions of type integer, then $e_1[e_2:e_3]$ is an expression of type list(t) (resp. array(t)). This extracts the subcollection of e_1 starting at position e_2 and ending at position e_3.

Example:

```
list (a,b,c,d) [1:3]
```

This returns list (b,c,d).

Example:

```
element (select x
            from Courses x
            where x.name="Math" and x.number="101").requires[0:2]
```

This returns the list consisting of the first three prerequisites of Math 101.

4.10.11.3 Getting the First and Last Elements of an Indexed Collection

If e is an expression of type list(t) or array(t), <op> is an operator from {first, last}, then <op>(e) is an expression of type t. This extracts the first and last element of a collection.

Example:

```
first(element(select x
                from Courses x
                where x.name="Math" and x.number="101").requires)
```

This returns the first prerequisite of Math 101.

4.10.11.4 Concatenating Two Indexed Collections

If e_1 and e_2 are expressions of type list(t_1) and list(t_2) (resp. array(t_1) and array(t_2)) where t_1 and t_2 are compatible, then e_1+e_2 is an expression of type list(lub(t_1, t_2)) (resp. array(lub(t_1, t_2))). This computes the concatenation of e_1 and e_2.

```
list (1,2) + list(2,3)
```

This query generates list (1,2,2,3).

4.10.11.5 Accessing an Element of a Dictionary from Its Key

If e_1 is an expression of type dictionary(k,v) and e_2 is an expression of type k, then $e_1[e_2]$ is an expression of type v. This extracts the value associated with the key e_2 in the dictionary e_1.

example:

```
theDict["foobar"]
```

returns the value that is associated with the key "foobar" in the dictionary theDict.

4.10.12 Binary Set Expressions

4.10.12.1 Union, Intersection, Difference

If e_1 is an expression of type set(t_1) or bag(t_1) and e_2 is an expression of type set(t_2) or bag(t_2) where t_1 and t_2 are compatible types, if <op> is an operator from {union, except, intersect}, then e_1 <op> e_2 is an expression of type set(lub(t_1, t_2)) if both expressions are of type set, bag(lub(t_1, t_2))) if any of them is of type bag. This computes set theoretic operations, union, difference, and intersection on e_1 and e_2, as defined in Chapter 2.

When the operand's collection types are different (bag and set), the set is first converted into a bag and the result is a bag.

Examples:

```
Student except TA
```

This returns the set of students who are not teaching assistants.

```
bag(2,2,3,3,3) union bag(2,3,3,3)
```

This bag expression returns bag(2,2,3,3,3,2,3,3,3).

```
bag(2,2,3,3,3) intersect bag(2,3,3,3)
```

The intersection of two bags yields a bag that contains the minimum for each of the multiple values. So the result is bag(2,3,3,3).

```
bag(2,2,3,3,3) except bag(2,3,3,3)
```

This bag expression returns bag(2).

4.10.12.2 Inclusion

If e_1 and e_2 are expressions that denote sets or bag of compatible types and if <op> is an operator from {<, <=, >, >=}, then e_1 <op> e_2 is an expression of type boolean.

When the operands are different kinds of collections (bag and set), the set is first converted into a bag.

$e_1 < e_2$ is true if e_1 is included in e_2 but not equal to e_2

$e_1 <= e_2$ is true if e_1 is included in e_2

Example:

```
set(1,2,3) < set(3,4,2,1) is true
```

4.10.13 Conversion Expressions

4.10.13.1 Extracting the Element of a Singleton

If e is an expression of type collection(t), element(e) is an expression of type t. This takes the singleton e and returns its element. If e is not a singleton, this raises an exception.

Example:

```
element(select x from Professors x where x.name = "Turing")
```

This returns the professor whose name is Turing (if there is only one).

4.10.13.2 Turning a List into a Set

If e is an expression of type list(t), listtoset(e) is an expression of type set(t). This converts the list into a set, by forming the set containing all the elements of the list.

Example:

```
listtoset (list(1,2,3,2))
```

This returns the set containing 1, 2, and 3.

4.10.13.3 Removing Duplicates

If e is an expression of type col(t), where col is set or bag, then distinct(e) is an expression of type set(t) whose value is the same collection after removing the duplicated elements. If e is an expression of type col(t), where col is either list or array, then distinct(e) is an expression of type col(t) obtained by keeping the first occurrence for each element of the list.

Examples:

```
distinct(list(1, 4, 2, 3, 2, 4, 1))
```

This returns list(1, 4, 2, 3).

4.10.13.4 Flattening a Collection of Collections

If e is a collection-valued expression, flatten(e) is an expression. This converts a collection of collections of t into a collection of t. So flattening operates at the first level only.

Assuming the type of e to be col_1<col_2<t>>, the result of flatten(e) is:

- If col_2 is a set (resp. a bag), the union of all col_2<t> is done and the result is set<t> (resp. bag<t>).
- If col_2 is a list or an array and col_1 is a list or an array, the concatenation of all col_2<t> is done following the order in col_1 and the result is col_2<t>, which is

thus a list or an array. Of course duplicates, if any, are maintained by this operation.

- If col_2 is a list or an array and col_1 is a set (resp. a bag), the lists or arrays are converted into sets (resp. bags), the union of all these sets (resp. bags) is done, and the result is a set<t> (resp. bag<t>).

Examples:

```
flatten(list(set(1,2,3), set(3,4,5,6), set(7)))
```

This returns the set containing 1,2,3,4,5,6,7.

```
flatten(list(list(1,2), list(1,2,3)))
```

This returns list(1,2,1,2,3).

```
flatten(set(list(1,2), list(1,2,3)))
```

This returns the set containing 1,2,3.

4.10.13.5 Typing an Expression

If e is an expression of type t and t' is a type name, and t and t' are comparable (either t>=t' or t<=t'), then (t')e is an expression of type t'. This expression has two impacts

(1) At compile time, it is a statement for the interpreter/compiler type checker to notify that e should be understood as of type t'.

(2) At run time it asserts that e is indeed of type t' (or a subtype of it) and will return the result of e in this case, or an exception in all other cases.

This mechanism allows the user to execute queries that would otherwise be rejected as incorrectly typed. For instance

```
select s.salary
from Student s
where s in (select sec.assistant from Sections sec)
```

Because s is restricted in the where clause to teaching assistants that teach a section, this query will indeed return the salaries of these people. However, the type checker has no means to check that the s in Student have indeed always a salary field, and the query will be rejected at compile time.

If we write

```
select ((Employee) s).salary
from Student s
where s in (select sec.assistant from Sections sec)
```

then the type checker knows that s has to be of Employee type and the query is accepted as type correct. Note that at run time, each occurrence of s in the select clause will be checked for its type.

4.10.14 Function Call

If f is a function of type (t_1, t_2,..., t_n -> t), if e_1, e_2,..., e_n are expressions of type t_1, t_2,..., t_n, then f(e_1, e_2,..., e_n) is an expression of type t whose value is the value returned by the function, or the object nil, when the function does not return any value. The first form calls a function without a parameter, while the second one calls a function with the parameters e_1, e_2,..., e_n.

OQL does not define in which language the body of such a function is written. This allows one to extend the functionality of OQL without changing the language.

4.10.15 Scope Rules

The *from* part of a select-from-where query introduces explicit or implicit variables to range over the filtered collections. An example of an explicit variable is

```
select ... from Persons p ...
```

while an implicit declaration would be

```
select ... from Persons ...
```

The scope of these variables spreads over all the parts of the select-from-where expression, including nested subexpressions.

The *group by* part of a select-from-where-group_by query introduces the name *partition* along with possible explicit attribute names that characterize the partition. These names are visible in the corresponding *having* and *select* parts, including nested subexpressions within these parts.

Inside a scope, you use these variable names to construct path expressions and reach properties (attributes and operations) when these variables denote complex objects. For instance, in the scope of the first from clause above, you access the age of a person by p.age.

When the variable is implicit, like in the second from clause, you directly use the name of the collection by Persons.age.

However, when no ambiguity exists, you can use the property name directly as a shortcut, without using the variable name to open the scope (this is made implicitly), writing simply: age. There is no ambiguity when a property name is defined for one and only one object denoted by a visible variable.

To summarize, a name appearing in a (nested) query is looked up as follows:

- a variable in the current scope, or
- a named query introduced by the *define* clause, or

- a named object, i.e., an entry point in the database, or
- an attribute name or an operation name of a variable in the current scope, when there is no ambiguity, i.e., this property name belongs to only one variable in the scope

Example:

Assuming that in the current schema the names Persons and Cities are defined.

```
select scope1
from   Persons,
       Cities c
where exists(select scope2 from children as child)
       or count (select scope3, (select scope4 from partition)
                 from children p,
                      scope5 v
                 group by age: scope6
              )
```

In *scope1*, we see these names: Persons, c, Cities, all property names of class Person and class City as long as they are not present in both classes, and they are not called "Persons", "c", or "Cities"; otherwise they have to be explicitly disambiguated.

In *scope2*, we see these names: child, Persons, c, Cities, the property names of the class City that are not properties of the class Person. No attributes of the class Person can be accessed directly since they are ambiguous between "child" and "Persons".

Scope3 and *scope4* are the same, and we see these names: age, partition, p, v, and the same names from *scope1*, except "age", "partition", "p", and "v", if they exist. No attributes of the class Person can be accessed directly since they are ambiguous between "p" and "Persons".

In *scope5*, we see the name p and the same names from *scope1*, except "p", if it exists. No attributes of the class Person can be accessed directly since they are ambiguous between "p" and "Persons".

In *scope6*, we see these names: p, v, Persons, c, Cities, the property names of the class City that are not properties of the class Person. No attribute of the class Person can be accessed directly since they are ambiguous between "p" and "Persons".

4.11 Syntactical Abbreviations

OQL defines an orthogonal expression language, in the sense that all operators can be composed with each other as long as the types of the operands are correct. To achieve this property, we have defined a functional language with simple operators such as "+"

or composite operators such as "select from where", "group_by", and "order_by", which always deliver a result in the same type system and thus can be recursively operated with other operations in the same query.

In order to accept the whole DML query part of SQL, as a valid syntax for OQL, we have added ad-hoc constructions each time SQL introduces a syntax that cannot be considered in the category of true operators. This section gives the list of these constructions that we call "abbreviations," since they are completely equivalent to a functional OQL expression. At the same time, we give the semantics of these constructions, since all operators used for this description have been previously defined.

4.11.1 Structure Construction

The structure constructor has been introduced in Section 4.10.4.2. An alternate syntax is allowed in two contexts: select clause and group-by clause. In both contexts, the SQL syntax is accepted, along with the one already defined.

select *projection* {, *projection*} ...
select ... **group by** *projection* {, *projection*}

where *projection* is one of these forms:

1. expression **as** identifier
2. identifier: expression
3. expression

This is an alternate syntax for

struct(identifier: expression {, identifier: expression})

If there is only one *projection* and the syntax (3) is used in a select clause, then it is not interpreted as a structure construction, but rather the expression stands as is. Furthermore, a (3) expression is only valid if it is possible to infer the name of the variable for the corresponding attribute. This requires that the expression denote a path expression (possibly of length one) ending by a property whose name is then chosen as the identifier.

Example:

```
select p.name, salary, student_id
from Professors p, p.teaches
```

This query returns a bag of structures:

```
bag<struct(name: string, salary: float, student_id: integer)>
```

Both Professor and Student classes have the attribute "name". Therefore it must be disambiguated. On the contrary, only professors have salaries, and only students have student_ids.

4.11.2 Aggregate Operators

These operators have been introduced in Section 4.10.7.4. SQL adopts a notation that is not functional for them. So OQL accepts this syntax, too. If we define *aggregate* as one of **min**, **max**, **count**, **sum**, and **avg**,

select count(*) from ... is equivalent to
count(select * from ...)

select *aggregate*(query) from ... is equivalent to
aggregate(select query from ...)

select *aggregate*(distinct query) from ... is equivalent to
aggregate(distinct(select query from ...))

4.11.3 Composite Predicates

If e_1 and e_2 are expressions, e_2 is a collection, e_1 has the type of its elements, if *relation* is a relational operator (=, !=, <, <=, > , >=), then e_1 *relation* some e_2 and e_1 *relation* any e_2 and e_1 *relation* all e_2 are expressions whose value is a boolean.

The two first predicates are equivalent to

exists x in e_2: e_1 *relation* x

The last predicate is equivalent to

for all x in e_2: e_1 *relation* x

Example:

10 < some (8,15, 7, 22) is true

4.11.4 String Literal

OQL accepts single quotes as well to delineate a string (see Section 4.10.3.1), like SQL does. This introduces an ambiguity for a string with one character, which then has the same syntax as a character literal. This ambiguity is solved by context.

4.12 OQL BNF

The OQL grammar is given using a rather informal BNF notation.

- { symbol } is a sequence of 0 or n symbol(s).
- *[*symbol*]* is an optional symbol. Do not confuse this with the separators [].
- **keyword** is a terminal of the grammar.
- xxx_name is the syntax of an identifier.
- xxx_literal is self-explanatory, e.g., "a string" is a string_literal.
- bind_argument stands for a parameter when embedded in a programming language, e.g., $3i.

The nonterminal **query** stands for a valid query expression. The grammar is presented as recursive rules producing valid queries. This explains why most of the time this nonterminal appears on the left side of ::=. Of course, each operator expects its "query" operands to be of the right types. These type constraints have been introduced in the previous sections.

These rules must be completed by the priority of OQL operators, which is given after the grammar. Some syntactical ambiguities are solved semantically from the types of the operands.

4.12.1 Grammar

4.12.1.1 Axiom (see Section 4.10.1, Section 4.10.2)

query_program ::= {define_query;} query
define_query ::= **define** identifier **as** query

4.12.1.2 Basic (see Section 4.10.3)

query ::= **nil**
query ::= **true**
query ::= **false**
query ::= integer_literal
query ::= float_literal
query ::= character_literal
query ::= string_literal
query ::= entry_name
query ::= query_name
query ::= bind_argument[1]
query ::= from_variable_name
query ::= (query)

4.12.1.3 Simple Expression (see Section 4.10.5)

query ::= query + query[2]
query ::= query - query
query ::= query * query
query ::= query / query
query ::= - query
query ::= query **mod** query
query ::= **abs** (query)
query ::= query || query

---

1. A bind argument allows one to bind expressions from a programming language to a query when embedded into this language (see chapters on language bindings).
2. The operator + is also used for list and array concatenation.

4.12.1.4 Comparison (see Section 4.10.5)

query ::= query comparison_operator query
query ::= query **like** string_literal
comparison_operator ::= =
comparison_operator ::= !=
comparison_operator ::= >
comparison_operator ::= <
comparison_operator ::= >=
comparison_operator ::= <=

4.12.1.5 Boolean Expression (see Section 4.10.5)

query ::= **not** query
query ::= query **and** query
query ::= query **or** query

4.12.1.6 Constructor (see Section 4.10.4)

query ::= type_name (*[*query*]*)
query ::= **type_name** (identifier: query {,identifier: query})
query ::= **struct** (identifier: query {, identifier: query})
query ::= **set** (*[*query {, query}*]*)
query ::= **bag** (*[*query {,query}*]*)
query ::= **list** (*[*query {,query}*]*)
query ::= (query, query {, query})
query ::= *[***list***]*(query .. query)
query ::= **array** (*[*query {,query}*]*)

4.12.1.7 Accessor (see Section 4.10.6, Section 4.10.11, Section 4.10.14, Section 4.10.15)

query ::= query dot attribute_name
query ::= query dot relationship_name
query ::= query dot operation_name(query {,query})
dot ::= **. | ->**
query ::= ***** query
query ::= query **[**query**]**
query ::= query **[**query**:**query**]**
query ::= **first** (query)
query ::= **last** (query)
query ::= function_name(*[*query {,query}*]*)

4.12.1.8 Collection Expression (see Section 4.10.7, Section 4.11.3)

query ::= for **all** identifier **in** query: query
query ::= **exists** identifier **in** query: query
query ::= **exists**(query)
query ::= **unique**(query)
query ::= query **in** query
query ::= query comparison_operator quantifier query
quantifier ::= **some**
quantifier ::= **any**
quantifier ::= **all**
query ::= **count** (query)
query ::= **count** (*)
query ::= **sum** (query)
query ::= **min** (query)
query ::= **max** (query)
query ::= **avg** (query)

4.12.1.9 Select Expression (see Section 4.10.8, Section 4.10.9, Section 4.10.10)

query ::= **select** *[* **distinct** *]* projection_attributes
    from variable_declaration {, variable_declaration}
    *[***where** query*]*
    *[***group by** partition_attributes*]*
    *[***having** query*]*
    *[***order by** sort_criterion {, sort_criterion}*]*
projection_attributes ::= projection {, projection}
projection_attributes ::= *
projection ::= query
projection ::= identifier: query
projection ::= query **as** identifier
variable_declaration ::= query *[[* **as** *]* identifier*]*
partition_attributes ::= projection {, projection}
sort_criterion ::= query *[*ordering*]*
ordering ::= **asc**
ordering ::= **desc**

4.12.1.10 Set Expression (see Section 4.10.12)

query ::= query **intersect** query
query ::= query **union** query
query ::= query **except** query

4.12.1.11 Conversion (see Section 4.10.13)

query ::= **listtoset** (query)
query ::= **element** (query)
query ::= **distinct**(e)
query ::= **flatten** (query)
query ::= (class_name) query

4.12.2 Operator Priorities

The following operators are sorted by decreasing priority. Operators on the same line have the same priority and group left-to-right.

() [] . ->
not - (unary) + (unary)
in
*** / mod intersect**
+ - union except ||
< > <= >= < some < any < all (etc. ... for all comparison operators)
= != like
and exists for all
or
.. :
,
(identifier) This is the cast operator.
order
having
group by
where
from
select

Chapter 5

C++ Binding

5.1 Introduction

This chapter defines the C++ binding for ODL/OML.

ODL stands for Object Definition Language. It is the declarative portion of C++ ODL/OML. The C++ binding of ODL is expressed as a library that provides classes and functions to implement the concepts defined in the ODMG Object Model. OML stands for Object Manipulation Language. It is the language used for retrieving objects from the database and modifying them. The C++ OML syntax and semantics are those of standard C++ in the context of the standard class library.

ODL/OML specifies only the logical characteristics of objects and the operations used to manipulate them. It does not discuss the physical storage of objects. It does not address the clustering or memory management issues associated with the stored physical representation of objects or access structures like indices used to accelerate object retrieval. In an ideal world these would be transparent to the programmer. In the real world they are not. An additional set of constructs called *physical pragmas* is defined to give the programmer some direct control over these issues, or at least to enable a programmer to provide "hints" to the storage management subsystem provided as part of the ODBMS runtime. Physical pragmas exist within the ODL and OML. They are added to object type definitions specified in ODL, expressed as OML operations, or shown as optional arguments to operations defined within OML. Because these pragmas are not in any sense a stand-alone language, but rather a set of constructs added to ODL/OML to address implementation issues, they are included within the relevant subsections of this chapter.

The chapter is organized as follows. Section 5.2 discusses the ODL. Section 5.3 discusses the OML. Section 5.4 discusses OQL—the distinguished subset of OML that supports associative retrieval. Associative retrieval is access based on the values of the properties of objects rather than on their IDs or names. Section 5.6 provides an example program.

5.1.1 Language Design Principles

The programming language–specific bindings for ODL/OML are based on one basic principle: The programmer feels that there is one language, not two separate languages with arbitrary boundaries between them. This principle has two corollaries that are evident in the design of the C++ binding defined in the body of this chapter:

1. There is a single unified type system across the programming language and the database; individual instances of these common types can be persistent or transient.
2. The programming language–specific binding for ODL/OML respects the syntax and semantics of the base programming language into which it is being inserted.

5.1.2 Language Binding

The C++ binding maps the Object Model into C++ by introducing a set of classes that can have both persistent and transient instances. These classes are informally referred to as "persistence-capable classes" in the body of this chapter. These classes are distinct from the normal classes defined by the C++ language, all of whose instances are transient; that is, they don't outlive the execution of the process in which they were created. Where it is necessary to distinguish between these two categories of classes, the former are called "persistence-capable classes"; the latter are referred to as "transient classes."

The C++ to ODBMS language binding approach described by this standard is based on the smart pointer or "Ref-based" approach. For each persistence-capable class T, an ancillary class d_Ref<T> is defined. Instances of persistence-capable classes are then referenced using parameterized references, e.g.,

```
(1) d_Ref<Professor>     profP;
(2) d_Ref<Department>  deptRef;
(3) profP->grant_tenure();
(4) deptRef = profP->dept;
```

Statement (1) declares the object profP as an instance of the type d_Ref<Professor>. Statement (2) declares deptRef as an instance of the type d_Ref<Department>. Statement (3) invokes the grant_tenure operation defined on class Professor, on the instance of that class referred to by profP. Statement (4) assigns the value of the dept attribute of the professor referenced by profP to the variable deptRef.

Instances of persistence-capable classes may contain embedded members of C++ built-in types, user-defined classes, or pointers to transient data. Applications may refer to such embedded members using C++ pointers (*) or references (&) only during the execution of a transaction.

In this chapter we use the following terms to describe the places where the standard is formally considered undefined or allows for an implementor of one of the bindings to make implementation-specific decisions with respect to implementing the standard. The terms are

> *Undefined:* The behavior is unspecified by the standard. Implementations have complete freedom (can do anything or nothing), and the behavior need not be documented by the implementor or vendor.
>
> *Implementation-defined:* The behavior is specified by each implementor/vendor. The implementor/vendor is allowed to make implementation-specific decisions about the behavior. However, the behavior must be well defined and fully documented and published as part of the vendor's implementation of the standard.

Figure 5-1 shows the hierarchy of languages involved, as well as the preprocess, compile, and link steps that generate an executable application.

5.1.3 Mapping the ODMG Object Model into C++

Although C++ provides a powerful data model that is close to the one presented in Chapter 2, it is worth trying to explain more precisely how concepts introduced in Chapter 2 map into concrete C++ constructs.

5.1.3.1 Object and Literal

An ODMG object type maps into a C++ class. Depending on how a C++ class is instantiated, the result can be an ODMG object or an ODMG literal. A C++ object embedded as a member within an enclosing class is treated as an ODMG literal. This is explained by the fact that a block of memory is inserted into the enclosing object and belongs entirely to it. For instance, one cannot copy the enclosing object without getting a copy of the embedded one at the same time. In this sense the embedded object cannot be considered as having an identity, since it acts as a literal.

5.1.3.2 Structure

The Object Model notion of a *structure* maps into the C++ construct *struct* or *class* embedded in a class.

5.1.3.3 Implementation

C++ has implicit the notion of dividing a class definition into two parts: its interface (public part) and its implementation (protected and private members and function definitions). However, in C++ only one implementation is possible for a given class.

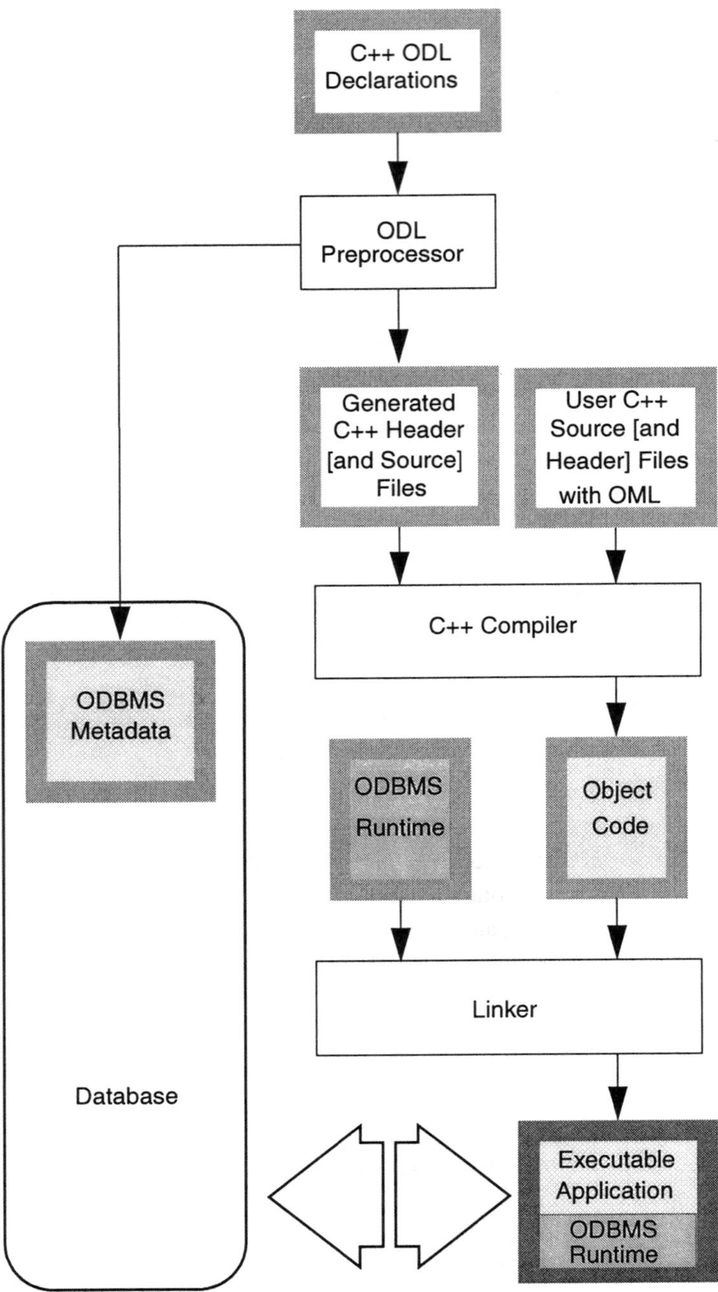

Figure 5-1. Language Hierarchy

5.1.3.4 Collection Classes

The ODMG Object Model includes collection type generators, collection types, and collection instances. Collection type generators are represented as *template classes* in C++. Collection types are represented as collection classes, and collection instances are represented as instances of these collection classes. To illustrate these three categories:

```
template<class T> class d_Set : public d_Collection<T> { ... };
class Ship { ... };
d_Set<d_Ref<Ship> > Cunard_Line;
```

d_Set<T> is a collection template class. d_Set<d_Ref<Ship> > is a collection class. And Cunard_Line is a particular collection, an instance of the class d_Set<d_Ref<Ship> >.

The subtype/supertype hierarchy of collection types defined in the ODMG Object Model is directly carried over into C++. The type d_Collection<T> is an abstract class in C++ with no direct instances. It is instantiable only through its derived classes. The only differences between the collection classes in the C++ binding and their counterparts in the Object Model are the following:

- Named operations in the Object Model are mapped to C++ function members.
- For some operations, the C++ binding includes both the named function and an overloaded infix operation, e.g., d_Set::union_with also has the form operator+=. The statements s1.union_with(s2) and s1 += s2 are functionally equivalent.
- Operations that return a boolean in the Object Model are modeled as function members that return a d_Boolean in the C++ binding.
- The create and delete operations defined in the Object Model have been replaced with C++ constructors and destructors.

5.1.3.5 Array

C++ provides a syntax for creating and accessing a contiguous and indexable sequence of objects. This has been chosen to map partially to the ODMG Array collection. To complement it, a d_Varray C++ class is also provided, which implements an array whose upper bound may vary.

5.1.3.6 Relationship

Relationships are not directly supported by C++. Instead, they are supported in ODMG by including instances of specific template classes that provide the maintenance of the relationship.

The relation itself is implemented as a reference (one-to-one relation) or as a collection (one-to-many relation) embedded in the object.

5.1.3.7 Extents

The class d_Extent<T> provides an interface to the extent for a persistence-capable class T in the C++ binding.

5.1.3.8 Keys

Key declarations are not supported by C++.

5.1.3.9 Names

The previous releases only allowed one name per object in the C++ binding. Now an object can have multiple names. The bind operation in the Object Model is implemented in C++ with the set_object_name and rename_object methods to maintain backward compatibility with previous releases of the C++ binding.

5.1.4 Use of C++ Language Features

5.1.4.1 Prefix

The global names in the ODMG interface will have a prefix of d_. The intention is to avoid name collisions with other names in the global namespace. The ODMG will keep the prefix even after C++ namespaces are generally available.

5.1.4.2 Namespaces

The namespace feature added to C++ did not have generally available implementations at the time this specification was written. In the future the ODMG plans to utilize namespaces and intends to use odmg as its namespace name.

5.1.4.3 Exception Handling

When error conditions are detected, an instance of class d_Error is thrown using the standard C++ exception mechanism. Class d_Error is derived from the class exception defined in the C++ standard.

5.1.4.4 Preprocessor Identifier

A preprocessor identifier, __ODMG_93__, is defined for conditional compilation. With ODMG 2.0 the following symbol:

```
#define __ODMG__ 20
```

is defined. The value of this symbol indicates the specific ODMG release, for example, 20 (release 2.0), 21 (release 2.1), or 30 (release 3.0).

5.1.4.5 Implementation Extensions

Implementations must provide the full function signatures for all the interface methods specified in the chapter and may provide variants on these methods, with additional parameters. Each additional parameter must have a default value. This allows applications that do not use the additional parameters to be portable.

5.2 C++ ODL

This section defines the C++ Object Definition Language. C++ ODL provides a description of the database schema as a set of object classes—including their attributes, relationships, and operations—in a syntactic style that is consistent with that of the declarative portion of a C++ program. Instances of these classes can be manipulated through the C++ OML.

Following is an example declaring type Professor:

```
extern const char _professors[ ];
extern const char _advisor [ ];

class Professor : public d_Object {
public:
// properties:
    d_UShort                                age;
    d_UShort                                id_number;
    d_String                                office_number;
    d_String                                name;
    d_Rel_Ref<Department, _professors>      dept;
    d_Rel_Set<Student, _advisor>            advisees;
// operations:
    void                                    grant_tenure();
    void                                    assign_course(Course &);
private:
            ...
};

const char _professors [ ] = "professors";
const char _advisor [ ] = "advisor";
```

The syntax for a C++ ODL class declaration is identical to a C++ class declaration. Attribute declarations map to a restricted set of C++ data member declarations. The variables _professors and _advisor are used for establishing an association between the two ends of a relationship.

Static data members of classes are not contained within each individual instance but are of static storage class. Thus static data members are not stored in the database, but are supported for persistence-capable classes. Supertypes are specified using the standard C++ syntax within the class header, e.g., class Professor : public Employee. Though this specification may use public members for ease and brevity, private and protected members are supported.

5.2.1 Attribute Declarations

Attribute declarations are syntactically identical to data member declarations within C++. Because notions of attributes as objects are not yet defined and included in this standard, attributes and data members are not and cannot be syntactically distinguished. In this standard, an attribute cannot have properties (e.g., unit of measure) and there is no way to specialize the get_value and set_value operations defined on the type (e.g., to raise an event when a value is changed).

Standard C++ syntax and semantics for class definitions are supported. However, compliant implementations need not support the following data types within persistent classes:

- unions
- bit fields
- references(&)

as members. Unions and bit fields pose problems when supporting heterogeneous environments. The semantics of references is that they are initialized once at creation; all subsequent operations are directed to the referenced object. References within persistent objects cannot be reinitialized when brought from the database into memory and their initialization value would, in general, not be valid across process boundaries. A set of special classes is defined within the ODMG specification to contain references to persistent objects.

In addition to all primitive data types, except those noted above, structures and class objects can be members. There are several structured literal types that are provided. These include:

- d_String
- d_Interval
- d_Date
- d_Time
- d_Timestamp

Examples:

```
struct University_Address {
        d_UShort    PO_box;
        d_String    university;
        d_String    city;
        d_String    state;
        d_String    zip_code;
};
```

```
class Student : public d_Object {
public:
    d_String            name;
    d_Date              birth_date;
    Phone_Number        dorm_phone;
    University_Address  address;
    d_List<d_String>    favorite_friends;
};
```

The attribute name takes a d_String as its value. The attribute dorm_phone takes a user-defined type Phone_Number as its value. The attribute address takes a structure. The attribute favorite_friends takes a d_List of d_String as its value. The following sections contain descriptions of the provided literal types.

5.2.1.1 Fixed-Length Types

In addition to the C++ built-in data types, such as the signed, unsigned, and floating point numeric data types, the following fixed-length types will be supported for use in defining attributes of persistence capable classes.

Type Name	Range	Description
d_Short	16 bit	signed integer
d_Long	32 bit	signed integer
d_UShort	16 bit	unsigned integer
d_ULong	32 bit	unsigned integer
d_Float	32 bit	IEEE Std 754-1985 single-precision floating point
d_Double	64 bit	IEEE Std 754-1985 double-precision floating point
d_Char	8 bit	ASCII
d_Octet	8 bit	no interpretation
d_Boolean	d_True or d_False	defines d_True (nonzero value) and d_False (zero value)

Unlike the C++ built-in types, these types have the same range and interpretation on all platforms and environments. Use of these types is recommended when developing applications targeted for heterogeneous environments. Note that like all other global names described in this chapter, these types will be defined within the ODMG namespace when that feature becomes available.

Any ODMG implementation that allows access to a database from applications that have been constructed with different assumptions about the range or interpretation of the C++ built-in types may require the use of the fixed-length data types listed above when defining attributes of persistent objects. The behavior of the database system in such a heterogeneous environment when the C++ built-in types are used for persistent data attributes is undefined.

ODMG implementations will allow but not require the use of the fixed-length data types when used in homogeneous environments.

For any given C++ language environment or platform, these fixed-length data types may be defined as identical to a built-in C++ data type that conforms to the range and interpretation requirements. Since a given C++ built-in data type may meet the requirements in some environments but not in others, portable application code should not assume any correspondence or lack of correspondence between the fixed-length data types and similar C++ built-in data types. In particular, function overloads should not be disambiguated solely on the difference between a fixed-length data type and a closely corresponding C++ built-in data type. Also, different implementations of a virtual function should use signatures that correspond exactly to the declaration in the base class with respect to use of fixed-length data types versus C++ built-in data types.

5.2.1.2 d_String

The following class defines a literal type to be used for string attributes. It is intended that this class is used strictly for storing strings in the database, as opposed to being a general string class with all the functionality of a string class normally used for transient strings in an application.

Initialization, assignment, copying, and conversion to and from C++ character strings are supported. The comparison operators are defined on d_String to compare with either another d_String or a C++ character string. One can also access an element in the d_String via an index and also determine the length of the d_String.

Definition:

```
class d_String {
public:
                            d_String();
                            d_String(const d_String &);
                            d_String(const char *);
                            ~d_String();
        d_String &          operator=(const d_String &);
        d_String &          operator=(const char *);
                            operator const char *() const;
        char &              operator[](unsigned long index);
        unsigned long       length() const;
```

```
friend d_Boolean     operator==(const d_String &sL, const d_String &sR);
friend d_Boolean     operator==(const d_String &sL, const char *pR);
friend d_Boolean     operator==(const char *pL, const d_String &sR);
friend d_Boolean     operator!= (const d_String &sL, const d_String &sR);
friend d_Boolean     operator!= (const d_String &sL, const char *pR);
friend d_Boolean     operator!= (const char *pL, const d_String &sR);
friend d_Boolean     operator<  (const d_String &sL, const d_String &sR);
friend d_Boolean     operator<  (const d_String &sL, const char *pR);
friend d_Boolean     operator<  (const char *pL, const d_String &sR);
friend d_Boolean     operator<=(const d_String &sL, const d_String &sR);
friend d_Boolean     operator<=(const d_String &sL, const char *pR);
friend d_Boolean     operator<=(const char *pL, const d_String &sR);
friend d_Boolean     operator>  (const d_String &sL, const d_String &sR);
friend d_Boolean     operator>  (const d_String &sL, const char *pR);
friend d_Boolean     operator>  (const char *pL, const d_String &sR);
friend d_Boolean     operator>=(const d_String &sL, const d_String &sR);
friend d_Boolean     operator>=(const d_String &sL, const char *pR);
friend d_Boolean     operator>=(const char *pL, const d_String &sR);
};
```

Class d_String is responsible for freeing the string that gets returned by operator const char *.

5.2.1.3 d_Interval

The d_Interval class is used to represent a duration of time. It is also used to perform arithmetic operations on the d_Date, d_Time, and d_Timestamp classes. This class corresponds to the day-time interval as defined in the SQL standard.

Initialization, assignment, arithmetic, and comparison functions are defined on the class, as well as member functions to access the time components of its current value.

The d_Interval class accepts nonnormalized input, but normalizes the time components when accessed. For example, the constructor would accept 28 hours as input, but then calling the day function would return a value of 1 and the hour function would return a value of 4. Arithmetic would work in a similar manner.

Definition:

```
class d_Interval {
public:
                    d_Interval(int day = 0, int hour = 0,int min = 0, float sec = 0.0);
                    d_Interval(const d_Interval &);
    d_Interval &    operator=(const d_Interval &);
    int             day() const;
```

```
        int             hour() const;
        int             minute() const;
        float           second() const;
        d_Boolean       is_zero() const;
        d_Interval &    operator+=(const d_Interval &);
        d_Interval &    operator-=(const d_Interval &);
        d_Interval &    operator*=(int);
        d_Interval &    operator/=(int);
        d_Interval      operator-() const;
    friend d_Interval   operator+(const d_Interval &L, const d_Interval &R);
    friend d_Interval   operator-(const d_Interval &L, const d_Interval &R);
    friend d_Interval   operator*(const d_Interval &L, int R);
    friend d_Interval   operator*(int L, const d_Interval &R);
    friend d_Interval   operator/ (const d_Interval &L, int R);
    friend d_Boolean    operator==(const d_Interval &L, const d_Interval &R);
    friend d_Boolean    operator!= (const d_Interval &L, const d_Interval &R);
    friend d_Boolean    operator< (const d_Interval &L, const d_Interval &R);
    friend d_Boolean    operator<=(const d_Interval &L, const d_Interval &R);
    friend d_Boolean    operator> (const d_Interval &L, const d_Interval &R);
    friend d_Boolean    operator>=(const d_Interval &L, const d_Interval &R);
    };
```

5.2.1.4 d_Date

The d_Date class stores a representation of a date consisting of a year, month, and day. It also provides enumerations to denote weekdays and months.

Initialization, assignment, arithmetic, and comparison functions are provided. Implementations may have additional functions available to support converting to and from the type used by the operating system to represent a date. Functions are provided to access the components of a date. There are also functions to determine the number of days in a month, etc. The static function current returns the current date. The next and previous functions advance the date to the next specified weekday.

Definition:

```
class d_Date {
public:
    enum Weekday {
        Sunday = 0,      Monday = 1,     Tuesday = 2,    Wednesday = 3,
        Thursday = 4,    Friday = 5,     Saturday = 6
    };
    enum Month {
```

```
        January = 1,   February = 2,   March = 3,   April = 4,   May = 5,   June = 6,
        July = 7,   August = 8,   September = 9,   October = 10,   November = 11,
        December = 12
    };
                        d_Date();            // sets to current date
                        d_Date(unsigned short year, unsigned short day_of_year);
                        d_Date(unsigned short year, unsigned short month,
                               unsigned short day);
                        d_Date(const d_Date &);
                        d_Date(const d_Timestamp &);
    d_Date &            operator=(const d_Date &);
    d_Date &            operator=(const d_Timestamp &);
    unsigned short      year() const;
    unsigned short      month() const;
    unsigned short      day() const;
    unsigned short      day_of_year() const;
    Weekday             day_of_week() const;
    Month               month_of_year() const;
    d_Boolean           is_leap_year() const;
static  d_Boolean       is_leap_year(unsigned short year);
static  d_Date          current();
    d_Date &            next(Weekday);
    d_Date &            previous(Weekday);
    d_Date &            operator+=(const d_Interval &);
    d_Date &            operator+=(int ndays);
    d_Date &            operator++();         // prefix  ++d
    d_Date              operator++(int);      // postfix  d++
    d_Date &            operator-=(const d_Interval &);
    d_Date &            operator-=(int ndays);
    d_Date &            operator--();         // prefix --d
    d_Date              operator--(int);      // postfix  d--
friend  d_Date          operator+(const d_Date &L, const d_Interval &R);
friend  d_Date          operator+(const d_Interval &L, const d_Date &R);
friend  d_Interval      operator-(const d_Date &L, const d_Date &R);
friend  d_Date          operator-(const d_Date &L, const d_Interval &R);
friend  d_Boolean       operator==(const d_Date &L, const d_Date &R);
friend  d_Boolean       operator!= (const d_Date &L, const d_Date &R);
friend  d_Boolean       operator<  (const d_Date &L, const d_Date &R);
friend  d_Boolean       operator<=(const d_Date &L, const d_Date &R);
friend  d_Boolean       operator>  (const d_Date &L, const d_Date &R);
friend  d_Boolean       operator>=(const d_Date &L, const d_Date &R);
```

```
    d_Boolean          is_between(const d_Date &, const d_Date &) const;
friend d_Boolean       overlaps(const d_Date &psL, const d_Date &peL,
                                const d_Date &psR, const d_Date &peR);
friend d_Boolean       overlaps(const d_Timestamp &sL, const d_Timestamp &eL,
                                const d_Date &sR, const d_Date &eR);
friend d_Boolean       overlaps(const d_Date &sL, const d_Date &eL,
                                const d_Timestamp &sR, const d_Timestamp &eR);
static int             days_in_year(unsigned short year);
       int             days_in_year() const;
static int             days_in_month(unsigned short yr, unsigned short month);
       int             days_in_month() const;
static d_Boolean       is_valid_date(unsigned short year, unsigned short month,
                                     unsigned short day);
};
```

If an attempt is made to set a d_Date object to an invalid value, a d_Error exception object of kind d_Error_DateInvalid is thrown and the value of the d_Date object is undefined.

The functions next, previous, operator+=, and operator-= alter the object and return a reference to the current object. The post increment and decrement operators return a new object by value.

The overlaps functions take two periods (start and end), each period denoted by a start and end time, and determines whether the two time periods overlap. The is_between function determines whether the d_Date value is within a given period.

5.2.1.5 d_Time

The d_Time class is used to denote a specific time, which is internally stored in Greenwich Mean Time (GMT). Initialization, assignment, arithmetic, and comparison operators are defined. There are also functions to access each of the components of a time value. Implementations may have additional functions available to support converting to and from the type used by the operating system to represent a time.

The enumeration Time_Zone is made available to denote a specific time zone. Time zones are numbered according to the number of hours that must be added or subtracted from local time to get the time in Greenwich, England (GMT). Thus the value of GMT is 0. A Time_Zone name of GMT6 indicates a time of 6 hours greater than GMT, and thus 6 must be subtracted from it to get GMT. Conversely, GMT_8 means that the time is 8 hours earlier than GMT (read the underscore as a minus). A default time zone value is maintained and is initially set to the local time zone. It is possible to change the default time zone value as well as reset it to the local value.

Definition:

```
class d_Time {
public:
     enum Time_Zone {
          GMT   = 0,  GMT12 = 12,    GMT_12 = –12,
          GMT1 = 1,   GMT_1 = –1,    GMT2 = 2,       GMT_2 = –2,
          GMT3 = 3,   GMT_3 =  –3,   GMT4 = 4,       GMT_4 = –4,
          GMT5 = 5,   GMT_5 = –5,    GMT6 = 6,       GMT_6 = –6,
          GMT7 = 7,   GMT_7 = –7,    GMT8 = 8,       GMT_8 = –8,
          GMT9 = 9,   GMT_9 = –9,    GMT10 = 10,     GMT_10 = –10,
          GMT11 = 11, GMT_11 = –11,
          USeastern = –5,  UScentral = –6, USmountain = –7, USpacific = –8
     };
static   void             set_default_Time_Zone(Time_Zone);
static   void             set_default_Time_Zone_to_local();
                          d_Time();
                          d_Time(unsigned short hour,
                                    unsigned short minute, float sec = 0.0f);
                          d_Time(unsigned short hour, unsigned short minute,
                                    float sec, short tzhour, short tzminute);
                          d_Time(const d_Time &);
                          d_Time(const d_Timestamp &);
     d_Time &             operator=(const d_Time &);
     d_Time &             operator=(const d_Timestamp &);
     unsigned short       hour() const;
     unsigned short       minute() const;
     Time_Zone            time_zone() const;
     float                second() const;
     short                tz_hour() const;
     short                tz_minute() const;
static   d_Time           current();
     d_Time &             operator+=(const d_Interval &);
     d_Time &             operator–=(const d_Interval &);
friend  d_Time            operator+(const d_Time &L, const d_Interval &R);
friend  d_Time            operator+(const d_Interval &L, const d_Time &R);
friend  d_Interval        operator–(const d_Time &L, const d_Time &R);
friend  d_Time            operator–(const d_Time &L, const d_Interval &R);
friend  d_Boolean         operator==(const d_Time &L, const d_Time &R);
friend  d_Boolean         operator!= (const d_Time &L, const d_Time &R);
friend  d_Boolean         operator<  (const d_Time &L, const d_Time &R);
```

```
friend d_Boolean    operator<=(const d_Time &L, const d_Time &R);
friend d_Boolean    operator> (const d_Time &L, const d_Time &R);
friend d_Boolean    operator>=(const d_Time &L, const d_Time &R);
friend d_Boolean    overlaps(const d_Time &psL, const d_Time &peL,
                             const d_Time &psR, const d_Time &peR);
friend d_Boolean    overlaps(const d_Timestamp &sL, const d_Timestamp &eL,
                             const d_Time &sR, const d_Time &eR);
friend d_Boolean    overlaps(const d_Time &sL, const d_Time &eL,
                             const d_Timestamp &sR, const d_Timestamp &eR);
};
```

All arithmetic on d_Time is done on a modulo 24-hour basis. If an attempt is made to set a d_Time object to an invalid value, a d_Error exception object of kind d_Error_TimeInvalid is thrown and the value of the d_Time object is undefined.

The default d_Time constructor initializes the object to the current time. The overlaps functions take two periods, each denoted by a start and end time, and determines whether the two time periods overlap.

5.2.1.6 d_Timestamp

A d_Timestamp consists of both a date and time.

Definition:

```
class d_Timestamp {
public:
                    d_Timestamp();      // sets to the current date/time
                    d_Timestamp(unsigned short year, unsigned short month=1,
                          unsigned short day = 1, unsigned short hour = 0,
                          unsigned short minute = 0, float sec = 0.0);
                    d_Timestamp(const d_Date &);
                    d_Timestamp(const d_Date &, const d_Time &);
                    d_Timestamp(const d_Timestamp &);
    d_Timestamp &   operator=(const d_Timestamp &);
    d_Timestamp &   operator=(const d_Date &);
    const d_Date &  date() const;
    const d_Time &  time() const;
    unsigned short  year() const;
    unsigned short  month() const;
    unsigned short  day() const;
    unsigned short  hour() const;
    unsigned short  minute() const;
    float           second() const;
    short           tz_hour() const;
    short           tz_minute() const;
```

```
static  d_Timestamp  current();
        d_Timestamp &  operator+=(const d_Interval &);
        d_Timestamp &  operator-=(const d_Interval &);
friend  d_Timestamp  operator+(const d_Timestamp &L, const d_Interval &R);
friend  d_Timestamp  operator+(const d_Interval &L, const d_Timestamp &R);
friend  d_Timestamp  operator-(const d_Timestamp &L, const d_Interval &R);
friend  d_Interval   operator-(const d_Timestamp &L, const d_Timestamp &R);
friend  d_Boolean    operator==(const d_Timestamp &L, const d_Timestamp &R);
friend  d_Boolean    operator!= (const d_Timestamp &L, const d_Timestamp &R);
friend  d_Boolean    operator<  (const d_Timestamp &L, const d_Timestamp &R);
friend  d_Boolean    operator<=(const d_Timestamp &L, const d_Timestamp &R);
friend  d_Boolean    operator>  (const d_Timestamp &L, const d_Timestamp &R);
friend  d_Boolean    operator>=(const d_Timestamp &L, const d_Timestamp &R);
friend  d_Boolean    overlaps(const d_Timestamp &sL, const d_Timestamp &eL,
                         const d_Timestamp &sR, const d_Timestamp &eR);
friend  d_Boolean    overlaps(const d_Timestamp &sL, const d_Timestamp &eL,
                         const d_Date &sR, const d_Date &eR);
friend  d_Boolean    overlaps(const d_Date &sL, const d_Date &eL,
                         const d_Timestamp &sR, const d_Timestamp &eR);
friend  d_Boolean    overlaps(const d_Timestamp &sL, const d_Timestamp &eL,
                         const d_Time &sR, const d_Time &eR);
friend  d_Boolean    overlaps(const d_Time &sL, const d_Time &eL,
                         const d_Timestamp &sR, const d_Timestamp &eR);
};
```

If an attempt is made to set the value of a d_Timestamp object to an invalid value, a d_Error exception object of kind d_Error_TimestampInvalid is thrown and the value of the d_Timestamp object is undefined.

5.2.2 Relationship Traversal Path Declarations

Relationships do not have syntactically separate definitions. Instead, the *traversal paths* used to cross relationships are defined within the bodies of the definitions of each of the two object types that serve a role in the relationship. For example, if there is a one-to-many relationship between professors and the students they have as advisees, then the traversal path advisees is defined within the type definition of the object type Professor, and the traversal path advisor is defined within the type definition of the object type Student.

A relationship traversal path declaration is similar to an attribute declaration, but with the following differences. Each end of a relationship has a relationship traversal path. A traversal path declaration is an attribute declaration and must be of type

- d_Rel_Ref<T, const char *> (which has the interface of d_Ref<T>)
- d_Rel_Set<T, const char *> (which has the interface of d_Set<d_Ref<T> >)
- d_Rel_List<T, const char *> (which has the interface of d_List<d_Ref<T> >)

for some persistent class T. The second template argument should be a variable that contains the name of the attribute in the other class, which serves as the inverse role in the relationship. Both classes in a relationship must have a member of one of these types, and the members of the two classes must refer to each other. If the second template argument has a name that does not correspond to a data member in the referenced class, a d_Error exception object of kind d_Error_MemberNotFound is thrown. If the second template argument does refer to a data member, but the data member is the wrong type, i.e., it is not of type d_Rel_Ref, d_Rel_Set, or d_Rel_List, a d_Error exception object of kind d_Error_MemberIsOfInvalidType is thrown.

Studying the relationships in the examples below will make this clear.

Examples:

```
extern const char _dept [ ],      _professors [ ] ;
extern const char _advisor [ ],   _advisees [ ] ;
extern const char _classes [ ],   _enrolled [ ] ;

class Department : public d_Object {
public:
     d_Rel_Set<Professor, _dept>               professors;
};
class Professor : public d_Object {
public:
     d_Rel_Ref<Department, _professors>  dept;
     d_Rel_Set<Student, _advisor>              advisees;
};
class Student : public d_Object {
public:
     d_Rel_Ref<Professor, _advisees>         advisor;
     d_Rel_Set<Course, _enrolled>              classes;
};
class Course : public d_Object {
public:
     d_Rel_Set<Student, _classes>              students_enrolled;
};
const char _dept [ ] = "dept";
const char _professors [ ] = "professors";
```

```
const char _advisor [ ] = "advisor";
const char _advisees [ ] = "advisees";
const char _classes [ ] = "classes" ;
const char _enrolled [ ] = "students_enrolled";
```

The second template parameter is based on the address of the variable, not on the string contents. Thus a different variable is required for each role, even if the member name happens to be the same. The string contents must match the name of the member in the other class involved in the relationship.

The referential integrity of bidirectional relationships is automatically maintained. If a relationship exists between two objects and one of the objects gets deleted, the relationship is considered to no longer exist and the inverse traversal path will be altered to remove the relationship.

5.2.3 Operation Declarations

Operation declarations in C++ are syntactically identical to *function member* declarations. For example, see grant_tenure and assign_course defined for class Professor in Section 5.2.

5.3 C++ OML

This section describes the C++ binding for the OML. A guiding principle in the design of C++ OML is that the syntax used to create, delete, identify, reference, get/set property values, and invoke operations on a persistent object should be, so far as possible, no different than that used for objects of shorter lifetimes. A single expression may freely intermix references to persistent and transient objects.

While it is our long-term goal that nothing can be done with persistent objects that cannot also be done with transient objects, this standard treats persistent and transient objects slightly differently. Queries and transaction consistency apply only to persistent objects.

5.3.1 Object Creation, Deletion, Modification, and References

Objects can be created, deleted, and modified. Objects are created in C++ OML using the new operator, which is overloaded to accept additional arguments specifying the lifetime of the object. An optional storage pragma allows the programmer to specify how the newly allocated object is to be clustered with respect to other objects.

The static member variable d_Database::transient_memory is defined in order to allow libraries that create objects to be used uniformly to create objects of any lifetime. This variable may be used as the value of the database argument to operator new to create objects of transient lifetime.

```
static d_Database * const d_Database::transient_memory;
```

The formal ODMG forms of the C++ new operator are

```
(1) void * operator new(size_t size);
(2) void * operator new(size_t size, const d_Ref_Any &clustering,
                        const char* typename);
(3) void * operator new(size_t size, d_Database *database,
                        const char* typename);
```

These operators have d_Object scope. (1) is used for creation of transient objects derived from d_Object. (2) and (3) create persistent objects. In (2) the user specifies that the newly created object should be placed "near" the existing clustering object. The exact interpretation of "near" is implementation-defined. An example interpretation would be "on the same page if possible." In (3) the user specifies that the newly created object should be placed in the specified database, but no further clustering is specified.

The size argument, which appears as the first argument in each signature, is the size of the representation of an object. It is determined by the compiler as a function of the class of which the new object is an instance, not passed as an explicit argument by a programmer writing in the language.

If the database does not have the schema information about a class when new is called, a d_Error exception object of kind d_Error_DatabaseClassUndefined is thrown.

Examples:

```
     d_Database *yourDB, *myDB; // assume these get initialized properly
(1)  d_Ref<Schedule> temp_sched1 = new Schedule;
(2)  d_Ref<Professor> prof2 = new(yourDB,"Professor") Professor;
(3)  d_Ref<Student> student1 = new(myDB, "Student") Student;
(4)  d_Ref<Student> student2 = new(student1, "Student") Student;
(5)  d_Ref<Student> temp_student =
         new(d_Database::transient_memory, "Student") Student;
```

Statement (1) creates a transient object temp_sched1. Statements (2)–(4) create persistent objects. Statement (2) creates a new instance of class Professor in the database yourDB. Statement (3) creates a new instance of class Student in the database myDB. Statement (4) does the same thing, except that it specifies that the new object, student2, should be placed close to student1. Statement (5) creates a transient object temp_student.

5.3.1.1 Object Deletion

Objects, once created, can be deleted in C++ OML using the d_Ref::delete_object member function. Using the delete operator on a pointer to a persistent object will also delete the object, as in standard C++ practice. Deleting an object is permanent, subject to transaction commit. The object is removed from memory and, if it is a persistent object, from the database. The d_Ref instance or pointer still exists in memory, but its reference value is undefined. An attempt to access the deleted object is implementation defined.

Example:

```
d_Ref<anyType> obj_ref;
 ...  // set obj_ref to refer to a persistent object
obj_ref.delete_object();
```

C++ requires the operand of delete to be a pointer, so the member function delete_object was defined to delete an object with just a d_Ref<T> reference to it.

5.3.1.2 Object Modification

The state of an object is modified by updating its properties or by invoking operations on it. Updates to persistent objects are made visible to other users of the database when the transaction containing the modifications commits.

Persistent objects that will be modified must communicate to the runtime ODBMS process the fact that their states will change. The ODBMS will then update the database with these new states at transaction commit time. Object change is communicated by invoking the d_Object::mark_modified member function, which is defined in Section 5.3.4 and is used as follows:

```
obj_ref->mark_modified();
```

The mark_modified function call is included in the constructor and destructor methods for persistence-capable classes, i.e., within class d_Object. The developer should include the call in any other methods that modify persistent objects, before the object is actually modified.

As a convenience, the programmer may omit calls to mark_modified on objects where classes have been compiled using an optional C++ OML preprocessor switch; the system will automatically detect when the objects are modified. In the default case, mark_modified calls are required, because in some ODMG implementations performance will be better when the programmer explicitly calls mark_modified. However, each time a persistent object is modified by a member update function provided explicitly by the ODMG classes, the mark_modified call is not necessary since it is done automatically.

5.3.1.3 Object References

Objects, whether persistent or not, may refer to other objects via object references. In C++ OML object references are instances of the template class d_Ref<T> (see Section 5.3.5). All accesses to persistent objects are made via methods defined on classes d_Ref, d_Object, and d_Database. The dereference operator –> is used to access members of the persistent object "addressed" by a given object reference. How an object reference is converted to a C++ pointer to the object is implementation-defined.

A dereference operation on an object reference always guarantees that the object referred to is returned or a d_Error exception object of kind d_Error_RefInvalid is thrown. The behavior of a reference is as follows. If an object reference refers to a persistent object that exists but is not in memory when a dereference is performed, it will be retrieved automatically from disk, mapped into memory, and returned as the result of the dereference. If the referenced object does not exist, a d_Error exception object of kind d_Error_RefInvalid is thrown. References to transient objects work exactly the same (at least on the surface) as references to persistent objects.

Any object reference may be set to a null reference or *cleared* to indicate the reference does not refer to an object.

The rules for when an object of one lifetime may refer to an object of another lifetime are a straightforward extension of the C++ rules for its two forms of transient objects—procedure coterminus and process coterminus. An object can always refer to another object of longer lifetime. An object can only refer to an object of shorter lifetime as long as the shorter-lived object exists.

A persistent object is retrieved from disk upon activation. It is the application's responsibility to initialize the values of any of that object's pointers to transient objects. When a persistent object is committed, the ODBMS sets its embedded d_Refs to transient objects to the null value.

5.3.1.4 Object Names

A database application generally will begin processing by accessing one or more critical objects and proceeding from there. These objects are in some sense "root" objects, in that they lead to interconnected webs of other objects. The ability to name an object and retrieve it later by that name facilitates this start-up capability. Named objects are also convenient in many other situations.

There is a single, flat name scope per database; thus all names in a particular database are unique. A name is not explicitly defined as an attribute of an object. The operations for manipulating names are defined in the d_Database class in Section 5.3.8.

5.3.2 Properties

5.3.2.1 Attributes

C++ OML uses standard C++ for accessing attributes. For example, assume prof has been initialized to reference a professor and we wish to modify its id_number:

```
prof->id_number = next_id;
cout << prof->id_number;
```

Modifying an attribute's value is considered a modification to the enclosing object instance. One must call mark_modified for the object before it is modified.

The C++ binding allows persistence-capable classes to embed instances of C++ classes, including other persistence-capable classes. However, embedded objects are not considered "independent objects" and have no object identity of their own. Users are not permitted to get a d_Ref to an embedded object. Just as with any attribute, modifying an embedded object is considered a modification to the enclosing object instance, and mark_modified for the enclosing object must be called before the embedded object is modified.

5.3.2.2 Relationships

The ODL specifies which relationships exist between object classes. Creating, traversing, and breaking relationships between instances are defined in the C++ OML. Both to-one and to-many traversal paths are supported by the OML. The integrity of relationships is maintained by the ODBMS.

The following diagrams will show graphically the effect of adding, modifying, and deleting relationships among classes. Each diagram is given a name to reflect the cardinality and resulting effect on the relationship. The name will begin with 1-1, 1-m, or m-m to denote the cardinality and will end in either N (no relationship), A (add a relationship), or M (modify a relationship). When a relationship is deleted, this will result in a state of having no relationship (N). A solid line is drawn to denote the explicit operation performed by the program, and a dashed line shows the side effect operation performed automatically by the ODBMS to maintain referential integrity.

The following template class allows one to specify a to-one relationship to a class T.

```
template <class T, const char *Member> class d_Rel_Ref : public d_Ref<T> { };
```

The template d_Rel_Ref<T,M> supports the same interface as d_Ref<T>. Implementations will redefine some functions to provide support for referential integrity.

The application programmer must introduce two const char * variables, one used at each end of the relationship to refer to the other end of the relationship, thus establishing the association of the two ends of the relationship. The variables must be initialized with the name of the attribute at the other end of the relationship.

Assume the following 1-1 relationship exists between class A and class B:

```
extern const char _ra [ ], _rb [ ] ;
class A {
    d_Rel_Ref<B, _ra>    rb;
};
```

```
class B {
        d_Rel_Ref<A, _rb>     ra;
};
const char _ra [ ] = "ra";
const char _rb [ ] = "rb";
```

Note that class A and B could be the same class, as well. In each of the diagrams below, there will be an instance of A called a or aa and an instance of B called b or bb. In the following scenario 1-1N there is no relationship between a and b.

1-1N: No relationship

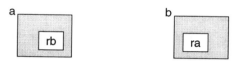

Then, adding a relationship between a and b via

```
a.rb = &b;
```

results in the following:

1-1A: Add a relationship

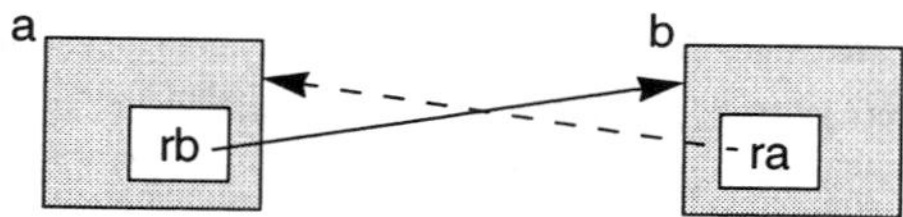

The solid arrow indicates the operation specified by the program, and the dashed line shows what operation gets performed automatically by the ODBMS.

Assume now the previous diagram (1-1A) represents the current state of the relationship between a and b. If the program executes the statement:

```
a.rb.clear ();
```

the result will be no relationship, as shown in 1-1N.

Assume we have the relationship depicted in 1-1A. If we now execute

```
a.rb = &bb;
```

we obtain the following:

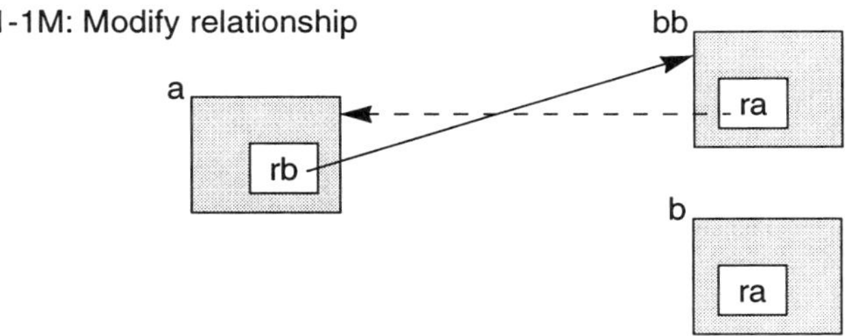

Notice that b.ra no longer refers to A and bb.ra is set automatically to reference a.

Whenever the operand to initialization or assignment represents a null reference, the result will be no relationship as in 1-1N. In the case of assignment, if there had been a relationship, it is removed. If the relationship is currently null (is_null would return true), then doing an assignment would add a relationship, unless the assignment operand was null as well.

If there is currently a relationship with an object, then doing the assignment will modify the relationship as in 1-1M. If the assignment operand is null, then the existing relationship is removed.

When an object involved in a relationship is deleted, all the relationships that the object was involved in will be removed as well.

There are two other cardinalities to consider: one-to-many and many-to-many. With one-to-many and many-to-many relationships, the set of operations allowed are based upon whether the relationship is an unordered set or positional.

The following template class allows one to specify an unordered to-many relationship with a class T:

```
template <class T, const char *M> class d_Rel_Set : public d_Set<d_Ref<T> > { }
```

The template d_Rel_Set<T,M> supports the same interface as d_Set<d_Ref<T> >. Implementations will redefine some functions in order to support referential integrity.

Assuming an unordered one-to-many set relationship between class A and class B:

```
extern const char _ra [ ], _sb [ ] ;

class A {
     d_Rel_Set<B, _ra>     sb;
};
class B {
     d_Rel_Ref<A, _sb>     ra;
};
```

```
const char _ra[ ] = "ra";
const char _sb[ ] = "sb";
```

Assume we have the following instances a and b with no relationship.

1-mN: No relationship

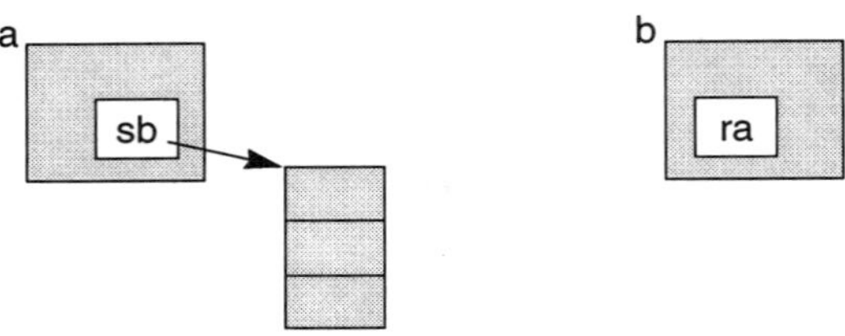

a.sb has 3 elements, but they are referring to instances of B other than b.

Now suppose we add a relationship between a and b by executing the statement

```
a.sb.insert_element (&b);
```

This results in the following:

1-mA: Add a relationship

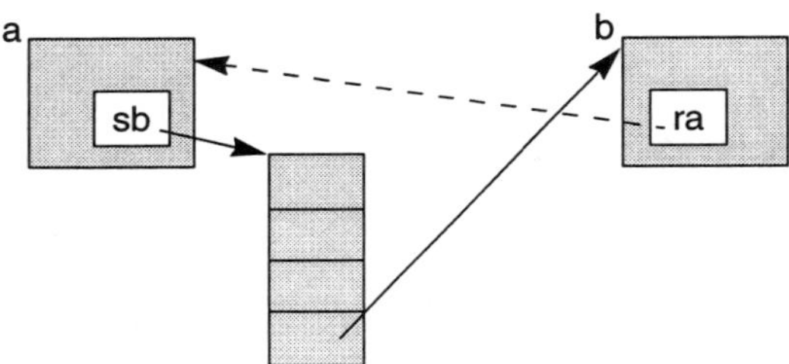

The b.ra traversal path gets set automatically to reference a. Conversely, if we execute the statement

```
b.ra = &a;
```

an element would have automatically been added to a.sb to refer to b. But only one of the two operations needs to be performed by the program; the ODBMS automatically updates the inverse traversal path.

Given the situation depicted in 1-mA, if we execute either

a.sb.remove_element (&b) or b.ra.clear ();

the result would be that the relationship between a and b would be deleted and the state of a and b would be as depicted in 1-mN.

Now assume we have the relationship between a and b as shown in 1-mA. If we execute the following statement:

```
b.ra = &aa;
```

this results in the following:

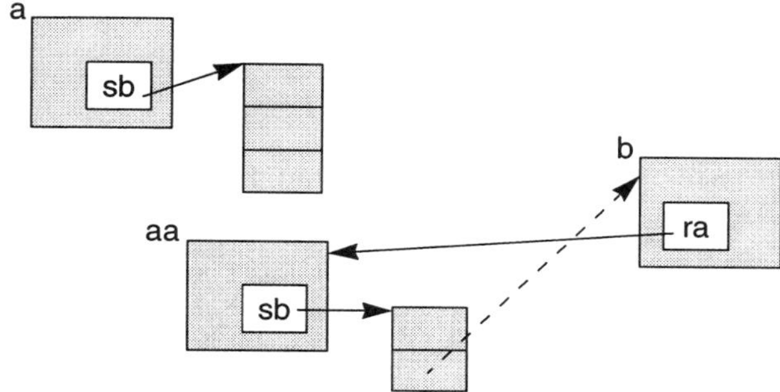

After the statement executes, b.ra refers to aa, and as a side effect, the element within a.sb that had referred to b is removed and an element is added to aa.sb to refer to b.

The d_List class represents a *positional* collection, whereas the d_Set class is an unordered collection. Likewise, the d_Rel_List<T, Member> template is used for representing relationships that are positional in nature.

```
template <class T, const char *M> class d_Rel_List : public d_List<d_Ref<T> > { };
```

The template d_Rel_List<T,M> has the same interface as d_List<d_Ref<T> >.

Assuming a positional to-many relationship between class A and class B:

```
extern const char _ra [ ] , _listB [ ] ;

class A {
     d_Rel_List<B, _ra>          listB;
};
class B {
     d_Rel_Ref<A, _listB>        ra;
};
const char _ra [ ] = "ra";
const char _listB [ ] = "listB";
```

The third relationship cardinality to consider is many-to-many. Suppose we have the following relationship between A and B:

```
extern const char _sa [ ], _sb [ ] ;

class A {
     d_Rel_Set<B, _sa>    sb;
};
```

```
class B {
    d_Rel_Set<A, _sb>    sa;
};
const char _sa [ ] = "sa";
const char _sb [ ] = "sb";
```

Initially, there will be no relationship between instances a and b though a and b have relationships with other instances.

m-mN: No relationship

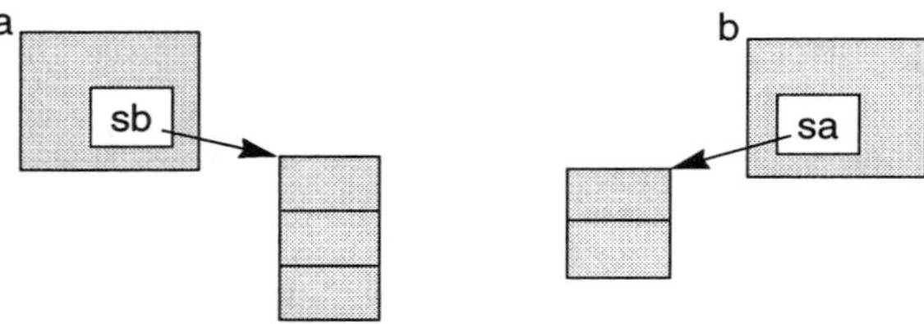

The following statement will add a relationship between a and b:

```
a.sb.insert_element (&b);
```

This will result in the following:

m-mA: Add a relationship

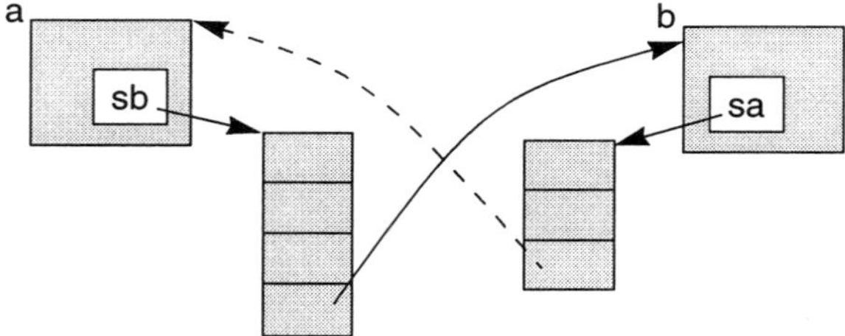

In addition to an element being added to a.sb to reference b, there is an element automatically added to b.sa that references a.

Executing either

a.sb.remove_element(&b) or b.sa.remove_element(&a)

would result in the relationship being removed between a and b, and the result would be as depicted in m-mN.

Last, we consider the modification of a many-to-many relationship. Assume the prior state is the situation depicted in m-mA, and assume that sb represents a positional relationship. The following statement will modify an existing relationship that exists between a and b, changing a to be related to bb.

```
a.sb.replace_element_at( &bb, 3);
```

This results in the following object relationships:

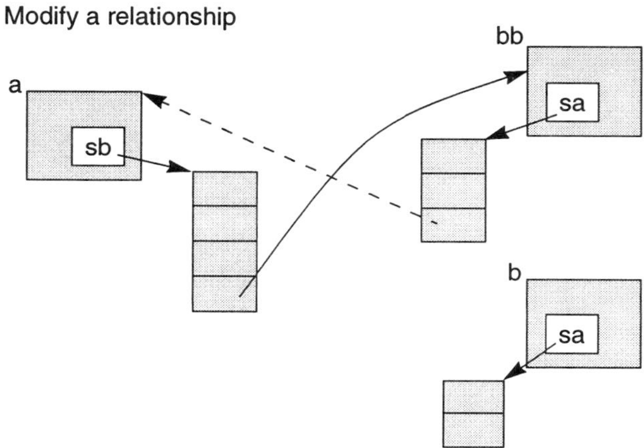

The result of this operation is that the element in b.sa that referenced a is removed and an element is added to bb.sa to reference a.

The initializations and assignments that have an argument of type d_Rel_Set<T,Member> or d_Set<d_Ref<T> > are much more involved than the simple diagrams above because they involve performing the corresponding operation for every element of the set versus doing it for just one element. The remove_all function removes every member of the relationship, also removing the back reference for each referenced member. If the assignment operators have an argument that represents an empty set, the assignment will have the same effect as the remove_all function.

Below are some more examples based on the classes used throughout the chapter.

Examples:

```
d_Ref<Professor> p;
d_Ref<Student> Sam;
d_Ref<Department> english_dept;
// initialize p, Sam, and english_dept references
p->dept = english_dept;  // create 1:1 relationship
p->dept.clear();         // clear the relationship
p->advisees.insert_element(Sam); // add Sam to the set of students that are p's
                                 // advisees; same effect as 'Sam->advisor = p'
p->advisees.remove_element(Sam); // remove Sam from the set of students that
                                 // are p's advisees, also clears Sam->advisor
```

5.3.3 Operations

Operations are defined in the OML as they are generally implemented in C++. Operations on transient and persistent objects behave entirely consistently with the operational context defined by standard C++. This includes all overloading, dispatching, function call structure and invocation, member function call structure and invocation, argument passing and resolution, error handling, and compile time rules.

5.3.4 d_Object Class

The class d_Object is introduced and defined as follows:

Definition:

```
class d_Object {
public:
                        d_Object();
                        d_Object(const d_Object &);
virtual                 ~d_Object();
     d_Object &         operator=(const d_Object &);
     void               mark_modified(); // mark the object as modified
     void *             operator new(size_t size);
     void *             operator new(size_t size, const d_Ref_Any &cluster,
                                  const char *typename);
     void *             operator new(size_t size, d_Database *database,
                                  const char *typename);
     void               operator delete(void *);
virtual    void         d_activate();
virtual    void         d_deactivate();
};
```

This class is introduced to allow the type definer to specify when a class is capable of having persistent as well as transient instances. Instances of classes derived from d_Object can be either persistent or transient. A class A that is persistence-capable would inherit from class d_Object:

```
class My_Class : public d_Object {...};
```

The delete operator can be used with a pointer to a persistent object to delete the object; the object is removed from both the application cache and the database, which is the same behavior as Ref<T>::delete_object.

An application needs to initialize and manage the transient members of a persistent object as the object enters and exits the application cache. Memory may need to be allocated and deallocated when these events occur, for example. The d_activate function is called when an object enters the application cache, and d_deactivate is called when the object exits the application cache. Normally C++ code uses the constructor and destructor to perform initialization and destruction, but in an ODMG implementation the constructor only gets called when an object is first created and the destructor is called at the point the object is deleted from the database. The following diagram depicts the calls made throughout the lifetime of an object.

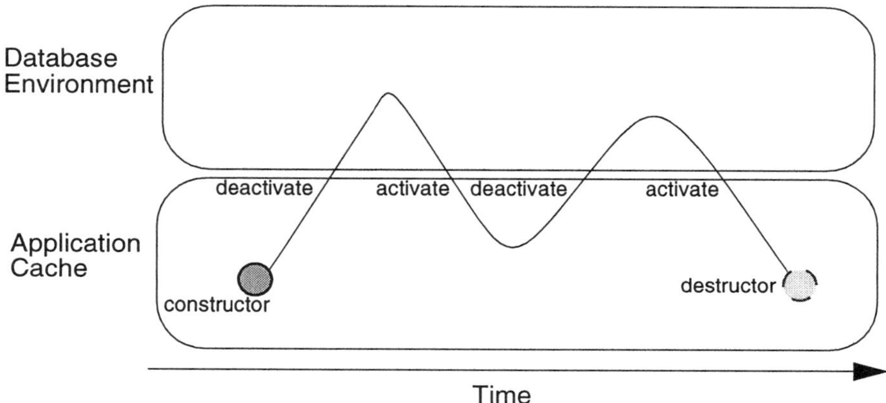

The object first gets initialized by the constructor. At the point the object exits the application cache, the d_deactivate function gets called. When the object reenters the application cache, d_activate gets called. This may get repeated many times, as the object moves in and out of an application cache. Eventually, the object gets deleted, in which case only the destructor gets called, not d_deactivate.

5.3.5 Reference Classes

Objects may refer to other objects through a smart pointer or reference called a d_Ref. A d_Ref<T> is a reference to an instance of type T. There is also a d_Ref_Any class defined that provides a generic reference to any type.

A d_Ref is a template class defined as follows:

Definition:

```
template <class T> class d_Ref {
public:
                    d_Ref();
                    d_Ref(T *fromPtr);
                    d_Ref(const d_Ref<T> &);
                    d_Ref(const d_Ref_Any &);
                    ~d_Ref();
                    operator d_Ref_Any() const;
    d_Ref<T> &      operator=(T *);
    d_Ref<T> &      operator=(const d_Ref<T>&);
```

```
        void            clear();
        T *             operator->() const;    // dereference the reference
        T &             operator*() const;
        T *             ptr() const;
        void            delete_object();  // delete referred object from memory
                                          // and the database
    // boolean predicates to check reference
        d_Boolean       operator!() const;
        d_Boolean       is_null() const;
    // do these d_Refs and pointers refer to the same objects?
    friend d_Boolean    operator==(const d_Ref<T> &refL, const d_Ref<T> &refR );
    friend d_Boolean    operator==(const d_Ref<T> &refL, const T *ptrR );
    friend d_Boolean    operator==(const T *ptrL, const d_Ref<T> &refR );
    friend d_Boolean    operator==(const d_Ref<T> &L, const d_Ref_Any &R);
    friend d_Boolean    operator!=(const d_Ref<T> &refL, const d_Ref<T> &refR);
    friend d_Boolean    operator!=(const d_Ref<T> &refL, const T *ptrR);
    friend d_Boolean    operator!=(const T *ptrL, const d_Ref<T> &refR);
    friend d_Boolean    operator!=(const d_Ref<T> &refL, const d_Ref_Any &anyR);
    };
```

References in many respects behave like C++ pointers but provide an additional mechanism that guarantees integrity in references to persistent objects. Although the syntax for declaring a d_Ref is different than for declaring a pointer, the usage is, in most cases, the same due to overloading; e.g., d_Refs may be dereferenced with the * operator, assigned with the = operator, etc. A d_Ref to a class may be assigned to a d_Ref to a superclass. d_Refs may be subclassed to provide specific referencing behavior.

There is one anomaly that results from the ability to do conversions between d_Ref<T> and d_Ref_Any. The following code will compile without error, and a d_Error exception object of kind d_Error_TypeInvalid is thrown at run-time versus statically at compile time. Suppose that X and Y are two unrelated classes:

```
d_Ref<X>    x;
d_Ref<Y>    y(x);
```

The initialization of y via x will be done via a conversion to d_Ref_Any. One should avoid such initializations in their application.

The pointer or reference returned by operator–> or operator * is only valid until either the d_Ref is deleted, the end of the outermost transaction, or until the object it points to is deleted. The pointer returned by ptr is only valid until the end of the outermost transaction or until the object it points to is deleted. The value of a d_Ref after a transaction commit or abort is undefined. If an attempt is made to dereference a null d_Ref<T>, a d_Error exception object of kind d_Error_RefNull is thrown. Calling delete_object with a null d_Ref is silently ignored, as it is with a pointer in C++.

The following template class allows one to specify a to-one relationship to a class T:

```
template <class T, const char *Member> class d_Rel_Ref : public d_Ref<T> { };
```

The template d_Rel_Ref<T,M> supports the same interface as d_Ref<T>. Implementations will redefine some functions to provide support for referential integrity.

A class d_Ref_Any is defined to support a reference to any type. Its primary purpose is to handle generic references and allow conversions of d_Refs in the type hierarchy. A d_Ref_Any object can be used as an intermediary between any two types d_Ref<X> and d_Ref<Y> where X and Y are different types. A d_Ref<T> can always be converted to a d_Ref_Any; there is a function to perform the conversion in the d_Ref<T> template. Each d_Ref<T> class has a constructor and assignment operator that takes a reference to a d_Ref_Any.

The d_Ref_Any class is defined as follows:

Definition:

```
class d_Ref_Any {
public:
                        d_Ref_Any();
                        d_Ref_Any(const d_Ref_Any &);
                        d_Ref_Any(d_Object *);
                        ~d_Ref_Any();
        d_Ref_Any &      operator=(const d_Ref_Any &);
        d_Ref_Any &      operator=(d_Object *);
        void            clear();
        void            delete_object();

// boolean predicates checking to see if value is null or not
        d_Boolean       operator!() const;
        d_Boolean       is_null() const;

friend  d_Boolean       operator==(const d_Ref_Any &, const d_Ref_Any &);
friend  d_Boolean       operator==(const d_Ref_Any &, const d_Object *);
friend  d_Boolean       operator==(const d_Object *, const d_Ref_Any &);
friend  d_Boolean       operator!=(const d_Ref_Any &, const d_Ref_Any &);
friend  d_Boolean       operator!=(const d_Ref_Any &, const d_Object *);
friend  d_Boolean       operator!=(const d_Object *, const d_Ref_Any &);
};
```

The operations defined on d_Ref<T> that are not dependent on a specific type T have been provided in the d_Ref_Any class.

5.3.6 Collection Classes

Collection templates are provided to support the representation of a collection whose elements are of an arbitrary type. A conforming implementation must support at least the following subtypes of d_Collection:

- d_Set
- d_Bag
- d_List
- d_Varray
- d_Dictionary

The C++ class definitions for each of these types are defined in the subsections that follow. Iterators are defined as a final subsection.

The following discussion uses the d_Set class in its explanation of collections, but the description applies for all concrete classes derived from d_Collection.

Given an object of type T, the declaration

```
d_Set<T> s;
```

defines a d_Set collection whose elements are of type T. If this set is assigned to another set of the same type, both the d_Set object itself and each of the elements of the set are copied. The elements are copied using the copy semantics defined for the type T. A common convention will be to have a collection that contains d_Refs to persistent objects—for example,

```
d_Set<d_Ref<Professor> > faculty;
```

The d_Ref class has shallow copy semantics. For a d_Set<T>, if T is of type d_Ref<C> for some persistence-capable class C, only the d_Ref objects are copied, not the C objects that the d_Ref objects reference.

This holds in any scope; in particular, if s is declared as a member inside a class, the set itself will be embedded inside an instance of this class. When an object of this enclosing class is copied into another object of the same enclosing class, the embedded set is copied, too, following the copy semantics defined above. This must be differentiated from the declaration

```
d_Ref<d_Set<T> >  ref_set;
```

which defines a reference to a d_Set. When such a reference is defined as a property of a class, that means that the set itself is an independent object that lies outside an instance of the enclosing class. Several objects may then share the same set, since copying an object will not copy the set, but just the reference to it. These are illustrated in Figure 5-2.

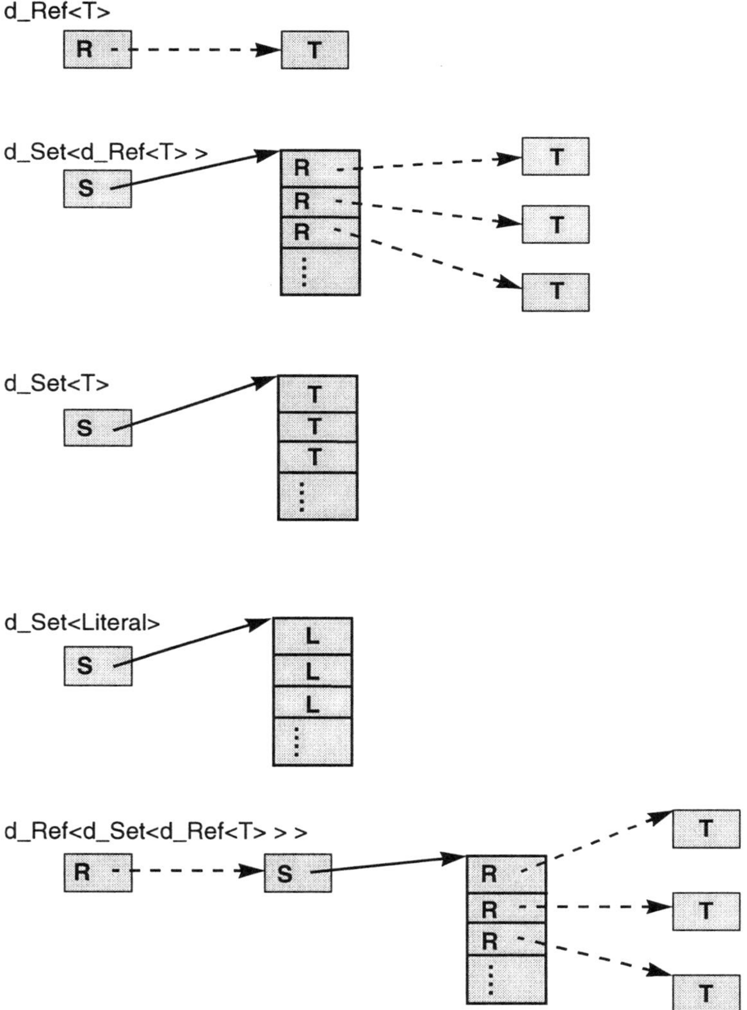

Figure 5-2. Collections, Embedded and with d_Ref

Collection elements may be of any type. Every type T that will become an element of a given collection must support the following operations:

```
class T {
public:
        T();
        T(const T &);
        ~T();
```

```
    T &          operator=(const T &);
  friend int     operator==(const T&, const T&);
  };
```

This is the complete set of functions required for defining the copy semantics for a given type. For types requiring ordering, the following operation must also be provided:

```
  friend d_Boolean     operator<(const T&, const T&);
```

Note that the C++ compiler will automatically generate a copy constructor and assignment operator if the class designer does not declare one. Note that the d_Ref<T> class supports these operations, except for operator<.

Collections of literals, including both atomic and structured literals, are defined as part of the standard. This includes both primitive and user-defined types; e.g., d_Set<int>, d_Set<struct time_t> will be defined with the same behavior.

Figure 5-2 illustrates various types involving d_Sets, d_Refs, a literal type L (int for example) and a persistent class T. The d_Set object itself is represented by a box that then refers to a set of elements of the specified type. A solid arrow is used to denote containment of the set elements within the d_Set object. d_Refs have a dashed arrow pointing to the referenced object of type T.

5.3.6.1 Class d_Collection

Class d_Collection is an abstract class in C++ and cannot have instances. It is derived from d_Object, allowing instances of concrete classes derived from d_Collection to be stand-alone persistent objects.

Definition:

```
template <class T> class d_Collection : public d_Object {
public:
virtual                    ~d_Collection();
     d_Collection<T> &     assign_from(const d_Collection<T> &);
friend d_Boolean          operator==( const d_Collection<T> &cL,
                                      const d_Collection<T> &cR);
friend d_Boolean          operator!=( const d_Collection<T> &cL,
                                      const d_Collection<T> &cR);
     unsigned long        cardinality() const;
     d_Boolean            is_empty() const;
     d_Boolean            is_ordered() const;
     d_Boolean            allows_duplicates() const;
     d_Boolean            contains_element(const T &element) const;
```

```
    void              insert_element(const T &elem);
    void              remove_element(const T &elem);
    void              remove_all();
    void              remove_all(const T &elem);
    d_Iterator<T>     create_iterator() const;
    d_Iterator<T>     begin() const;
    d_Iterator<T>     end() const;
    T                 select_element(const char *OQL_predicate) const;
    d_Iterator<T>     select(const char * OQL_predicate) const;
    int               query(d_Collection<T> &, const char *OQL_pred) const;
    d_Boolean         exists_element(const char* OQL_predicate) const;
protected:
                      d_Collection(const d_Collection<T> &);
    d_Collection<T> &  operator=(const d_Collection<T> &);
                      d_Collection();
};
```

Note that the d_Collection class provides the operation assign_from in place of operator= because d_Collection assignment is relatively expensive. This will prevent the often gratuitous use of assignment with collections.

The member function remove_element() removes one element that is equal to the argument from the collection. For ordered collections this will be the element that is equal to the value that would be first encountered if performing a forward iteration of the collection. The remove_all() function removes all of the elements from the collection. The remove_all(const T&) function removes all of the elements in the collection that are equal to the supplied value.

The destructor is called for an element whenever the element is removed from the collection. This also applies when the collection itself is assigned to or removed. If the element type of the collection is d_Ref<T> for some class T, the destructor of d_Ref<T> is called, but not the destructor of T.

The equality can be evaluated of two instances of any collection class derived from d_Collection that have the same element type. When comparing an instance of d_Set to either an instance of d_Set, d_Bag, d_List, or d_Varray, they are only equal if they have the same cardinality and the same elements. When comparing an instance of d_Bag to an instance of d_Bag, d_List, or d_Varray, they are equal if they have the same cardinality and the same number of occurrences of each element value. The ordering of the elements in the d_List or d_Varray does not matter; they are treated like a d_Bag. An instance of d_List or d_Varray is equal to another instance of d_List or d_Varray if they have the same cardinality and the element at each position is equal.

The create_iterator function returns an iterator pointing at the first element in the collection. The begin and end functions are supplied for compatibility with the C++ Standard Template Library (STL) algorithms. The function begin returns an iterator positioned at the first element of iteration. As defined in STL, the end function returns an iterator value that is "past the end" of iteration and is not dereferenceable.

5.3.6.2 Class d_Set

A d_Set<T> is an unordered collection of elements of type T with no duplicates.

Definition:

```
template <class T> class d_Set : public d_Collection<T> {
public:
                        d_Set();
                        d_Set(const d_Set<T> &);
                        ~d_Set();
        d_Set<T> &      operator=(const d_Set<T> &);
        d_Set<T> &      union_of(const d_Set<T> &sL, const d_Set<T> &sR);
        d_Set<T> &      union_with(const d_Set<T> &s2);
        d_Set<T> &      operator+=(const d_Set<T> &s2);        // union_with
        d_Set<T>        create_union(const d_Set<T> &s) const;
 friend d_Set<T>        operator+(const d_Set<T> &s1, const d_Set<T> &s2);
        d_Set<T> &      intersection_of(const d_Set<T> &sL, const d_Set<T> &sR);
        d_Set<T> &      intersection_with(const d_Set<T> &s2);
        d_Set<T> &      operator*=(const d_Set<T> &s2);        // intersection_with
        d_Set<T>        create_intersection(const d_Set<T> &s) const;
 friend d_Set<T>        operator*(const d_Set<T> &s1, const d_Set<T> &s2);
        d_Set<T> &      difference_of(const d_Set<T> &sL, const d_Set<T> &sR);
        d_Set<T> &      difference_with(const d_Set<T> &s2);
        d_Set<T> &      operator-=(const d_Set<T> &s2);        // difference_with
        d_Set<T>        create_difference(const d_Set<T> &s) const;
 friend d_Set<T>        operator-(const d_Set<T> &s1, const d_Set<T> &s2);
        d_Boolean       is_subset_of(const d_Set<T> &s2) const;
        d_Boolean       is_proper_subset_of(const d_Set<T> &s2) const;
        d_Boolean       is_superset_of(const d_Set<T> &s2) const;
        d_Boolean       is_proper_superset_of(const d_Set<T> &s2) const;
};
```

Note that all operations defined on type d_Collection are inherited by type d_Set, e.g., insert_element, remove_element, select_element, and select.

Examples:

- creation:

```
d_Database db;              // assume we open a database
d_Ref<Professor> Guttag; // assume we set this to a professor
d_Ref<d_Set<d_Ref<Professor> > > my_profs =
                                   new(&db) d_Set<d_Ref<Professor> >;
```

- insertion:

```
my_profs->insert_element(Guttag);
```

- removal:

```
my_profs->remove_element(Guttag);
```

- deletion:

```
my_profs.delete_object();
```

For each of the set operations (union, intersection, and difference) there are three ways of computing the resulting set. These will be explained using the union operation. Each one of the union functions has two set operands and computes their union. They vary in how the set operands are passed and how the result is returned, to support different interface styles. The union_of function is a member function that has two arguments, which are references to d_Set<T>. It computes the union of the two sets and places the result in the d_Set object with which the function was called, removing the original contents of the set. The union_with function is also a member and places its result in the object with which the operation is invoked, removing its original contents. The difference is that union_with uses its current set contents as one of the two operands being unioned, thus requiring only one operand passed to the member function. Both union_of and union_with return a reference to the object with which the operation was invoked. The union_with function has a corresponding operator+= function defined. On the other hand, create_union creates and returns a new d_Set instance by value that contains the union, leaving the two original sets unaltered. This function also has a corresponding operator+ function defined.

The following template class allows one to specify an unordered to-many relationship with a class T:

```
template <class T, const char *M> class d_Rel_Set : public d_Set<d_Ref<T> > { }
```

The template d_Rel_Set<T,M> supports the same interface as d_Set<d_Ref<T> >. Implementations will redefine some functions in order to support referential integrity.

5.3.6.3 Class d_Bag

A d_Bag<T> is an unordered collection of elements of type T that does allow for duplicate values.

Definition:

```
template <class T> class d_Bag : public d_Collection<T> {
public:
                        d_Bag();
                        d_Bag(const d_Bag<T> &);
                        ~d_Bag();
     d_Bag<T> &         operator=(const d_Bag<T> &);
     unsigned long      occurrences_of(const T &element) const;
     d_Bag<T> &         union_of(const d_Bag<T> &bL, const d_Bag<T> &bR);
     d_Bag<T> &         union_with(const d_Bag<T> &b2);
     d_Bag<T> &         operator+=(const d_Bag<T> &b2); // union_with
     d_Bag<T>           create_union(const d_Bag<T> &b) const;
friend d_Bag<T>         operator+(const d_Bag<T> &b1, const d_Bag<T> &b2);
     d_Bag<T> &         intersection_of(const d_Bag<T> &bL, const d_Bag<T> &bR);
     d_Bag<T> &         intersection_with(const d_Bag<T> &b2);
     d_Bag<T> &         operator*=(const d_Bag<T> &b2);  // intersection_with
     d_Bag<T>           create_intersection(const d_Bag<T>&b) const;
friend d_Bag<T>         operator*(const d_Bag<T> &b1, const d_Bag<T> &b2);
     d_Bag<T> &         difference_of(const d_Bag<T> &bL, const d_Bag<T> &bR);
     d_Bag<T> &         difference_with(const d_Bag<T> &b2);
     d_Bag<T> &         operator-=(const d_Bag<T> &b2); // difference_with
     d_Bag<T>           create_difference(const d_Bag<T> &b) const;
friend d_Bag<T>         operator-(const d_Bag<T> &b1, const d_Bag<T> &b2);
};
```

The union, intersection, and difference operations are described in the section above on the d_Set class.

5.3.6.4 Class d_List

A d_List<T> is an ordered collection of elements of type T and does allow for duplicate values. The beginning d_List index value is 0, following the convention of C and C++.

Definition:

```
template <class T> class d_List : public d_Collection<T> {
public:
                        d_List( );
                        d_List(const d_List<T> &);
                        ~d_List( );
```

```
    d_List<T> &      operator=(const d_List<T> &);
    T                retrieve_first_element() const;
    T                retrieve_last_element() const;
    void             remove_first_element();
    void             remove_last_element();
    T                operator[ ](unsigned long position) const;
    d_Boolean        find_element(const T &element,
                                  unsigned long &position) const;
    T                retrieve_element_at(unsigned long position) const;
    void             remove_element_at(unsigned long position);
    void             replace_element_at(const T &element,
                                        unsigned long position);
    void             insert_element_first(const T &element);
    void             insert_element_last(const T &element);
    void             insert_element_after(const T & element,
                                          unsigned long position);
    void             insert_element_before(const T &element,
                                           unsigned long position);
    d_List<T>        concat(const d_List<T> &listR) const;
friend d_List<T>     operator+(const d_List<T> &listL, const d_List<T> &listR);
    d_List<T> &      append(const d_List<T> &listR);
    d_List<T> &      operator+=(const d_List<T> &listR);
};
```

The insert_element function (inherited from d_Collection <T>) inserts a new element at the end of the list. The subscript operator (operator[]) has the same semantics as the member function retrieve_element_at. The concat function creates a new d_List<T> that contains copies of the elements from the original list, followed by copies of the elements from listR. The original lists are not affected. Similarly, operator+ creates a new d_List<T> that contains copies of the elements in listL and listR and does not change either list. The append function and operator+= both copy elements from listR and adds them after the last element of the list. The modified list is returned as the result.

The d_Rel_List<T, Member> template is used for representing relationships that are positional in nature:

```
template <class T, const char *M> class d_Rel_List : public d_List<d_Ref<T> > { };
```

The template d_Rel_List<T,M> has the same interface as d_List<d_Ref<T> >.

5.3.6.5 Class Array

The Array type defined in Section 2.3.6 is implemented by the built-in array defined by the C++ language. This is a single-dimension, fixed-length array.

5.3.6.6 Class d_Varray

A d_Varray<T> is a one-dimensional array of varying length containing elements of type T. The beginning d_Varray index value is 0, following the convention of C and C++.

Definition:

```
template <class T> class d_Varray : public d_Collection<T> {
public:
                    d_Varray();
                    d_Varray(unsigned long length);
                    d_Varray(const d_Varray<T> &);
                    ~d_Varray();
    d_Varray<T> &   operator= (const d_Varray<T> &);
    void            resize(unsigned long length);
    T               operator[](unsigned long index) const;
    d_Boolean       find_element(const T &element,
                            unsigned long &index) const;
    T               retrieve_element_at(unsigned long index) const;
    void            remove_element_at(unsigned long index);
    void            replace_element_at(const T &element,
                                   unsigned long index);
};
```

The insert_element function (inherited from d_Collection <T>) inserts a new element by increasing the d_Varray length by one and placing the new element at this new position in the d_Varray.

Examples:

```
d_Varray<d_Double>  vector(1000);
vector.replace_element_at(3.14159, 97);
vector.resize(2000);
```

5.3.6.7 Class d_Dictionary

The d_Dictionary<K,V> class is an unordered collection of key-value pairs, with no duplicate keys. A key-value pair is represented by an instance of d_Association<K,V>.

```
template <class K, class V> class d_Association
{
public:
    K       key;
    V       value;
            d_Association(const K &k, const V &v) : key(k), value(v) { }
};
```

The d_Dictionary<K,V> inherits from class d_Collection<T> and thus supports all of its base class operations. The insert_element, remove_element, and contains_element operations inherited from d_Collection<T> are valid for d_Dictionary<K,V> types when a d_Association<K,V> is specified as the argument. The contains_element function returns true if both the key and value specified in the d_Association parameter are contained in the dictionary.

```
template <class K, class V>
class d_Dictionary : public d_Collection<d_Association<K,V> > {
public:
                            d_Dictionary();
                            d_Dictionary(const d_Dictionary<K,V> &);
                            ~d_Dictionary();
    d_Dictionary<K,V> &     operator=(const d_Dictionary<K,V> &);
    void                    bind(const K&, const V&);
    void                    unbind(const K&);
    V                       lookup(const K&) const;
    d_Boolean               contains_key(const K&) const;
};
```

Iterating over a d_Dictionary<K,V> object will result in the iteration over a sequence of d_Association<K,V> instances. Each get_element operation, executed on an instance of d_Iterator<T>, returns an instance of d_Association<K,V>. If insert_element inherited from d_Collection is called and a duplicate key is found, its value is replaced with the new value passed to insert_element. The bind operation works the same as insert_element except the key and value are passed separately. When remove_element inherited from d_Collection is called, both the key and value must be equal for the element to be removed. An exception error of d_Error_ElementNotFound is thrown if the d_Association is not found in the dictionary. The function unbind removes the element with the specified key.

5.3.6.8 Class d_Iterator

A template class, d_Iterator<T>, defines the generic behavior for iteration. All iterators use a consistent protocol for sequentially returning each element from the collection over which the iteration is defined. A template class has been used to give us type-safe iterators, i.e., iterators that are guaranteed to return an instance of the type of the element of the collection over which the iterator is defined. Normally, an iterator is initialized by the create_iterator method on a collection class.

The template class d_Iterator<T> is defined as follows:

```
template <class T> class d_Iterator {
public:
                            d_Iterator();
                            d_Iterator(const d_Iterator<T> &);
                            ~d_Iterator();
    d_Iterator<T> &         operator=(const d_Iterator<T> &);
friend  d_Boolean           operator==(const d_Iterator<T> &, const d_Iterator<T> &);
friend  d_Boolean           operator!=(const d_Iterator<T> &, const d_Iterator<T> &);
    void                    reset();
    d_Boolean               not_done() const;
    void                    advance();
    d_Iterator<T> &         operator++();
    d_Iterator<T>           operator++(int);
    d_Iterator<T> &         operator--();
    d_Iterator<T>           operator--(int);
    T                       get_element() const;
    T                       operator*() const;
    void                    replace_element(const T &);
    d_Boolean               next(T &objRef);
};
```

When an iterator is constructed, it is either initialized with another iterator or set to null. When an iterator is constructed via the create_iterator function defined in d_Collection, the iterator is initialized to point to the first element, if there is one. Iterator assignment is also supported. A reset function is provided to reinitialize the iterator to the start of iteration for the same collection. The replace_element function can only be used with d_List or d_Varray.

The not_done function allows one to determine whether there are any more elements in the collection to be visited in the iteration. It returns 1 if there are more elements and 0 if iteration is complete. The advance function moves the iterator forward to the next element in the collection. The prefix and postfix forms of the increment operator ++ have been overloaded to provide an equivalent advance operation. One can also move backward through the collection by using the decrement operator --. However, using the -- decrement operator on an iterator of an unordered collection will throw a d_Error exception object of kind d_Error_IteratorNotBackward. If an attempt is made to either advance an iterator once it has already reached the end of a collection or move backward once the first element has been reached, a d_Error exception object of kind d_Error_IteratorExhausted is thrown. An attempt to use an iterator with a different collection than the collection it is associated with causes a d_Error exception object of kind d_Error_IteratorDifferentCollections to be thrown.

The get_element function and operator* return the value of the current element. If there is no current element, a d_Error exception object of kind d_Error_IteratorExhausted is thrown. There would be no current element if iteration had been completed (not_done return of 0) or if the collection had no elements.

The next function provides a facility for checking the end of iteration, advancing the iterator and returning the current element, if there is one. Its behavior is as follows:

```
template <class T> d_Boolean d_Iterator<T>::next(T &objRef)
{
    if( !not_done() ) return 0;   // no more elements, return false
    objRef = get_element();       // assign current element into output parameter
    advance();                    // advance to the next element
    return 1;                     // return true, that there is a next element
}
```

These operations allow for two styles of iteration, using either a while or for loop.

Example:

Given the class Student, with extent students:

```
(1) d_Iterator<d_Ref<Student> > iter = students.create_iterator();
    d_Ref<Student> s;
(2) while( iter.next(s) ) {
        ....
    }
```

Note that calling get_element after calling next will return a different element (the next element, if there is one). This is due to the fact that next will access the current element and then advance the iterator before returning.

Or equivalently with a for loop:

```
(3) d_Iterator<d_Ref<Student> > iter = students.create_iterator();
(4) for( ; iter.not_done(); ++iter) {
(5)     d_Ref<Student> s = iter.get_element();
        ....
    }
```

Statement (1) defines an iterator iter that ranges over the collection students. Statement (2) iterates through this collection, returning a d_Ref to a Student on each successive call to next, binding it to the loop variable s. The body of the while statement is then executed once for each student in the collection students. In the for loop (3) the iterator is initialized, iteration is checked for completion, and the iterator is advanced. Inside the for loop the get_element function can be called to get the current element.

5.3.6.9 Collections and the Standard Template Library

The C++ Standard Template Library (STL) provides an extensible set of containers, i.e., collections and algorithms that work together in a seamless way. The ODMG C++ language binding extends STL with persistence-capable versions of STL's container classes, each of which may be operated on by all template algorithms in the same manner as transient containers. A conforming implementation must provide at least the following persistence-capable STL container types, derived from d_Object:

- d_set
- d_multiset
- d_vector
- d_list
- d_map
- d_multimap

The names of these containers have the ODMG prefix (d_) and have interfaces that correspond to the STL set, multiset, vector, list, map, and multimap containers, respectively.

The C++ STL may be used to operate on the collection classes derived from d_Collection defined in the C++ OML. STL algorithms traverse container data structures using iterator objects, which are compatible with the d_Iterator<T> objects defined in the C++ OML. Specifically, d_Iterator<T> objects conform to the STL specification of constant iterators of the bidirectional_iterator category, though an implementation may provide more powerful iterators in some circumstances.

5.3.7 Transactions

Transaction semantics are defined in the object model explained in Chapter 2.

Transactions can be started, committed, aborted, and checkpointed. It is important to note that *all access, creation, modification, and deletion of persistent objects must be done within a transaction.*

Transactions are implemented in C++ as objects of class d_Transaction. The class d_Transaction defines the operation for starting, committing, aborting, and checkpointing transactions. These operations are

```
class d_Transaction {
public:
                          d_Transaction();
                          ~d_Transaction();
     void                 begin();
     void                 commit();
     void                 abort();
     void                 checkpoint();
// Thread operations
     void                 join();
     void                 leave();
     d_Boolean            is_active() const;
static d_Transaction *    current();
private:
                          d_Transaction(const d_Transaction &);
     d_Transaction &      operator=(const d_Transaction &);
};
```

Transactions must be explicitly created and started; they are not automatically started on database open, upon creation of a d_Transaction object, or following a transaction commit or abort.

The begin function starts a transaction. Calling begin multiple times on the same transaction object, without an intervening commit or abort, causes a d_Error exception object of kind d_Error_TransactionOpen to be thrown on second and subsequent calls. If a call is made to commit, checkpoint, or abort on a transaction object and a call had not been initially made to begin, a d_Error exception object of kind d_Error_TransactionNotOpen is thrown.

Calling commit commits to the database all persistent objects modified (including those created or deleted) within the transaction and releases any locks held by the transaction. Implementations may choose to maintain the validity of d_Refs to persistent objects across transaction boundaries. The commit operation does not delete the transaction object.

Calling checkpoint commits objects modified within the transaction since the last checkpoint to the database. The transaction retains all locks it held on those objects at the time the checkpoint was invoked. All d_Refs and pointers remain unchanged.

Calling abort aborts changes to objects and releases the locks, and does not delete the transaction object.

The destructor aborts the transaction if it is active.

The boolean function is_active returns d_True if the transaction is active; otherwise it returns d_False.

In the current standard, transient objects are not subject to transaction semantics. Committing a transaction does not remove transient objects from memory. Aborting a transaction does not restore the state of modified transient objects.

d_Transaction objects are not long-lived (beyond process boundaries) and cannot be stored to the database. This means that transaction objects may not be made persistent and that the notion of "long transactions" is not defined in this specification.

In summary the rules that apply to object modification (necessarily, during a transaction) are

1. Changes made to persistent objects within a transaction can be "undone" by aborting the transaction.
2. Transient objects are standard C++ objects.
3. Persistent objects created within the scope of a transaction are handled consistently at transaction boundaries: stored to the database and removed from memory (at transaction commit) or deleted (as a result of a transaction abort).

A thread must explicitly create a transaction object or associate itself with an existing transaction object by calling join. The member function join attaches the caller's thread to the transaction and the thread is detached from any other transaction it may be associated with. Calling begin on a transaction object without doing a prior join implicitly joins the transaction to the calling thread. All subsequent operations by the thread, including reads, writes, and implicit lock acquisitions, are done under the thread's current transaction.

Calling leave detaches the caller's thread from the d_Transaction instance without attaching the thread to another transaction. The static function current can be called to access the current d_Transaction object that the thread is associated with; null is returned if the thread is not associated with a transaction.

If a transaction is associated with multiple threads, all of these threads are affected by any data operations or transaction operations (begin, commit, checkpoint, abort). Concurrency control on data among threads is up to the client program in this case. In contrast, if threads use separate transactions, the database system maintains ACID transaction properties just as if the threads were in separate address spaces. Programmers must not pass objects from one thread to another running under a different transaction; ODMG does not define the results of doing this.

There are three ways in which threads can be used with transactions:

1. An application program may have exactly one thread doing database operations, under exactly one transaction. This is the simplest case, and it represents the vast majority of database applications today. Other applications on

separate machines or in separate address spaces may access the same database under separate transactions. A thread can create multiple instances of d_Transaction and can alternate between them by calling join.

2. There may be multiple threads, each with its own separate transaction. This is useful for writing a service accessed by multiple clients on a network. The database system maintains ACID transaction properties just as if the threads were in separate address spaces. Programmers must not pass objects from one thread to another thread running under a different transaction; ODMG does not define the results of doing this.

3. Multiple threads may share one or more transactions. Using multiple threads per transaction is only recommended for sophisticated programming because concurrency control must be performed by the application.

5.3.8 d_Database Operations

There is a predefined type d_Database. It supports the following methods:

```
class d_Database {
public:
static d_Database * const transient_memory;
    enum access_status { not_open, read_write, read_only, exclusive };
                        d_Database();
    void                open(   const char * database_name,
                                access_status status = read_write);
    void                close();
    void                set_object_name(const d_Ref_Any &theObject,
                                        const char* theName);
    void                rename_object(  const char * oldName,
                                        const char * newName);
    d_Ref_Any           lookup_object(const char * name) const;
private:
                        d_Database(const d_Database &);
    d_Database &        operator=(const d_Database &);
};
```

The database object, like the transaction object, is transient. Databases cannot be created programmatically using the C++ OML defined by this standard. Databases must be opened before starting any transactions that use the database, and closed after ending these transactions.

To open a database, use d_Database::open, which takes the name of the database as its argument. This initializes the instance of the d_Database object.

```
database->open("myDB");
```

Method open locates the named database and makes the appropriate connection to the database. You must open a database before you can access objects in that database. Attempts to open a database when it has already been opened will result in the throwing of a d_Error exception object of kind d_Error_DatabaseOpen. Extensions to the open method will enable some ODBMSs to implement default database names and/or implicitly open a default database when a database session is started. Some ODBMSs may support opening logical as well as physical databases. Some ODBMSs may support being connected to multiple databases at the same time.

To close a database, use d_Database::close:

```
database->close();
```

Method close does appropriate clean-up on the named database connection. After you have closed a database, further attempts to access objects in the database will cause a d_Error exception object of kind d_Error_DatabaseClosed to be thrown. The behavior at program termination if databases are not closed or transactions are not committed or aborted is undefined.

The *name* methods allow manipulating names of objects. The set_object_name method assigns a character string name to the object referenced. If the string supplied as the name argument is not unique within the database, a d_Error exception object of kind d_Error_NameNotUnique will be thrown. Each call to set_object_name for an object adds an additional name to the object. If a value of 0 is passed as the second parameter to set_object_name, all of the names associated with the object are removed.

The rename_object method changes the name of an object. If the new name is already in use, a d_Error exception object of kind d_Error_NameNotUnique will be thrown and the old name is retained. A name can be removed by passing 0 as the second parameter to rename_object. Names are not automatically removed when an object is deleted. If a call is made to lookup_object with the name of a deleted object, a null d_Ref_Any is returned. Previous releases removed the names when the object was deleted.

An object is accessed by name using the d_Database::lookup_object member function. A null d_Ref_Any is returned if no object with the name is found in the database.

Example:

```
d_Ref<Professor> prof = myDatabase->lookup_object("Newton");
```

If a Professor instance named "Newton" exists, it is retrieved and a d_Ref_Any is returned by lookup_object. The d_Ref_Any return value is then used to initialize prof. If the object named "Newton" is not an instance of Professor or a subclass of Professor, a d_Error exception object of kind d_Error_TypeInvalid is thrown during this initialization.

If the definition of a class in the application does not match the database definition of the class, a d_Error exception object of kind d_Error_DatabaseClassMismatch is thrown.

5.3.9 Class d_Extent<T>

The class d_Extent<T> provides an interface to the extent of a persistence-capable class T in the C++ binding.

d_Extent provides nearly the same interface as the d_Collection class.

```
template <class T> class d_Extent
{
public:
                              d_Extent (const d_Database* base,
                                        d_Boolean include_subclasses = d_True);
    virtual                   ~d_Extent ();
    unsigned long             cardinality() const;
    d_Boolean                 is_empty() const;
    d_Boolean                 allows_duplicates() const;
    d_Boolean                 is_ordered() const;
    d_Iterator<T>             create_iterator() const;
    d_Iterator<T>             begin() const;
    d_Iterator<T>             end() const;
    d_Ref<T>                  select_element (const char * OQL_pred) const;
    d_Iterator<T>             select (const char * OQL_pred) const;
    int                       query(d_Collection<d_Ref<T> > &,
                                        const char* OQL_pred) const;
    d_Boolean                 exists_element (const char * OQL_pred) const;
protected:
                              d_Extent (const d_Extent<T> &);
    d_Extent<T> &             operator=(const d_Extent<T> &);
};
```

The database schema definition contains a parameter for each persistent class specifying whether the ODBMS should maintain an extent for the class. This parameter can be set using the schema API or a database tool that enables specification of the schema.

The content of a d_Extent<T> is automatically maintained by the ODBMS. The d_Extent class therefore has neither insert nor remove methods. d_Extents themselves are not persistence-capable and cannot be stored in the database. This explains why d_Extent is not derived from d_Collection; since d_Collection is in turn derived from d_Object, this would imply that extents are also persistence-capable. However, semantically d_Extent is equivalent to d_Set.

If a user wants to maintain an extent they can define a d_Set<d_Ref<T> > that is stored in the database, as in the example in Section 5.6.

The class d_Extent supports polymorphism when the constructor argument include_subclasses is a true value. If type B is a subtype of A a d_Extent for A includes all instances of A and B.

The association of a d_Extent to a type is performed by instantiating the template with the appropriate type. Every d_Extent instance must be associated with a database by passing a d_Database pointer to the constructor.

```
d_Extent<Person>      PersonExtent(database);
```

Passing the database pointer to the constructor instead of operator new (as with d_Object) allows the user to instantiate a d_Extent instance on the stack. If no extent has been defined in the database schema for the class, an exception is thrown.

Comparison operators like operator== and operator!= or the subset and superset methods of d_Set do not make sense for d_Extent, since all instances of a d_Extent for a given type have the same content.

5.3.10 Exceptions

Instances of d_Error contain state describing the cause of the error. This state is composed of a number, representing the kind of error, and optional additional information. This additional information can be appended to the error object by using operator<<. If the d_Error object is caught, more information can be appended to it if it is to be thrown again. The complete state of the object is returned as a human-readable character string by the what function.

The d_Error class is defined as follows:

```
class d_Error : public exception {
public:
    typedef d_Long    kind;
                      d_Error();
                      d_Error(const d_Error &);
                      d_Error(kind the_kind);
                      ~d_Error();
    kind              get_kind();
    void              set_kind(kind the_kind);
    const char *      what() const throw();

    d_Error &         operator<<(d_Char);
    d_Error &         operator<<(d_Short);
```

```
    d_Error &        operator<<(d_UShort);
    d_Error &        operator<<(d_Long);
    d_Error &        operator<<(d_ULong);
    d_Error &        operator<<(d_Float);
    d_Error &        operator<<(d_Double);
    d_Error &        operator<<(const char *);
    d_Error &        operator<<(const d_String &);
    d_Error &        operator<<(const d_Error &);
};
```

The null constructor initializes the kind property to d_Error_None. The class d_Error is responsible for releasing the string that is returned by the member function what.

The following constants are defined for error kinds used in this standard. Note that each of these names has a prefix of d_Error_.

Error Name	Description
None	No error has occurred.
DatabaseClassMismatch	The definition of a class in the application does not match the database definition of the class.
DatabaseClassUndefined	The database does not have the schema information about a class.
DatabaseClosed	The database is closed; objects cannot be accessed.
DatabaseOpen	The database is already open.
DateInvalid	An attempt was made to set a d_Date object to an invalid value.
ElementNotFound	An attempt was made to access an element that is not in the collection.
IteratorDifferentCollections	An iterator, passed to a member function of a collection, is not associated with the collection.
IteratorExhausted	An attempt was made to either advance an iterator once it already reached the end of a collection or move backward once the first element has been reached.
IteratorNotBackward	An attempt has been made to iterate backward with either a d_Set<T> or d_Bag<T>.
NameNotUnique	An attempt was made to associate an object with a name that is not unique in the database.

Error Name	Description
PositionOutOfRange	A position within a collection has been supplied that exceeds the range of the index (0, cardinality - 1).
QueryParameterCountInvalid	The number of arguments used to build a query with the d_OQL_Query object does not equal the number of arguments supplied in the query string.
QueryParameterTypeInvalid	Either the parameters specified in the query or the return value type does not match the types in the database.
RefInvalid	An attempt was made to dereference a d_Ref that references an object that does not exist.
RefNull	An attempt was made to dereference a null d_Ref.
TimeInvalid	An attempt has been made to set a d_Time object to an invalid value.
TimestampInvalid	An attempt has been made to set a d_Timestamp object to an invalid value.
MemberIsOfInvalidType	The second template argument of either d_Rel_Ref, d_Rel_Set, or d_Rel_List references a data member that is not of type d_Rel_Ref, d_Rel_Set, or d_Rel_List.
MemberNotFound	The second template argument of either d_Rel_Ref, d_Rel_Set, or d_Rel_List references a data member that does not exist in the referenced class.
TransactionNotOpen	A call has been made to either commit or abort without a prior call to begin.
TransactionOpen	d_Transaction::begin has been called multiple times on the same transaction object, without an intervening commit or abort.
TypeInvalid	A d_Ref<T> was initialized to reference an object that is not of type T or a subclass of T.

The following table indicates which functions throw these exceptions.

Error Name	Raised By
DatabaseClassMismatch	d_Database::lookup_object
DatabaseClassUndefined	d_Object::new
DatabaseClosed	d_Database::close
DatabaseOpen	d_Database::open
DateInvalid	Any method that alters the date value

Error Name	Raised By
IteratorExhausted	d_Iterator functions get_element, ++, --,operator *
NameNotUnique	d_Database::set_object_name
PositionOutOfRange	d_List::operator[ ], d_Varray::operator[ ]
QueryParameterCountInvalid	d_oql_execute
QueryParameterTypeInvalid	d_oql_execute
RefInvalid	d_Ref<T> functions operator–>, operator *
RefNull	d_Ref<T> functions operator–>, operator *
TimeInvalid	Any method that alters the time value
TimestampInvalid	Any method that alters the timestamp value
TransactionOpen	d_Transaction::begin
TypeInvalid	d_Ref constructor

5.4 C++ OQL

Chapter 4 outlined the Object Query Language. In this section the OQL semantics are mapped into the C++ language.

5.4.1 Query Method on Class Collection

The d_Collection class has a query member function whose signature is:

```
int query(d_Collection<T> &result, const char* predicate) const;
```

This function filters the collection using the predicate and assigns the result to the first parameter. It returns a code different from 0, if the query is not well formed. The predicate is given as a string with the syntax of the *where* clause of OQL. The predefined variable this is used inside the predicate to denote the current element of the collection to be filtered.

Example:

Given the class Student, as defined in Chapter 3, with extent referenced by Students, compute the set of students who take math courses:

```
d_Bag<d_Ref<Student> >  mathematicians;
Students–>query(mathematicians,
                    "exists s in this.takes: s.section_of.name = \"math\" ");
```

5.4.2 d_oql_execute Function

An interface is provided to gain access to the complete functionality of OQL from a C++ program. There are several steps involved in the specification and execution of the OQL query. First, a query gets *constructed* via an object of type d_OQL_Query.

Once a query has been constructed, the query is *executed*. Once constructed, a query can be executed multiple times with different argument values.

The function to execute a query is called d_oql_execute; it is a free-standing template function, not part of any class definition:

```
template<class T> void     d_oql_execute(d_OQL_Query &query, T &result);
```

The first parameter, *query*, is a reference to a d_OQL_Query object specifying the query to execute. The second parameter, *result*, is used for returning the result of the query. The type of the query result must match the type of this second parameter, or a d_Error exception object of kind d_Error_QueryParameterTypeInvalid is thrown. Type checking of the input parameters according to their use in the query is done at runtime. Similarly, the type of the result of the query is checked. Any violation of type would cause a d_Error exception object of kind d_Error_QueryParameterTypeInvalid to be thrown. If the query returns a persistent object of type T, the function returns a d_Ref<T>. If the query returns a structured literal, the value of it is assigned to the value of the object or collection denoted by the *result* parameter.

If the result of the query is a large collection, a function d_oql_execute can be used. This function returns an iterator on the result collection instead of the collection itself. The behavior of this standalone function is exactly the same as the d_oql_execute function.

```
template<class T> void d_oql_execute (d_OQL_Query &q, d_Iterator<T> &results);
```

The << operator has been overloaded for d_OQL_Query to allow construction of the query. It concatenates the value of the right operand onto the end of the current value of the d_OQL_Query left operand. These functions return a reference to the left operand so that invocations can be cascaded.

Note that instances of d_OQL_Query contain either a partial or a complete OQL query. An ODMG implementation will contain ancillary data structures to represent a query both during its construction and once it is executed. The d_OQL_Query destructor will appropriately remove any ancillary data when the object gets deleted.

The d_OQL_Query class is defined as follows:

Definition:

```
class d_OQL_Query {
public:
                              d_OQL_Query();
                              d_OQL_Query(const char *s);
                              d_OQL_Query(const d_String &s);
                              d_OQL_Query(const d_OQL_Query &q);
                              ~d_OQL_Query();
```

```
    d_OQL_Query &        operator=(const d_OQL_Query &q);
    void                 clear();

  friend d_OQL_Query &   operator<<(d_OQL_Query &q, const char *s);
  friend d_OQL_Query &   operator<<(d_OQL_Query &q, const d_String &s);
  friend d_OQL_Query &   operator<<(d_OQL_Query &q, d_Char c);
  friend d_OQL_Query &   operator<<(d_OQL_Query &q, d_Octet uc);
  friend d_OQL_Query &   operator<<(d_OQL_Query &q, d_Short s);
  friend d_OQL_Query &   operator<<(d_OQL_Query &q, d_UShort us);
  friend d_OQL_Query &   operator<<(d_OQL_Query &q, int i);
  friend d_OQL_Query &   operator<<(d_OQL_Query &q, unsigned int ui);
  friend d_OQL_Query &   operator<<(d_OQL_Query &q, d_Long l);
  friend d_OQL_Query &   operator<<(d_OQL_Query &q, d_ULong ul);
  friend d_OQL_Query &   operator<<(d_OQL_Query &q, d_Float f);
  friend d_OQL_Query &   operator<<(d_OQL_Query &q, d_Double d);
  friend d_OQL_Query &   operator<<(d_OQL_Query &q, const d_Date &d);
  friend d_OQL_Query &   operator<<(d_OQL_Query &q, const d_Time &t);
  friend d_OQL_Query &   operator<<(d_OQL_Query &q, const d_Timestamp &);
  friend d_OQL_Query &   operator<<(d_OQL_Query &q, const d_Interval &i);
  template<class T> friend d_OQL_Query &   operator<<(d_OQL_Query &q,
                                                  const d_Ref<T> &r);
  template<class T> friend d_OQL_Query & operator<<(d_OQL_Query &q,
                                                  const d_Collection<T> &c);
  };
```

Strings used in the construction of a query may contain parameters signified by the form *$i*, where *i* is a number referring to the ith subsequent right operand in the construction of the query; the first subsequent right operand would be referred to as $1. If any of the $i are not followed by a right operand construction argument at the point d_oql_execute is called, a d_Error exception object of kind d_Error_QueryParameterCountInvalid is thrown. This exception will also be thrown if too many parameters are used in the construction of the query. If a query argument is of the wrong type, a d_Error exception object of kind d_Error_QueryParameterTypeInvalid is thrown.

The operation clear can be called to clear the values of any query parameters that have been provided to an instance of d_OQL_Query.

Once a query has been successfully executed via d_oql_execute, the arguments associated with the *$i* parameters are cleared and new arguments must be supplied. If any exceptions are thrown, the query arguments are not implicitly cleared and must be cleared explicitly by invoking clear. The original query string containing the *$i* parameters is retained across the call to d_oql_execute.

The d_OQL_Query copy constructor and assignment operator copy all the underlying data structures associated with the query, based upon the parameters that have been passed to the query at the point the operation is performed. If the original query object had two parameters passed to it, the object that is new or assigned to should have those same two parameters initialized. After either of these operations the two d_OQL_Query objects should be equivalent and have identical behavior.

Example:

Among the math students (as computed before in Section 5.4.1 into the variable mathematicians) who are teaching assistants and earn more than x, find the set of professors that they assist. Suppose there exists a named set of teaching assistants called "TA".

```
d_Bag<d_Ref<Student> >  mathematicians; // computed as above
d_Bag<d_Ref<Professor> >  assisted_profs;
double x = 50000.00;

d_OQL_Query q1 (
     "select t.assists.taught_by from t in TA where t.salary > $1 and t in $2");
q1 << x << mathematicians;
d_oql_execute(q1, assisted_profs);
```

After the above code has been executed, it could be followed by another query, passing in different arguments.

```
d_Set<d_Ref<Student> >  historians;      // assume this gets computed similar
                                          // to mathematicians
double y = 40000.00

q1 << y << historians;
d_oql_execute(q1, assisted_profs);
```

The ODMG OQL implementation may have parsed, compiled, and optimized the original query; it can now reexecute the query with different arguments without incurring the overhead of compiling and optimizing the query.

5.5 Schema Access

This section describes an interface for accessing the schema of an ODMG database via a C++ class library. The schema information is based on the Metadata described in Chapter 2. The C++ schema definition differs in some respects from the language-independent, abstract specification of the schema in ODL. Attempts have been made to make the schema access conform to C++ programming practices in order that the use of the API be intuitive for C++ programmers. C++-specific ODL extensions have been included in the API, in addition to the abstract ODL schema, since the C++ ODL is a superset of the ODMG ODL described in Chapter 2.

The schema access API is structured as an object-oriented framework. Only the interface methods through which meta-information is manipulated is defined, rather than defining the entire class structure and details of the internal implementation. The ODBMS implementation can choose the actual physical representation of the schema database. The ODL schema lists the classes that are used to describe a schema. It also uses ODL relationships to show how instances of these classes are interrelated. To allow maximum flexibility in an implementation of this model, methods are provided to traverse the relationships among instances of these classes, rather than mapping the ODL relationships directly to C++ data members.

The specification currently contains only the *read* interface portion of the schema API. The ODMG plans to extend the specification to include a full *read/write* interface enabling dynamic modification of the schema (e.g., creation and modification of classes). The initial *read-only* interface will substantially increase the flexibility and usability of the standard. The following application domains will be able to take advantage of this interface:

- Database tool development (e.g., class and object browsers, import/export utilities, Query By Example implementations)
- CASE tools
- Schema management tools
- Distributed computing and dynamic binding, object brokers (CORBA)
- Management of extended database properties (e.g. access control and user authorization)

This concept is analogous to the system table approach used by relational database systems. However, since it is a true object mapping, it also includes schema semantics (e.g., relationships between classes and properties), making it much easier to use.

5.5.1 The ODMG Schema Access Class Hierarchy

This section defines the types in the ODMG schema access class hierarchy. Subclasses are indented and placed below their base class. The names in square brackets denote additional base classes, if the class inherits from more than one class. Types in *italic code* font are abstract classes and cannot be directly instantiated; classes in code font can be instantiated. These classes are described in more detail in later sections using both C++ and ODL syntax.

- *d_Scope*
  d_Scope instances are used to form a hierarchy of meta objects. A *d_Scope* instance contains a list of *d_Meta_Object* instances, which are defined in the scope; operations to manage the list (e.g. finding a *d_Meta_Object* by its name) are provided. All meta objects are defined in a scope.

- *d_Meta_Object*
  Instances of *d_Meta_Object* are used to describe elements of the schema stored in the dictionary.
  - d_Module [*d_Scope*]
    d_Module instances manage domains in a dictionary. They are used to group and order *d_Meta_Object* instances, such as type/class descriptions, constant descriptions, subschemas (expressed as d_Module objects), etc.
  - d_Type
    d_Type is an abstract base class for all type descriptions.
    - d_Class [*d_Scope*]
      A d_Class instance is used to describe an application-defined class whose d_Attribute and d_Relationship instances represent the concrete state of an instance of that class. The state is stored in the database. All persistent-capable classes are described by a d_Class instance.
    - d_Ref_Type
      d_Ref_Type instances are used to describe types that are references to other objects. References can be pointers, references (like d_Ref<T>), or other language-specific references. The referenced object or literal can be shared by more than one reference, i.e., multiple references can reference the same object.
    - d_Collection_Type
      A d_Collection_Type describes a type whose instances group a set of elements in a collection. The collection elements must be of the same (base) type.
      - d_Keyed_Collection_Type
        A d_Keyed_Collection_Type describes a collection that can be accessed via keys.
    - d_Primitive_Type
      A d_Primitive_Type represents all built-in types, e.g., int (16, 32 bit), float, etc., as well as pre-defined ODMG literals such as d_String.
      - d_Enumeration_Type [*d_Scope*]
        d_Enumeration_Type describes a type whose domain is a list of identifiers.
    - d_Structure_Type [*d_Scope*]
      d_Structure_Type instances describe application-defined member values. The members are described by d_Attribute instances and

represent the state of the structure. Structures do not have object identity.

    - d_Alias_Type
      A d_Alias_Type describes a type that is equivalent to another *d_Type*, but has another name.

  - d_Property
    d_Property is an abstract base class for all *d_Meta_Object* instances that describe the state (abstract or concrete) of application-defined types.

    - d_Relationship
      Instances of d_Relationship describe relationships between persistent objects; in C++ these are expressed as d_Rel_Ref<T, MT>, d_Rel_Set<T, MT>, and d_Rel_List<T, MT> data members of a class.

    - d_Attribute
      A d_Attribute instance describes the concrete state of an object or structure.

  - d_Operation [*d_Scope*]
    d_Operation instances describe methods, including their return type, identifier, signature, and list of exceptions.

  - d_Exception
    d_Exception instances describe exceptions that are raised by operations represented by instances of d_Operation.

  - d_Parameter
    A d_Parameter describes a parameter of an operation. A parameter has a name, a type, and a mode (in, out, inout).

  - d_Constant
    A d_Constant describes a value that has a name and a type. The value may not be changed.

- d_Inheritance
  d_Inheritance is used to describe the bidirectional relationship between a base class and a subclass, as well as the type of inheritance used.

5.5.2 Schema Access Interface

The following interfaces describe the external C++ interface of an ODMG 2.0 schema repository. The interface is defined in terms of C++ classes with public methods, without exposing or suggesting any particular implementation.

In the following specification, some hints are provided as to how the ODL interface repository described in Chapter 2 has been mapped into the C++ interface.

All objects in the repository are subclasses of *d_Meta_Object* or *d_Scope*.

Interfaces that return a list of objects are expressed using iterator types, traversal of proposed relationships is expressed via methods that return iterators, access to attributes is provided using accessor functions.

An implementation of this interface is not required to use a particular implementation of the iterator type. We follow a design principle used in STL. Classes that have 1-to-n relationships to other classes define only a type to iterate over this relationship. A conformant implementation of the schema repository can implement these types by means of the d_Iterator type (but is not required to).

The iterator protocol must support at least the following methods. In subsequent sections this set of methods for iterator type *IterType* is referred to as a "constant forward iterator" over type T.

```
              IterType();
              IterType(const IterType &);
IterType &    operator=(const IterType &);
int           operator==(const IterType &) const;
int           operator!=(const IterType &) const;
IterType &    operator++();
IterType      operator++(int);
const T &     operator*() const;
```

The operator++ advances the iterator to the next element, and operator* retrieves the element. The iterator is guaranteed to always return the elements in the same order. The iterator in class d_Scope that iterates over instances of type d_Meta_Object would be of type d_Scope::meta_object_iterator.

The following names are used for embedded types that provide constant forward iteration.

Iterator Type Name	Element Type
alias_type_iterator	d_Alias_Type
attribute_iterator	d_Attribute
collection_type_iterator	d_Collection_Type
constant_iterator	d_Constant
exception_iterator	d_Exception
inheritance_iterator	d_Inheritance
keyed_collection_type_iterator	d_Keyed_Collection_Type
operation_iterator	d_Operation
parameter_iterator	d_Parameter
property_iterator	d_Property

Iterator Type Name	Element Type
ref_type_iterator	d_Ref_Type
relationship_iterator	d_Relationship
type_iterator	d_Type

Each class that iterates over elements of one of these types has an iterator type defined within the class with the corresponding name. This is denoted in the class interface with a line similar to the following:

```
typedef property_iterator; // this implies an iterator type with this name is defined
```

Properties and classes have access specifiers in C++. Several of the metaclass objects make use of the following enumeration:

```
typedef enum { d_PUBLIC, d_PROTECTED, d_PRIVATE } d_Access_Kind;
```

5.5.2.1 d_Scope

d_Scope instances are used to form a hierarchy of meta objects. A *d_Scope* contains a list of *d_Meta_Object* instances that are defined in the scope, as well as operations to manage the list. The method resolve is used to find a *d_Meta_Object* by name. All instances of *d_Meta_Object*, except d_Module, have exactly one *d_Scope* object. This represents a "defined in" relationship. The type *d_Scope*::meta_object_iterator defines a protocol to traverse this relationship in the other direction.

```
class d_Scope {
public:
    const d_Meta_Object &      resolve(const char *name) const;
    typedef                    meta_object_iterator;
    meta_object_iterator       defines_begin() const;
    meta_object_iterator       defines_end() const;
};
```

5.5.2.2 d_Meta_Object

Class *d_Meta_Object* has a name, an id and a comment attribute. Some instances of *d_Meta_Object* are themselves scopes (instances of *d_Scope*); that is, they define a namespace in which other *d_Meta_Object* instances can be identified (resolved) by name. They form a defines/defined_in relationship with other *d_Meta_Object* instances and are their defining scopes. The scope of a *d_Meta_Object* is obtained by the method defined_in.

```
class d_Meta_Object {
public:
    const char *               name() const;
    const char *               comment() const;
    const d_Scope &            defined_in() const;
};
```

5.5.2.3 d_Module

A d_Module manages domains in a dictionary. They are used to group and order *d_Meta_Object* instances such as type/class descriptions, constant descriptions, subschemas (expressed as d_Module objects), etc. A d_Module is also a *d_Scope* that provides client repository services. A module is the uppermost meta object in a naming hierarchy. The class d_Module provides methods to iterate over the various meta objects that can be defined in a module. It is an entry point for accessing instances of *d_Type*, d_Constant, and d_Operation. The *d_Type* objects returned by type_iterator can be asked for the set of d_Operations, *d_Properties*, etc. that describe operations and properties of the module. It is then possible to navigate further down in the hierarchy. For example, from d_Operation, the set of d_Parameter instances can be reached, and so on.

```
class d_Module : public d_Meta_Object, public d_Scope {
public:
    static const d_Module &    top_level(const d_Database &);

    typedef                    type_iterator;
    type_iterator              defines_types_begin() const;
    type_iterator              defines_types_end() const;

    typedef                    constant_iterator;
    constant_iterator          defines_constant_begin() const;
    constant_iterator          defines_constant_end() const;

    typedef                    operation_iterator;
    operation_iterator         defines_operation_begin() const;
    operation_iterator         defines_operation_end() const;
};
```

5.5.2.4 d_Type

d_Type meta objects are used to represent information about data types. They participate in a number of relationships with the other *d_Meta_Objects*. These relationships allow types to be easily administered within the repository and help to ensure the referential integrity of the repository as a whole.

Class *d_Type* is defined as follows:

```
class d_Type : public d_Meta_Object {
public:
    typedef                    alias_type_iterator;
    alias_type_iterator        used_in_alias_type_begin() const;
    alias_type_iterator        used_in_alias_type_end() const;
```

```
    typedef                          collection_type_iterator;
    collection_type_iterator         used_in_collection_type_begin() const;
    collection_type_iterator         used_in_collection_type_end() const;

    typedef                          keyed_collection_type_iterator;
    keyed_collection_type_iterator   used_in_keyed_collection_type_begin() const;
    keyed_collection_type_iterator   used_in_keyed_collection_type_end() const;

    typedef                          ref_type_iterator;
    ref_type_iterator                used_in_ref_type_begin() const;
    ref_type_iterator                used_in_ref_type_end() const;

    typedef                          property_iterator;
    property_iterator                used_in_property_begin() const;
    property_iterator                used_in_property_end() const;

    typedef                          operation_iterator;
    operation_iterator               used_in_operation_begin() const;
    operation_iterator               used_in_operation_end() const;

    typedef                          exception_iterator;
    exception_iterator               used_in_exception_begin() const;
    exception_iterator               used_in_exception_end() const;

    typedef                          parameter_iterator;
    parameter_iterator               used_in_parameter_begin() const;
    parameter_iterator               used_in_parameter_end() const;

    typedef                          constant_iterator;
    constant_iterator                used_in_constant_begin() const;
    constant_iterator                used_in_constant_end() const;
};
```

5.5.2.5 d_Class

A d_Class object describes an application-defined type whose attributes and relationships form the concrete state of an object of that type. The state is stored in the database. All persistent-capable classes are described by a d_Class instance.

d_Class objects are linked in a multiple inheritance graph by two relationships, inherits and derives. The relationship between two d_Class objects is formed by means of one connecting d_Inheritance object. A d_Class object also indicates whether the database maintains an extent for the class.

A class defines methods, data and relationship members, constants, and types; that is, the class is their defining scope.

Methods, data and relationship members, constants, and types are modeled by a list of related objects of type d_Operation, d_Attribute, d_Relationship, d_Constant, and *d_Type*. These descriptions can be accessed by name using the inherited method *d_Scope*::resolve. The methods resolve_operation, resolve_attribute, or resolve_constant can be used as shortcuts.

The inherited iterator *d_Meta_Object*::meta_object_iterator returns descriptions for methods, data members, relationship members, constants, and types. Methods, data members, relationship members, constants, and types are also accessible via special iterators. The following functions provide iterators that return their elements in their declaration order:

- base_class_list_begin
- defines_attribute_begin
- defines_operation_begin
- defines_constant_begin
- defines_relationship_begin
- defines_type_begin

The class d_Class is defined as follows:

```
class d_Class : public d_Type, public d_Scope {
public:
        typedef                 inheritance_iterator;
        inheritance_iterator    sub_class_list_begin() const;
        inheritance_iterator    sub_class_list_end() const;
        inheritance_iterator    base_class_list_begin() const;
        inheritance_iterator    base_class_list_end() const;

        d_Boolean               persistent_capable() const; // derived from d_Object?

        // these methods are used to return the characteristics of the class
        typedef                 operation_iterator;
        operation_iterator      defines_operation_begin() const;
        operation_iterator      defines_operation_end() const;
        const d_Operation &     resolve_operation(const char *name) const;

        typedef                 attribute_iterator;
        attribute_iterator      defines_attribute_begin() const;
```

```
    attribute_iterator       defines_attribute_end() const;
    const d_Attribute &      resolve_attribute(const char *name) const;

    typedef                  relationship_iterator;
    relationship_iterator    defines_relationship_begin() const;
    relationship_iterator    defines_relationship_end() const;
    const d_Relationship& resolve_relationship(const char *name) const;

    typedef                  constant_iterator;
    constant_iterator        defines_constant_begin() const;
    constant_iterator        defines_constant_end() const;
    const d_Constant &       resolve_constant(const char *name) const;

    typedef type_iterator;
    type_iterator            defines_type_begin() const;
    type_iterator            defines_type_end() const;
    const d_Type &           resolve_type(const char *name) const;

    d_Boolean                has_extent() const;
};
```

5.5.2.6 d_Ref_Type

d_Ref_Type instances are used to describe types that are references to other types. References can be pointers, references (like d_Ref<T>), or other language-specific references. The referenced object or literal can be shared by more than one reference.

```
class d_Ref_Type : public d_Type {
public:
    typedef enum { REF, POINTER } d_Ref_Kind;
    d_Ref_Kind                 ref_kind() const;
    const d_Type &             referenced_type() const;
};
```

5.5.2.7 d_Collection_Type

A d_Collection_Type describes a type that aggregates a variable number of elements of a single type and provides ordering, accessing, and comparison functionality.

```
class d_Collection_Type : public d_Type {
public:
    typedef enum {   LIST,
                     ARRAY,
                     BAG,
```

```
                         SET,
                         DICTIONARY,
                         STL_LIST,
                         STL_SET,
                         STL_MULTISET,
                         STL_VECTOR,
                         STL_MAP,
                         STL_MULTIMAP } d_Kind;

    d_Kind               kind() const;
    const d_Type &       element_type() const;
};
```

5.5.2.8 d_Keyed_Collection_Type

A d_Keyed_Collection_Type describes a collection type whose element can be accessed via keys. Examples are dictionaries and maps.

```
class d_Keyed_Collection_Type : public d_Collection_Type {
public:
    const d_Type &       key_type() const;
    const d_Type &       value_type() const;
};
```

5.5.2.9 d_Primitive_Type

d_Primitive_Type objects represent built-in types. These types are atomic; they are not composed of other types.

```
class d_Primitive_Type : public d_Type {
public:
    typedef enum {
              CHAR,
              SHORT,
              LONG,
              DOUBLE,
              FLOAT,
              USHORT,
              ULONG,
              OCTET,
              BOOLEAN,
              ENUMERATION } d_TypeId;

    d_TypeId             type_id() const;
};
```

5.5.2.10 d_Enumeration_Type

A d_Enumeration_Type describes a type whose domain is a list of identifiers.

An enumeration defines a scope for its identifiers. These identifiers are modeled by a list of related d_Constant objects. The d_Constant objects accessed via the iterator returned by defines_constant_begin are returned in their declaration order.

Constant descriptions can be accessed by name using the inherited method *d_Scope*::resolve. The method resolve_constant can also be used as a shortcut. The inherited iterator *d_Meta_Object*::meta_object_iterator returns enumeration member descriptions of type d_Constant.

The name of the constant descriptions is equivalent to the domain of the enumeration identifiers. All constants of an enumeration must be of the same discrete type. The enumeration identifiers are associated with values of this discrete type. For instance, an enumeration "days_of_week" has the domain "Monday," "Tuesday," "Wednesday," and so on. The enumeration description refers to a list of seven constant descriptions. The names of these descriptions are named "Monday," "Tuesday," "Wednesday," and so on. All these descriptions reference the same type description, here an object of type d_Primitive_Type with the name "int". The values of the constants are integers, e.g., 1, 2, 3, and so on up to 7, and can be obtained from the constant description.

```
class d_Enumeration_Type : public d_Primitive_Type, public d_Scope{
public:
    typedef constant_iterator;
    constant_iterator       defines_constant_begin() const;
    constant_iterator       defines_constant_end() const;
    const d_Constant &      resolve_constant(const char *name) const;
};
```

5.5.2.11 d_Structure_Type

d_Structure_Type describes application-defined aggregated values. The members represent the state of the structure. Structures have no identity.

A structure defines a scope for its members. These members are modeled using a list of related d_Attribute objects. The member descriptions can be accessed by name using the inherited method *d_Scope*::resolve. The method resolve_attribute can be used as a shortcut.

The inherited iterator *d_Meta_Object*::meta_object_iterator returns member descriptions of type d_Attribute. Structure members are also accessible via the iterator returned by defines_attribute_begin, which returns them during iteration in the order they are declared in the structure.

```
class d_Structure_Type : public d_Type, public d_Scope {
public:
      typedef                    attribute_iterator;
      attribute_iterator         defines_attribute_begin() const;
      attribute_iterator         defines_attribute_end() const;
      const d_Attribute &        resolve_attribute(const char *name) const;
};
```

5.5.2.12 d_Alias_Type

A d_Alias_Type describes a type that is equivalent to another type, but has another name. The description of the related type is returned by the method alias_type.

The defining scope of a type alias is either a module or a class; the inherited method *d_Meta_Object*::defined_in returns an object of class d_Class or d_Module.

```
class d_Alias_Type : public d_Type {
public:
      const d_Type &             alias_type() const;
};
```

5.5.2.13 d_Property

d_Property is an abstract base class for d_Attribute and d_Relationship. Properties have a name and a type. The name is returned by the inherited method *d_Meta_Object*::name. The type description can be obtained using the method type_of.

Properties are defined in the scope of exactly one structure or class. The inherited method *d_Meta_Object*::defined_in returns an object of class d_Structure_Type or d_Class, respectively.

```
class d_Property : public d_Meta_Object {
public:
      const d_Type &             type_of() const;
      d_Access_Kind              access_kind() const;
};
```

5.5.2.14 d_Attribute

d_Attribute describes a member of an object or a literal. An attribute has a name and a type. The name is returned by the inherited method *d_Meta_Object*::name. The type description of an attribute can be obtained using the inherited method d_Property::type_of.

Attributes may be read-only, in which case their values cannot be changed. This is described in the meta object by the method is_read_only. If an attribute is a static data member of a class, the method is_static returns d_True.

Attributes are defined in the scope of exactly one class or structure. The inherited method *d_Meta_Object*::defined_in returns an object of class d_Class or d_Structure_Type, respectively.

```
class d_Attribute : public d_Property {
public:
    d_Boolean        is_read_only() const;
    d_Boolean        is_static() const;
    unsigned long    dimension() const;
};
```

5.5.2.15 d_Relationship

d_Relationships model bilateral object references between participating objects. In practice, two relationship meta objects are required to represent each traversal direction of the relationship. Operations are defined implicitly to form and drop the relationship, as well as accessor operations for traversing the relationship. The inherited *d_Type* expresses the cardinality. It may be either a d_Rel_Ref, d_Rel_Set, or d_Rel_List; the method rel_kind returns a d_Rel_Kind enumeration indicating the type.

The defining scope of a relationship is a class. The inherited method *d_Meta_Object*::defined_in returns a d_Class object. The method defined_in_class can be used as a shortcut.

```
class d_Relationship : public d_Property {
public:
    typedef enum { REL_REF, REL_SET, REL_LIST } d_Rel_Kind;
    d_Rel_Kind                  rel_kind() const;
    const d_Relationship &      inverse() const;
    const d_Class &             defined_in_class() const;
};
```

5.5.2.16 d_Operation

d_Operation describes the behavior supported by application objects. Operations have a name, a return type, and a signature (list of parameters), which is modeled by the inherited method *d_Meta_Object*::name, a *d_Type* object returned by result_type, and a list of d_Parameter objects (accessible via an iterator). The d_Parameter objects are returned during iteration in the order that they are declared in the operation. Operations may raise exceptions. The list of possible exceptions is described by a list of d_Exception objects (accessible via an iterator).

Operations may have an access specifier. This is described by the method access_kind inherited from d_Property.

An operation defines a scope for its parameters. They can be accessed by name using the inherited method *d_Scope*::resolve. The method resolve_parameter can be used as a shortcut.

The inherited iterator *d_Meta_Object*::meta_object_iterator returns a parameter description of type d_Parameter. Parameters are also accessible via a special parameter_iterator.

The defining scope for an operation is either a class or a module.

The inherited method *d_Meta_Object*::defined_in returns a d_Class object.

```
class d_Operation : public d_Meta_Object, public d_Scope {
public:
      const d_Type &              result_type () const;
      d_Boolean                   is_static() const;

      typedef                     parameter_iterator;
      parameter_iterator          defines_parameter_begin() const;
      parameter_iterator          defines_parameter_end() const;
      const d_Parameter &         resolve_parameter(const char *name) const;

      typedef                     exception_iterator;
      exception_iterator          raises_exception_begin() const;
      exception_iterator          raises_exception_end() const;
      d_Access_Kind               access_kind() const;
};
```

If the operation is a static member function of a class, the method is_static returns d_True.

5.5.2.17 d_Exception

Operations may raise exceptions. A d_Exception describes such an exception. An exception has a name, which can be accessed using the inherited method *d_Meta_Object*::name, and a type whose description can be obtained using the method exception_type.

A single exception can be raised in more than one operation. The list of operation descriptions can be accessed via an iterator.

The defining scope of an exception is a module. The inherited method *d_Meta_Object*::defined_in returns a d_Module object. The method defined_in_module can be used as a shortcut.

```
class d_Exception : public d_Meta_Object {
```

```
public:
      const d_Type &          exception_type() const;
      typedef                 operation_iterator;
      operation_iterator      raised_in_operation_begin() const;
      operation_iterator      raised_in_operation_end() const;
      const d_Module &        defined_in_module() const;
};
```

5.5.2.18 d_Parameter

d_Parameter describes a parameter of an operation. Parameters have a name, a type, and a mode (in, out and inout). The name is returned by the inherited method *d_Meta_Object*::name.

The type description can be obtained by the method parameter_type. The mode is returned by the method mode.

Parameters are defined in the scope of exactly one operation, and the inherited method *d_Meta_Object*::defined_in returns an object of class d_Operation. The method defined_in_operation can be used as a shortcut.

```
class d_Parameter : public d_Meta_Object {
public:
      typedef enum { IN, OUT, INOUT } d_Mode;
      d_Mode                  mode() const;
      const d_Type &          parameter_type() const;
      const d_Operation &     defined_in_operation() const;
};
```

5.5.2.19 d_Constant

Constants provide a mechanism for statically associating values with names in the repository. Constants are used by enumerations to form domains. In this case, the name of a d_Constant is used as an identifier for an enumeration value. Its name is returned by the inherited method *d_Meta_Object*::name.

Constants are defined in the scope of exactly one module or class. The inherited method *d_Meta_Object*::defined_in returns an object of class d_Module or d_Class, respectively.

```
class d_Constant : public d_Meta_Object {
public:
      const d_Type &          constant_type() const;
      void *                  constant_value() const;
};
```

5.5.2.20 d_Inheritance

d_Inheritance is used to describe the bidirectional relationship between a base class and a subclass, as well as the type of inheritance used. An object of type d_Inheritance connects two objects of type d_Class.

Depending on the programming language, inheritance relationships can have properties. The schema objects that describe inheritance relationships are augmented with information to reproduce the language-specific extensions.

```
class d_Inheritance {
public:
    const d_Class &        derives_from() const;
    const d_Class &        inherits_to() const;

    d_Access_Kind          access_kind() const;
    d_Boolean              is_virtual() const;
};
```

5.6 Example

This section gives a complete example of a small C++ application. This application manages people records. A Person may be entered into the database. Then special events can be recorded: marriage, the birth of children, moving to a new address.

The application comprises two transactions: the first one populates the database, while the second consults and updates it.

The next section defines the schema of the database, as C++ ODL classes. The C++ program is given in the subsequent section.

5.6.1 Schema Definition

For the explanation of the semantics of this example, see Section 3.2.3. Here is the C++ ODL syntax:

```
// Schema Definition in C++ ODL
class City;             // forward declaration
struct Address {
    d_UShort            number;
    d_String            street;
    d_Ref<City>         city;
                        Address();
                        Address(d_UShort, const char*, const d_Ref<City> &);
};
```

```
extern const char _spouse [ ],  _parents [ ],  _children [ ];

class Person : public d_Object {
public:
// Attributes (all public, for this example)
     d_String                    name;
     Address                     address;
// Relationships
     d_Rel_Ref<Person, _spouse>  spouse;
     d_Rel_List<Person, _parents> children;
     d_Rel_List<Person, _children> parents;
// Operations
                                 Person(const char * pname);
     void                        birth(const d_Ref<Person> &child); // a child is born
     void                        marriage(const d_Ref<Person> &to_whom);
     d_Ref<d_Set<d_Ref<Person> > >ancestors() const; // returns ancestors
     void                        move(const Address &); // move to a new address
// Extent
static  d_Ref<d_Set<d_Ref<Person> > >   people; // a reference to class extent1
static  const char * const             extent_name;
};
class City : public d_Object {
public:
// Attributes
     d_ULong                         city_code;
     d_String                        name;
     d_Ref<d_Set<d_Ref<Person> > >   population;  // the people living in this city
// Operations
                                     City(int, const char*);
// Extension
static  d_Ref<d_Set<d_Ref<City> > >  cities;     // a reference to the class extent
static  const char * const           extent_name;
};
```

---

1. This (transient) static variable will be initialized at transaction begin time (see the application).

5.6.2 Schema Implementation

We now define the code of the operations declared in the schema. This is written in plain C++. We assume the C++ ODL preprocessor has generated a file, "schema.hxx", which contains the standard C++ definitions equivalent to the C++ ODL classes.

```
// Classes Implementation in C++
#include "schema.hxx"

const char _spouse [ ] = "spouse";
const char _parents [ ] = "parents";
const char _children [ ] = "children";

// Address structure:

Address::Address(d_UShort pnum, const char* pstreet,
                                const d_Ref<City> &pcity)
  :  number(pnumber),
     street(pstreet),
     city(pcity)
 { }

Address::Address()
  :  number(0),
     street(0),
     city(0)
 { }
// Person Class:
const char * const Person::extent_name = "people";
Person::Person(const char * pname)
  :  name(pname)
 {
     people->insert_element(this);  // Put this person in the extension
}
void Person::birth(const d_Ref<Person> &child)
 {                                    // Adds a new child to the children list
     children.insert_element_last(child);
     if(spouse)
          spouse->children.insert_element_last(child);
}
void Person::marriage(const d_Ref<Person> &to_whom)
 {                               // Initializes the spouse relationship
```

```
        spouse = with;              // with->spouse is automatically set to this person
    }
    d_Ref<d_Set<d_Ref<Person> > >  Person::ancestors()
    {                               // Constructs the set of all ancestors of this person
        d_Ref<d_Set<d_Ref<Person> > >  the_ancestors =
                                        new d_Set<d_Ref<Person> >;
        int i;
        for( i = 0; i < 2; i++)
            if( parents[i] ) {
                // The ancestors = parents union ancestors(parents)
                the_ancestors->insert_element(parents[i]);
                d_Ref<d_Set<d_Ref<Person> > >
                    grand_parents= parents[i]->ancestors();
                the_ancestors->union_with(*grand_parents);
                grand_parents.delete_object();
            }
        return the_ancestors;
    }
    void Person::move(const Address &new_address)
    {                               // Updates the address attribute of this person
        if(address.city)
            address.city->population->remove_element(this);
        new_address.city->population->insert_element(this);
        mark_modified();2
        address = new_address;
    }
    // City class:

    const char * const City::extent_name = "cities";

    City::City(d_ULong code, const char * cname)
      : city_code(code),
        name(cname)
    {
        cities->insert_element(this);       // Put this city into the extension
    }
```

2. Do not forget it! Notice that it is necessary only in the case where an attribute of the object is modified. When a relationship is updated, the object is automatically marked modified.

5.6.3 An Application

We now have the whole schema well defined and implemented. We are able to populate the database and play with it. In the following application, the transaction Load builds some objects into the database. Then the transaction Consult reads it, prints some reports from it, and makes updates. Each transaction is implemented inside a C++ function.

The database is opened by the main program, which then starts the transactions.

```
#include <iostream.h>
#include "schema.hxx"

static d_Database dbobj;
static d_Database * database = &dbobj;

void Load()
{                          // Transaction that populates the database
    d_Transaction load;
    load.begin();
    // Create both persons and cities extensions, and name them.

    Person::people = new(database) d_Set<d_Ref<Person> >;
    City::cities = new(database) d_Set<d_Ref<City> >;

    database->set_object_name(Person::people, Person::extent_name);
    database->set_object_name(City::cities, City::extent_name);

    // Construct 3 persistent objects from class Person.

    d_Ref<Person> God, Adam, Eve;

    God  = new(database, "Person") Person("God");
    Adam = new(database, "Person") Person("Adam");
    Eve  = new(database, "Person") Person("Eve");

// Construct an Address structure, Paradise, as (7 Apple Street, Garden),
// and set the address attributes of Adam and Eve.

    Address Paradise(7, "Apple", new(database, "City") City(0, "Garden"));

    Adam->move(Paradise);
    Eve->move(Paradise);
```

```
// Define the family relationships
      God->birth(Adam);
      Adam->marriage(Eve);
      Adam->birth(new(database, "Person") Person("Cain"));
      Adam->birth(new(database, "Person") Person("Abel"));

      load.commit();      // Commit transaction, putting objects into the database
}

static void print_persons(const d_Collection<d_Ref<Person> >& s)
{                               // A service function to print a collection of persons
      d_Ref<Person> p;
      d_Iterator<d_Ref<Person> > it = s.create_iterator();
      while( it.next(p) ) {
            cout << "--- " << p->name << " lives in ";
            if (p->address.city)
                  cout << p->address.city->name;
            else
                  cout << "Unknown";
            cout << endl;
      }
}

void Consult()
{                         // Transaction that consults and updates the database
      d_Transaction                 consult;
      d_List<d_Ref<Person> >  list;
      d_Bag<d_Ref<Person>>    bag;
      consult.begin();
      // Static references to objects or collections must be recomputed
      // after a commit
      Person::people = database->lookup_object(Person::extent_name);
      City::cities = database->lookup_object(City::extent_name);
      // Now begin the transaction
      cout << "All the people ....:" << endl;
      print_persons(*Person::people);
      cout << "All the people sorted by name ....:" << endl;
      d_oql_execute("select p from people order by name", list);
      print_persons(list);
      cout << "People having 2 children and living in Paradise ...:" << endl;
```

```
    d_oql_execute(list, "select p from p in people\
            where    p.address.city.name = \"Garden\"\
                     and count(p.children) = 2", bag);
    print_persons(bag);
    // Adam and Eve are moving ...
    Address Earth(13, "Macadam", new(database, "City") City(1, "St-Croix"));
    d_Ref<Person> Adam;
    d_oql_execute("element(select p from p in people\
            where p.name = \"Adam\")", Adam);
    Adam->move(Earth);
    Adam->spouse->move(Earth);
    cout << "Cain's ancestors ...:" << endl;
    d_Ref<Person> Cain = Adam->children.retrieve_element_at(0);
    print_persons(*(Cain->ancestors()));
    consult.commit();
}

main()
{
    database->open("family");
    Load();
    Consult();
    database->close();
}
```

Chapter 6

Smalltalk Binding

6.1 Introduction

This chapter defines the Smalltalk binding for the ODMG Object Model, ODL, and OQL. While no Smalltalk language standard exists at this time, ODMG member organizations participate in the X3J20 ANSI Smalltalk standards committee. We expect that as standards are agreed upon by that committee and commercial implementations become available that the ODMG Smalltalk binding will evolve to accommodate them. In the interests of consistency and until an official Smalltalk standard exists, we will map many ODL concepts to class descriptions as specified by Smalltalk80.

6.1.1 Language Design Principles

The ODMG Smalltalk binding is based upon two principles: it should bind to Smalltalk in a natural way that is consistent with the principles of the language, and it should support language interoperability consistent with ODL specification and semantics. We believe that organizations who specify their objects in ODL will insist that the Smalltalk binding honor those specifications. These principles have several implications that are evident in the design of the binding described in the body of this chapter.

1. There is a unified type system that is shared by Smalltalk and the ODBMS. This type system is ODL as mapped into Smalltalk by the Smalltalk binding.
2. The binding respects the Smalltalk syntax, meaning the Smalltalk language will not have to be modified to accommodate this binding. ODL concepts will be represented using normal Smalltalk coding conventions.
3. The binding respects the fact that Smalltalk is dynamically typed. Arbitrary Smalltalk objects may be stored persistently, including ODL-specified objects that will obey the ODL typing semantics.
4. The binding respects the dynamic memory management semantics of Smalltalk. Objects will become persistent when they are referenced by other persistent objects in the database and will be removed when they are no longer reachable in this manner.

6.1.2 Language Binding

The ODMG binding for Smalltalk is based upon the OMG Smalltalk IDL binding.[1] As ODL is a superset of IDL, the IDL binding defines a large part of the mapping required by this document. This chapter provides informal descriptions of the IDL binding topics and more formally defines the Smalltalk binding for the ODL extensions, including relationships, literals, and collections.

The ODMG Smalltalk binding can be automated by an ODL compiler that processes ODL declarations and generates a graph of *meta objects*, which model the schema of the database. These meta objects provide the type information that allows the Smalltalk binding to support the required ODL type semantics. The complete set of such meta objects defines the entire *schema* of the database and would serve much in the same capacity as an OMG Interface Repository. This chapter includes a Smalltalk binding for the Meta Object interfaces defined in Chapter 2.

In such a repository, the meta objects that represent the schema of the database may be programmatically accessed and modified by Smalltalk applications, through their standard interfaces. One such application, a *binding generator*, may be used to generate Smalltalk class and method skeletons from the meta objects. This binding generator would resolve the type/class mapping choices that are inherent in the ODMG Smalltalk binding.

The information in the meta objects is also sufficient to *regenerate* the ODL declarations for the portions of the schema that they represent. The relationships between these components are illustrated in Figure 6-1. A conforming implementation must support the Smalltalk output of this binding process; it need not provide automated tools.

6.1.3 Mapping the ODMG Object Model into Smalltalk

Although Smalltalk provides a powerful data model that is close to the one presented in Chapter 2, it remains necessary to precisely describe how the concepts of the ODMG Object Model map into concrete Smalltalk constructions.

6.1.3.1 Object and Literal

An ODMG object type maps into a Smalltalk class. Since Smalltalk has no distinct notion of literal objects, both ODMG objects and ODMG literals may be implemented by the same Smalltalk classes.

1. OMG Document 94-11-8, November 16, 1994.

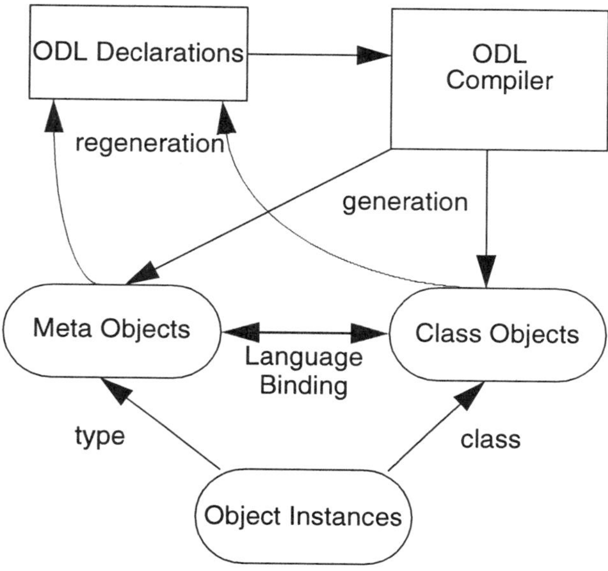

Figure 6-1. Smalltalk Language Binding

6.1.3.2 Relationship

This concept is not directly supported by Smalltalk and must be implemented by Smalltalk methods that support a standard protocol. The relationship itself is typically implemented either as an object reference (one-to-one relation) or as an appropriate Collection subclass (one-to-many, many-to-many relations) embedded as an instance variable of the object. Rules for defining sets of accessor methods are presented that allow all relationships to be managed uniformly.

6.1.3.3 Names

Objects in Smalltalk have a unique object identity, and references to objects may appear in a variety of naming contexts. The Smalltalk system dictionary contains globally accessible objects that are indexed by Symbols which name them. A similar protocol has been defined on the Database class for managing named persistent objects which exist within the database.

6.1.3.4 Extents

Extents are not supported by this binding. Instead, users may use the database naming protocol to explicitly register and access named Collections.

6.1.3.5 Keys

Key declarations are not supported by this binding. Instead, users may use the database naming protocol to explicitly register and access named Dictionaries.

6.1.3.6 Implementation

Everything in Smalltalk is implemented as an object. Objects in Smalltalk have instance variables that are private to the implementations of their methods. An instance variable refers to a single Smalltalk object, the class of which is available at runtime through the class method. This instance object may itself refer to other objects.

6.1.3.7 Collections

Smalltalk provides a rich set of Collection subclasses, including Set, Bag, List, Dictionary, and Array classes. Where possible, this binding has chosen to use existing methods to implement the ODMG Collection interfaces. Unlike statically typed languages, Smalltalk collections may contain heterogeneous elements whose type is only known at runtime. Implementations utilizing these collections must be able to enforce the homogeneous type constraints of ODL.

6.1.3.8 Database Administration

Databases are represented by instances of Database objects in this binding, and a protocol is defined for creating databases and for connecting to them. Some operations regarding database administration are not addressed by this binding and represent opportunities for future work.

6.2 Smalltalk ODL

6.2.1 OMG IDL Binding Overview

Since the Smalltalk/ODL binding is based upon the OMG Smalltalk/IDL binding, we include here some descriptions of the important aspects of the IDL binding that are needed in order to better understand the ODL binding that follows. These descriptions are not intended to be definitions of these aspects, however, and the reader should consult the OMG binding document directly for the actual definitions.

6.2.1.1 Identifiers

IDL allows the use of underscore characters in its identifiers. Since underscore characters are not allowed in all Smalltalk implementations, the Smalltalk/IDL binding provides a conversion algorithm. To convert an IDL identifier with underscores into a Smalltalk identifier, remove the underscore and capitalize the following letter (if it exists):

```
month_of_year
```

in IDL, becomes in Smalltalk:

```
monthOfYear
```

6.2.1.2 Interfaces

Interfaces define sets of operations that an instance that supports that interface must possess. As such, interfaces correspond to Smalltalk protocols. Implementors are free to map interfaces to classes as required to specify the operations that are supported by a Smalltalk object. In the IDL binding, all objects that have an IDL definition must implement a CORBAName method that returns the fully scoped name of an interface that defines all of its IDL behavior.

```
anObject CORBAName
```

6.2.1.3 Objects

Any Smalltalk object that has an associated IDL definition (by its CORBAName method) may be a CORBA object. In addition, many Smalltalk objects may also represent instances of IDL types as defined below.

6.2.1.4 Operations

IDL operations allow zero or more ***in*** parameters and may also return a functional result. Unlike Smalltalk, IDL operations also allow ***out*** and ***inout*** parameters to be defined, which allow more than a single result to be communicated back to the caller of the method. In the Smalltalk/IDL binding, holders for these output parameters are passed explicitly by the caller in the form of objects that support the CORBAParameter protocol (value, value:).

IDL operation signatures also differ in syntax from that of Smalltalk selectors, and the IDL binding specifies a mapping rule for composing default selectors from the operation and parameter names of the IDL definition. To produce the default Smalltalk operation selector, begin with the operation name. If the operation has only one parameter, append a colon. If the operation has more than one parameter, append a colon and then append each of the second to last parameter names, each followed by colon. The binding allows default selectors to be explicitly overridden, allowing flexibility in method naming.

```
current();
days_in_year(in ushort year);
from_hmstz(in ushort hour,
   ushort minute,
   in float second,
   in short tz_hour,
   in short tz_minute);
```

in IDL, become in Smalltalk:

```
current
daysInYear:
fromHmstz:minute:second:tzHour:tzMinute:
```

6.2.1.5 Constants

Constants, Exceptions, and Enums that are defined in IDL are made available to the Smalltalk programmer in a global dictionary CORBAConstants, which is indexed by the fully qualified scoped name of the IDL entity.

```
const Time_Zone USpacific = -8;
```

would be accessed by the Smalltalk:

```
(CORBAConstants at: #'::Time::USpacific)
```

6.2.1.6 Types

Since, in Smalltalk, everything is an object, there is no separation of objects and datatypes as exist in other hybrid languages such as C++. Thus it is necessary for some Smalltalk objects to fill dual roles in the binding. Since some objects in Smalltalk are more natural in this role than others, we will describe the simple type mappings first.

Simple Types

IDL allows several basic datatypes that are similar to literal valued objects in Smalltalk. While exact type-class mappings are not specified in the IDL binding for technical reasons, the following mappings comply:

- short, unsigned short, long, unsigned long — An appropriate Integer subclass (SmallInteger, LargePositiveInteger, LargeNegativeInteger, depending upon the value)
- float, double — Float and Double, respectively
- char — Character
- boolean — The Boolean values **true** and **false**
- octet — SmallInteger
- string — An appropriate String subclass
- any — Object (any class that supports CORBAName)

Compound Types

IDL has a number of data structuring mechanisms that have a less intuitive mapping to Smalltalk. The list below describes the *implicit* bindings for these types. Implementors are also free to provide *explicit* bindings for these types that allow other Smalltalk objects to be used in these roles. These explicit bindings are especially important in the ODL binding since the various Collections have an object-literal duality that is not present in IDL (e.g., ODL list sequences also have a List interface).

- Array — An appropriate Array subclass
- Sequence — An appropriate OrderedCollection subclass
- Structure — Implicit: A Dictionary containing the fields of the structure keyed by the structure fields as Symbols
- Structure — Explicit: A class supporting accessor methods to get and set of the structure fields
- Union — Implicit: Object (any class that supports CORBAName)
- Union — Explicit: A class that supports the CORBAUnion protocol (discriminator, discriminator:, value, and value: methods)
- Enum — A class that supports the CORBAEnum protocol (=, <, > methods). Implementations must ensure that the correct ordering is maintained and that instances of different enumeration types cannot be compared.

Binding Examples

```
union Number switch(boolean) {
   case TRUE:                long integerValue;
   case FALSE:               float realValue;
   };
struct Point{Number x; Number y;};
```

The implicit bindings for the above would allow a Point to be represented by a Dictionary instance containing the keys #x and #y and values that are instances of Integer or Float:

```
aPoint := Dictionary with: #x -> 452 with: #y -> 687.44
```

Alternatively, the binding allows the Smalltalk class Point to represent the struct Point{ } because it implements the selectors x, x:, y, and y:.

```
enum Weekday{Sunday, Monday, Tuesday, Wednesday, Thursday, Friday,
Saturday};
```

the Smalltalk values for Weekday enumerations would be provided by the implementation and accessed from the CORBAConstants global dictionary, as in:

```
(CORBAConstants at: #'::Date::Wednesday) >
   (CORBAConstants at: #'::Date::Tuesday)
```

6.2.1.7 Exceptions

IDL exceptions are defined within modules and interfaces, and are referenced by the operation signatures that raise them. Each exception may define a set of alternative results that are returned to the caller should the exception be raised by the operation. These values are similar to structures, and Dictionaries are used to represent exception values.

```
exception InvalidDate{};
```

would be raised by the following Smalltalk:

```
(CORBAConstants at: #'::DateFactory::InvalidDate')
   CORBARaiseWith: Dictionary new
```

6.2.2 Smalltalk ODL Binding Extensions

This section describes the binding of ODMG ODL to Smalltalk. ODL provides a description of the database schema as a set of interfaces, including their attributes, relationships, and operations. Smalltalk implementations consist of a set of object classes and their instances. The language binding provides a mapping between these domains.

6.2.2.1 Interfaces and Classes

In ODL, interfaces are used to represent the *abstract behavior* of an object and classes are used to model the *abstract state* of objects. Both types may be implemented by Smalltalk classes. In order to maintain the independence of ODMG ODL and OMG IDL type bindings, all uses of the method CORBAName in the IDL binding are replaced by the method ODLName in this definition. This method will return the name of the ODL interface or class that is bound to the object in the schema repository.

```
aDate ODLName
```

returns the string '::Date', which is the name of its ODL interface. Similarly, all uses of the CORBAConstants dictionary for constants, enums, and exceptions will be replaced by a global dictionary named ODLConstants in this definition. For example:

```
(ODLConstants at: #'::Date::Monday')
```

is a Weekday enum,

```
(ODLConstants at: #'::Time::USpacific')
```

equals -8, and

```
(ODLConstants at: #'::DateFactory::InvalidDate')
```

is an exception.

6.2.2.2 Attribute Declarations

Attribute declarations are used to define pairs of accessor operations that *get* and *set* attribute values. Generally, there will be a one-to-one correspondence between attributes defined within an ODL class and instance variables defined within the corresponding Smalltalk class, although this is not required. ODL attributes define the *abstract state* of their object when they appear within class definitions. When attributes appear within interface definitions, as in IDL they are merely a convenience mechanism for introducing get and set accessing operations.

For example:

```
attribute Enum Rank {full, associate, assistant} rank;
```

yields Smalltalk methods:

```
rank
rank: aProfessorRank
```

6.2.2.3 Relationship Declarations

Relationships define sets of accessor operations for adding and removing associations between objects. As with attributes, relationships are a part of an object's *abstract state*. The Smalltalk binding for relationships results in public methods to *form* and *drop* members from the relationship, plus public methods on the relationship target classes to provide access and private methods to manage the required referential integrity constraints. We begin the relationship binding by applying the Chapter 2 mapping rule from ODL relationships to equivalent IDL constructions, and then illustrate with a complete example.

Single-Valued Relationships

For single-value relationships such as

```
relationship  X  Y              inverse  Z;
```

we expand first to the IDL attribute and operations:

```
attribute     X  Y;
void          form_Y(in X target);
void          drop_Y(in X target);
```

which results in the following Smalltalk selectors:

```
Y
formY:
dropY:
Y:                              "private"
```

For example, from Chapter 3:

```
interface Course {
...
   relationship Professor is_taught_by
       inverse Professor::teaches;
 ...
}
```

yields Smalltalk methods (on the class Course):

```
formIsTaughtBy: aProfessor
dropIsTaughtBy: aProfessor
isTaughtBy
isTaughtBy:                     "private"
```

Multivalued Relationships

For a multivalued ODL relationship such as

```
relationship  set<X>            Y inverse Z;
```

we expand first to the IDL attribute and operations:

```
readonly attribute              set<X>  Y;
void               form_Y(in X target);
void               drop_Y(in X target);
void               add_Y(in X target);
void               remove_Y(in X target);
```

which results in the following Smalltalk selectors:

```
Y
formY:
dropY:
addY:            "private"
removeY:         "private"
```

For example, from Chapter 3:

```
interface Professor {
...
   relationship Set<Course> teaches
       inverse Course::is_taught_by;
...
}
```

yields Smalltalk methods (on class Professor):

```
formTeaches: aCourse
dropTeaches: aCourse
teaches
addTeaches: aCourse          "private"
removeTeaches: aCourse       "private"
```

Finally, to form the above relationship, the programmer could write:

```
| professor course |
professor := Professor new.
course := Course new.
professor formTeaches: course.
   -or-
course formIsTaughtBy: professor.
```

6.2.2.4 Collections

Chapter 2 introduced several new kinds of Collections that extend the IDL sequence to deal with the special needs of ODBMS users. The following shows the Smalltalk method selector that this binding defines for each of the Collection interfaces. Where possible, we have explicitly bound operations to commonly available Smalltalk80 selectors when the default operation binding rules would not produce the desired selector.

"interface Collection"	
size	"unsigned long cardinality()"
isEmpty	"boolean is_empty()"
isOrdered	"boolean is_ordered()"
allowsDuplicates	"boolean allows_duplicates()"
add: anObject	"void insert_element(...)"
remove: anObject	"void remove_element(...)"
includes: anObject	"boolean contains_element(...)"
createIterator: aBoolean	"Iterator create_iterator(...)"
createBidirectionalIterator: aBoolean	"BidirectionalIterator create_bidirectional_iterator(...)"
"interface Iterator"	
isStable	"boolean is_stable()"
atEnd	"boolean at_end()"
reset	"boolean reset()"
getElement	"any get_element()"
nextPosition	"void next_position()"
replaceElement: anAny	"void replace_element(...)"
"interface BidirectionalIterator"	
atBeginning	"boolean at_beginning()"
previousPosition	"void previous_position()"
"interface Set"	
createUnion: aSet	"Set create_union(...)"
createIntersection: aSet	"Set create_intersection(...)"
createDifference: aSet	"Set create_difference(...)"
isSubsetOf: aSet	"boolean is_subset_of(...)"
isProperSubsetOf: aSet	"boolean is_proper_subset_of(...)"
isSupersetOf: aSet	"boolean is_superset_of(...)"
isProperSupersetOf: aSet	"boolean is_proper_superset_of(...)"
"interface CollectionFactory"	
new: aLong	"Collection new_of_size(...)"
"interface Bag"	
occurrencesOf: anAny	"unsigned long occurrences_of(...)"
createUnion: aBag	"Bag create_union(...)"
createIntersection: aBag	"Bag create_intersection(...)"
createDifference: aBag	"Bag create_difference(...)"
"interface List"	
at: aULong put: anObject	"void replace_element_at(...)"
removeElementAt: aULong	"void remove_element_at(...)"
retrieveElementAt: aULong	"any retrieve_element_at(...)"
add: anObject after: aULong	"void insert_element_after(...)"
add: anObject before: aULong	"void insert_element_before(.)"
addFirst: anObject	"void insert_element_first(...)"
addLast: anObject	"void insert_element_last(...)"
removeFirst	"void remove_first_element()"
removeLast	"void remove_last_element()"
first	"any retrieve_first_element()"
last	"any retrieve_last_element()"
concat: aList	"List concat(...)"
append: aList	"void append(...)"

"interface Array"

replaceElementAt: aULong element: anAnyObject	"void replace_element_at(...)"
removeElementAt: aULong	"void remove_element_at(...)"
retrieveElementAt: aULong	"any retrieve_element_at(...)"
resize: aULong	"void resize(...)"

"interface Dictionary"

at: anObject put: anObject1	"void bind(...)"
removeKey: anObject	"void unbind(...)"
at: anObject	"any lookup(...)"
includesKey: anObject	"boolean contains_key(...)"

6.2.2.5 Structured Literals

Chapter 2 defined structured literals to represent Date, Time, Timestamp, and Interval values that must be supported by each language binding. The following section defines the binding from each operation to the appropriate Smalltalk selector.

"interface Date"

year	"ushort year()"
month	"ushort month()"
day	"ushort day()"
dayOfYear	"ushort day_of_year()"
monthOfYear	"Month month_of_year()"
dayOfWeek	"Weekday day_of_week()"
isLeapYear	"boolean is_leap_year()"
= aDate	"boolean is_equal(...)"
> aDate	"boolean is_greater(...)"
>= aDate	"boolean is_greater_or_equal(...)"
< aDate	"boolean is_less(...)"
<= aDate	"boolean is_less_or_equal(...)"
isBetween: aDate and: aDate1	"boolean is_between(...)"
next: aWeekday	"Date next(...)"
previous: aWeekday	"Date previous(...)"
addDays: along	"Date add_days(...)"
subtractDays: aLong	"Date subtract_days(...)"
subtractDate: aDate	"Date subtract_date(...)"

"interface DateFactory"

julianDate: aUShort julianDay: aUShort1	"Date julian_date(...)"
calendarDate: aUShort month: aUShort1 day: aUShort2	"Date calendar_date(...)"
isLeapYear: aUShort	"boolean is_leap_year(...)"
isValidDate: aUShort month: aUShort1 day: aUShort2	"boolean is_valid_date(...)"
daysInYear: aUShort	"unsigned short days_in_year(...)"
daysInMonth: aUShort month: aMonth	"unsigned short days_in_month(...)"
today	"Date current()"

```
"interface Interval"
    day                                  "ushort day()"
    hour                                 "ushort hour()"
    minute                               "ushort minute()"
    second                               "ushort second()"
    millisecond                          "ushort millisecond()"
    isZero                               "boolean is_zero()"
    plus: anInterval                     "Interval plus(...)"
    minus: anInterval                    "Interval minus(...)"
    product: aLong                       "Interval product(...)"
    quotient: aLong                      "Interval quotient(...)"
    isEqual: anInterval                  "boolean is_equal(...)"
    isGreater: anInterval                "boolean is_greater(...)"
    isGreaterOrEqual: anInterval         "boolean is_greater_or_equal(...)"
    isLess: anInterval                   "boolean is_less(...)"
    isLessOrEqual: anInterval            "boolean is_less_or_equal(...)"
"interface Time"
    hour                                 "ushort hour()"
    minute                               "ushort minute()"
    second                               "ushort second()"
    millisecond                          "ushort millisecond()"
    timeZone                             "Time_Zone time_zone()"
    tzHour                               "ushort tz_hour()"
    tzMinute                             "ushort tz_minute()"
    = aTime                              "boolean is_equal(...)"
    > aTime                              "boolean is_greater(...)"
    >= aTime                             "boolean is_greater_or_equal(...)"
    < aTime                              "boolean is_less(...)"
    <= aTime                             "boolean is_less_or_equal(...)"
    isBetween: aTime and: aTime1         "boolean is_between(...)"
    addInterval: anInterval              "Time add_interval(...)"
    subtractInterval: anInterval         "Time subtract_interval(...)"
    subtractTime: aTime                  "Interval subtract_time(...)"
"interface TimeFactory"
    defaultTimeZone                      "Time_Zone default_time_zone()"
    setDefaultTimeZone                   "void setDefault_time_zone(...)"
    fromHms: aUShort
        minute: aUShort1
        second: aFloat                   "Time from_hms(...)"
    fromHmstz: aUShort
        minute: aUShort1
        second: aFloat
        tzhour: aShort
        tzminute: aShort1                "Time from_hmstz(...)"
    current                              "Time current(...)"
"interface Timestamp"
    getDate                              "Date get_date()"
    getTime                              "Time get_time()"
    year                                 "ushort year()"
    month                                "ushort month()"
```

day	"ushort day()"
hour	"ushort hour()"
minute	"ushort minute()"
second	"ushort second()"
millisecond	"ushort millisecond()"
tzHour	"ushort tz_hour(...)"
tzMinute	"ushort tz_minute(...)"
plus: anInterval	"Interval plus(...)"
minus: anInterval	"Interval minus(...)"
isEqual: aTimestamp	"boolean is_equal(...)"
isGreater: aTimestamp	"boolean is_greater(...)"
isGreaterOrEqual: aTimestamp	"boolean is_greater_or_equal(...)"
isLess: aTimestamp	"boolean is_less(...)"
isLessOrEqual: aTimestamp	"boolean is_less_or_equal(...)"
isBetween: aTimestamp bStamp: aTimestamp1	"boolean is_between(...)"
"interface TimestampFactory"	
current	"Timestamp current()"
create: aDate aTime: aTime	"Timestamp create(...)"

6.3 Smalltalk OML

The Smalltalk Object Manipulation Language (OML) consists of a set of method additions to the classes Object and Behavior, plus the classes Database and Transaction. The guiding principle in the design of Smalltalk OML is that the syntax used to create, delete, identify, reference, get/set property values, and invoke operations on a persistent object should be no different from that used for objects of shorter lifetimes. A single expression may thus freely intermix references to persistent and transient objects. All Smalltalk OML operations are invoked by sending messages to appropriate objects.

6.3.1 Object Protocol

Since all Smalltalk objects inherit from class Object, it is natural to implement some of the ODMG language binding mechanisms as methods on this class. The following text defines the Smalltalk binding for the common operations on all objects defined in Chapter 2.

"interface Object"	
== anObject	"boolean same_as(...)"
copy	"Object copy()"
lock: aLockType	"void lock(...)"
tryLock: aLockType	"boolean try_lock(...)"
"interface ObjectFactory"	
new	"Object new()"

6.3.1.1 Object Persistence

Persistence is not limited to any particular subset of the class hierarchy, nor is it determined at object creation time. A transient object that participates in a relationship with a persistent object will become persistent when a transaction commit occurs. This approach is called *transitive persistence*. Named objects (see "Database Names" on page 216) are the roots from which the Smalltalk binding's transitive persistence policy is computed.

6.3.1.2 Object Deletion

In the Smalltalk binding, as in Smalltalk, there is no notion of explicit deletion of objects. An object is removed from the database during garbage collection if that object is not referenced by any other persistent object. The delete() operation from interface Object is not supported.

6.3.1.3 Object Locking

Objects activated into memory acquire the default lock for the active concurrency control policy. Optionally, a lock can be explicitly acquired on an object by sending the appropriate locking message to it. Two locking mode enumeration values are required to be supported: read and write. The OMG Concurrency service's LockSet interface is the source of the following method definitions.

To acquire a lock on an object that will block the process until success, the syntax would be

```
anObject lock: aLockMode.
```

To acquire a lock without blocking, the syntax would be

```
anObject tryLock: aLockMode. "returns a boolean indicating
                                 success or failure"
```

In these methods, the receiver is locked in the context of the current transaction. A lockNotGrantedSignal is raised by the lock: method if the requested lock cannot be granted. Locks are released implicitly at the end of the transaction, unless an option to retain locks is used.

6.3.1.4 Object Modification

Modified persistent Smalltalk objects will have their updated values reflected in the ODBMS at transaction commit. Persistent objects to be modified must be sent the message markModified. MarkModified prepares the receiver object by setting a write lock (if it does not already have a write lock) and marking it so that the ODBMS can detect that the object has been modified.

```
anObject markModified
```

It is conventional to send the markModified message as part of each method that sets an instance variable's value. Immutable objects, such as instances of Character and SmallInteger and instances such as **nil**, **true**, and **false**, cannot change their intrinsic values. The markModified message has no effect on these objects. Sending markModified to a transient object is also a null operation.

6.3.2 Database Protocol

An object called a Database is used to manage each connection with a database. A Smalltalk application must open a Database before any objects in that database are accessible. A Database object may only be connected to a single database at a time; however, a vendor may allow many concurrent Databases to be open on different databases simultaneously.

```
"interface Database"
   open: aString                        "void open(...)"
   close                                "void close()"
   bind: anObject name: aString         "void bind(...)"
   inbind:  aString                     "Object unbind(...)"
   lookup: aString                      "Object lookup(...)"
   schema                               "Module schema()"
```

6.3.2.1 Opening a Database

To open a new database, send the open: method to an instance of the Database class.

```
database := Database new.
... set additional parameters as required ...
database open: aDatabaseName
```

If the connection is not established, a connectionFailedSignal will be raised.

6.3.2.2 Closing a Database

To close a database, send the close message to the Database.

```
aDatabase close
```

This closes the connection to the particular database. Once the connection is closed, further attempts to access the database will raise a notConnectedSignal. A Database that has been closed may be subsequently reopened using the open method defined above.

6.3.2.3 Database Names

Each Database manages a persistent name space that maps string names to objects or collections of objects, which are contained in the database. The following paragraphs describe the methods that are used to manage this name space. In addition to being assigned an object identifier by the ODBMS, an individual object may be given a name that is meaningful to the programmer or end user. Each database provides methods for associating names with objects and for determining the names of given objects. Named objects become the roots from which the Smalltalk binding's transitive persistence policy is computed.

The bind:name: method is used to name any persistent object in a database.

```
aDatabase bind: anObject name: aString
```

The lookup:ifAbsent: method is used to retrieve the object that is associated with the given name. If no such object exists in the database, the absentBlock will be evaluated.

```
aDatabase lookup: aString ifAbsent: absentBlock
```

6.3.2.4 Schema Access

The schema of a database may be accessed by sending the schema method to a Database instance. This method returns an instance of a Module that contains (perhaps transitively) all of the meta objects that define the database's schema.

6.3.3 Transaction Protocol

```
"interface Transaction"
   begin                     "void begin()"
   commit                    "void commit()"
   abort                     "void abort()"
   checkpoint                "void checkpoint()"
   isOpen                    "boolean isOpen()"
   join                      "void join()"
   leave                     "void leave()"

"interface TransactionFactory"
   current                   "Transaction current()"
```

6.3.3.1 Transactions

Transactions are implemented in Smalltalk using methods defined on the class Transaction. Transactions are dynamically scoped and may be started, committed, aborted, checkpointed, joined, and left. The default concurrency policy is pessimistic concurrency control (see Locking, above), but an ODBMS may support additional policies as well. With the pessimistic policy all access, creation, modification, and deletion of persistent objects must be done within a transaction.

A transaction may be started by invoking the method begin on a Transaction instance.

```
aTransaction begin
```

A transaction is committed by sending it the commit message. This causes the transaction to commit, writing the changes to all persistent objects that have been modified within the context of the transaction to the database.

```
aTransaction commit
```

Transient objects are not subject to transaction semantics. Committing a transaction does not remove transient objects from memory, nor does aborting a transaction restore the state of modified transient objects. The method for executing block-scoped transactions (below) provides a mechanism to deal with transient objects.

A transaction may also be checkpointed by sending it the checkpoint message. This is equivalent to performing a commit followed by a begin, except that all locks are retained and the transaction's identity is preserved.

```
aTransaction checkpoint
```

Checkpointing can be useful in order to continue working with the same objects while ensuring that intermediate logical results are written to the database.

A transaction may be aborted by sending it the abort message. This causes the transaction to end, and all changes to persistent objects made within the context of that transaction will be rolled back in the database.

```
aTransaction abort
```

A transaction is open if it has received a begin but not a commit or a abort message. The open status of a particular Transaction may be determined by sending it the isOpen message.

```
aTransaction isOpen
```

A process thread must explicitly create a transaction object or associate itself with an existing transaction object. The join message is used to associate the current process thread with the target Transaction.

```
aTransaction join
```

The leave message is used to drop the association between the current process thread and the target Transaction.

```
aTransaction leave
```

The current message is defined on the Transaction class and is used to determine the transaction associated with the current process thread. The value returned by this method may be **nil** if there is no such association.

```
Transaction current
```

6.3.3.2 Block-Scoped Transactions

A transaction can also be scoped to a Block to allow for greater convenience and integrity. The following method on class Transaction evaluates aBlock within the context of a new transaction. If the transaction commits, the commitBlock will be evaluated after the commit has completed. If the transaction aborts, the abortBlock will be evaluated after the rollback has completed. The abortBlock may be used to undo any side effects of the transaction on transient objects.

```
Transaction perform: aBlock
   onAbort: abortBlock
   onCommit: commitBlock
```

Within the transaction block, the checkpoint message may be used without terminating the transaction.

6.3.3.3 Transaction Exceptions

Several exceptions that may be raised during the execution of a transaction are defined:

- The noTransactionSignal is raised if an attempt is made to access persistent objects outside of a valid transaction context.
- The inactiveSignal is raised if a transactional operation is attempted in the context of a transaction that has already committed or aborted.
- The transactionCommitFailedSignal is raised if a commit operation is unsuccessful.

6.4 Smalltalk OQL

Chapter 4 defined the Object Query Language. This section describe how OQL is mapped to the Smalltalk language. The current Smalltalk OQL binding is a loosely coupled binding modeled after the OMG Object Query Service Specification. A future binding may include one that is more tightly integrated with the Smalltalk language.

6.4.1 Query Class

Instances of the class Query have four attributes: queryResult, queryStatus, queryString, and queryParameters. The queryResult holds the object that was the result of executing the OQL query. The queryStatus holds the status of query execution. The queryString is the OQL query text to be executed. The queryParameters contains variable/value pairs to be bound to the OQL query at execution.

The Query class supports the following methods:

```
create: aQueryString params: aParameterList     "returns a Query"
evaluate: aQueryString params: aParameterList   "returns query result"
complete                                        "returns enum complete"
incomplete                                      "returns enum incomplete"
```

Instances of the Query class support the following methods:

```
prepare: aParameterList     "no result"
execute: aParameterList     "no result"
getResult                   "returns the query result"
getStatus                   "returns a QueryStatus"
```

The execute: and prepare: methods can raise the QueryProcessingError signal if an error in the query is detected. The queryString may include parameters specified by the form $variable, where variable is a valid Smalltalk integer. Parameter lists may be partially specified by Dictionaries and fully specified by Arrays or OrderedCollections.

Example:

Return all persons older than 45 who weigh less than 150. Assume there exists a collection of people called AllPeople.

```
| query result |
query := Query
   create: 'select name from AllPeople where age > $1 and weight < $2'
   params: #(45 150).
query execute: Dictionary new.
[query getStatus = Query complete] whileFalse: [Processor yield].
result := query getResult.
```

To return all persons older than 45 that weigh less than 170, the same Query instance could be reused. This would save the overhead of parsing and optimizing the query again.

```
query execute: (Dictionary with: 2->170).
[query getStatus = Query complete] whileFalse: [Processor yield].
result := query getResult.
```

The following example illustrates the simple, synchronous form of querying an OQL database. This query will return the bag of the names of customers from the same state as aCustomer.

```
Query
   evaluate: 'select c.name from AllCustomers c where c.address.state = $1'
   params: (Array with: aCustomer address state)
```

6.5 Schema Access

Chapter 2 defined Metadata that define the operations, attributes, and relationships between the meta objects in a database schema. The following text defines the Smalltalk binding for these interfaces.

```
"interface MetaObject"
   name                                  "attribute name"
   name: aString
   comment                               "attribute comment"
   comment: aString
   formDefinedIn: aDefiningScope         "relationship definedIn"
   dropDefinedIn: aDefiningScope
   definedIn
   definedIn: aDefiningScope
"interface Scope"
   bind: aString value: aMetaObject      "void bind(...)"
   resolve: aString                      "MetaObject resolve(...)"
   unBind: aString                       "MetaObject un_bind(...)"
"interface DefiningScope"
   formDefines: aMetaObject              "relationship defines"
```

```
    dropDefines: aMetaObject
    defines
    addDefines: aMetaObject
    removeDefines: aMetaObject
    createPrimitiveType: aPrimitiveKind
                                  "PrimitiveType create_primitive_type()"
    createCollectionType: aCollectionKind
        maxSize: anOperand
        subType: aType            "Collection create_collection_type(...)"
    createOperand: aString                  "Operand create_operand(...)"
    createMember: aString
        memberType: aType                   "Member create_member(...)"
    createCase: aString
        caseType: aType
        caseLabels: aCollection             "UnionCase create_case(...)"
    addConstant: aString
        value: anOperand                    "Constant add_constant(...)"
    addTypedef: aString alias: aType        "TypeDefinition add_typedef(...)"
    addEnumeration: aString
        elementNames: aCollection           "Enumeration add_enumeration(...)"
    addStructure: aString
        fields: anOrderedCollection         "Structure add_structure(...)"
    addUnion: aString
        switchType: aType
        cases: aCollection                  "Union add_union(...)"
    addException: aString
        result: aStructure                  "Exception add_exception(...)"
    removeConstant: aConstant               "void remove_constant(...)"
    removeTypedef: aTypeDefinition          "void remove_typedef(...)"
    removeEnumeration: anEnumeration        "void remove_enumeration(...)"
    removeStructure: aStructure             "void remove_structure(...)"
    removeUnion: aUnion                     "void remove_union(...)"
    removeException: anException            "void remove_exception(...)"
"interface Module"
    addModule: aString                      "Module add_module(...)"
    addInterface: aString
        inherits: aCollection               "Interface add_interface(...)"
    removeModule: aModule                   "void remove_module(...)"
    removeInterface: anInterface            "void remove_interface(...)"
"interface Operation"
    formSignature: aParameter               "relationship signature"
    dropSignature: aParameter
    signature
    addSignature: aParameter
    removeSignature: aParameter
    formResult: aType                       "relationship result"
    dropResult: aType
    result
    result: aType
```

```
    formExceptions: anException          "relationship exceptions"
    dropExceptions: anException
    exceptions
    addExceptions: anException
    removeExceptions: anException
"interface Exception"
    formResult: aStructure               "relationship result"
    dropResult: aStructure
    result
    result: aStructure

    formOperations: anOperation          "relationship operations"
    dropOperations: anOperation
    operations
    addOperations: anOperation
    removeOperations: anOperation
"interface Constant"
    formHasValue: anOperand              "relationship hasValue"
    dropHasValue: anOperand
    hasValue
    hasValue: anOperand

    formType: aType                      "relationship type"
    dropType: aType
    type
    type: aType

    formReferencedBy: aConstOperand      "relationship referencedBy"
    dropReferencedBy: aConstOperand
    referencedBy
    addReferencedBy: aConstOperand
    removeReferencedBy: aConstOperand

    formEnumeration: anEnumeration       ""relationship enumeration"
    dropEnumeration: anEnumeration
    enumeration
    enumeration: anEnumeration

    value                                "any value(...)"
"interface Property"
    formType: aType                      "relationship type"
    dropType: aType
    type
    type: aType
"interface Attribute"
    isReadOnly                           "attribute isReadOnly"
    isReadOnly: aBoolean
"interface Relationship"
    formTraversal: aRelationship         "relationship traversal"
    dropTraversal: aRelationship
    traversal
    traversal: aRelationship

    getCardinality                       "Cardinality getCardinality(...)"
```

```
"interface TypeDefinition"
    formAlias: aType                          "relationship alias"
    dropAlias: aType
    alias
    alias: aType
"interface Type"
    formCollections: aCollection              "relationship collections"
    dropCollections: aCollection
    collections
    addCollections: aCollection
    removeCollections: aCollection
    formSpecifiers: aSpecifier                "relationship specifiers"
    dropSpecifiers: aSpecifier
    specifiers
    addSpecifiers: aSpecifier
    removeSpecifiers: aSpecifier
    formUnions: aUnion                        "relationship unions"
    dropUnions: aUnion
    unions
    addUnions: aUnion
    removeUnions: aUnion
    formOperations: anOperation               "relationship operations"
    dropOperations: anOperation
    operations
    addOperations: anOperation
    removeOperations: anOperation
    formProperties: aProperty                 "relationship properties"
    dropProperties: aProperty
    properties
    addProperties: aProperty
    removeProperties: aProperty
    formConstants: aConstant                  "relationship constants"
    dropConstants: aConstant
    constants
    addConstants: aConstant
    removeConstants: aConstant
    formTypeDefs: aTypeDefinition             "relationship typeDefs"
    dropTypeDefs: aTypeDefinition
    typeDefs
    addTypeDefs: aTypeDefinition
    removeTypeDefs: aTypeDefinition
"interface PrimitiveType"
    kind                                      "attribute kind"
    kind: aPrimitiveKind
"interface Interface"
    formInherits: anInheritance               "relationship inherits"
    dropInherits: anInheritance
    inherits
```

```
    addInherits: anInheritance
    removeInherits: anInheritance
    formDerives: anInheritance               "relationship derives"
    dropDerives: anInheritance
    derives
    addDerives: anInheritance
    removeDerives: anInheritance
    addAttribute: aString attrType: aType    "Attribute add_attribute(...)"
    addRelationship: aString
        relType: aType
        relTraversal: aRelationship          "Relationship add_relationship(...)"
    addOperation: aString
        opResult: aType
        opParams: anOrderedCollection
        opRaises: anOrderedCollection1       "Operation add_operation(...)"
    removeAttribute: anAttribute             "void remove_attribute(...)"
    removeRelationship: aRelationship        "void remove_relationship(...)"
    removeOperation: anOperation             "void remove_operation(...)"
"interface Inheritance"
    formDerivesFrom: anInterface             "relationship derivesFrom"
    dropDerivesFrom: anInterface
    derivesFrom
    derivesFrom: anInterface
    formInheritsTo: anInterface              "relationship inheritsTo"
    dropInheritsTo: anInterface
    inheritsTo
    inheritsTo: anInterface
"interface Class"
    extents                                  "attribute extents"
    extents: anOrderedCollection
    formExtender: aClass                     "relationship extender"
    dropExtender: aClass
    extender
    extender: aClass
    formExtensions: aClass                   "relationship extensions"
    dropExtensions: aClass
    extensions
    addExtensions: aClass
    removeExtensions: aClass
"interface Collection"
    kind                                     "attribute kind"
    kind: aCollectionKind
    formMaxSize: anOperand                   "relationship maxSize"
    dropMaxSize: anOperand
    maxSize
    maxSize: anOperand
    formSubtype: aType                       "relationship subtype"
    dropSubtype: aType
```

subtype subtype: aType	
isOrdered bound	"boolean isOrdered(...)" "unsigned long bound(...)"
"interface Enumeration"	
formElements: aConstant dropElements: aConstant elements addElements: aConstant removeElements: aConstant	"relationship elements"
"interface Structure"	
formFields: aMember dropFields: aMember fields addFields: aMember removeFields: aMember	"relationship fields"
formExceptionResult: anException dropExceptionResult: anException exceptionResult exceptionResult: anException	"relationship exceptionResult"
"interface Union"	
formSwitchType: aType dropSwitchType: aType switchType switchType: aType	"relationship switchType"
formCases: aUnionCase dropCases: aUnionCase cases addCases: aUnionCase removeCases: aUnionCase	"relationship cases"
"interface Specifier"	
name name: aString	"attribute name"
formType: aType dropType: aType type type: aType	"relationship type"
"interface Member"	
formStructureType: aStructure dropStructureType: aStructure structureType structureType: aStructure	"relationship structure_type"
"interface UnionCase"	
formUnionType: aUnion dropUnionType: aUnion unionType unionType: aUnion	"relationship union_type"

formCaseLabels: anOperand	"relationship caseLabels"
dropCaseLabels: anOperand	
caseLabels	
addCaseLabels: anOperand	
removeCaseLabels: anOperand	
"interface Parameter"	
parameterMode	"attribute parameterMode"
parameterMode: aDirection	
formOperation: anOperation	"relationship operation"
dropOperation: anOperation	
operation	
operation: anOperation	
"interface Operand"	
formOperandIn: anExpression	"relationship OperandIn"
dropOperandIn: anExpression	
operandIn	
operandIn: anExpression	
dropValueOf: aConstant	"relationship valueOf"
valueOf	
valueOf: aConstant	
formSizeOf: aCollection	"relationship sizeOf"
dropSizeOf: aCollection	
sizeOf	
sizeOf: aCollection	
formCaseIn: aUnionCase	"relationship caseIn"
dropCaseIn: aUnionCase	
caseIn	
caseIn: aUnionCase	
value	"any value(...)"
"interface Literal"	
literalValue	"attribute literalValue"
literalValue: anAnyObject	
"interface ConstOperand"	
formReferences: aConstant	relationship references"
dropReferences: aConstant	
references	
references: aConstant	
"interface Expression"	
operator	"attribute operator"
operator: aString	
formHasOperands: anOperand	"relationship hasOperands"
dropHasOperands: anOperand	
hasOperands	
addHasOperands: anOperand	
removeHasOperands: anOperand	

6.6 Future Directions

Many people believe that keys and extents are an essential ingredient of database query processing. Implicit extents and keys would be preferable to explicit mechanisms involving named Collections, yet there are challenging engineering issues that must be faced to rationalize these capabilities with the notions of transitive persistence and dynamic storage management herein presented.

A uniform set of Database administration operations would facilitate application portability and allow system administration tools to be constructed that could work uniformly across multiple vendors' database products.

This binding has only touched upon the need for interface regeneration mechanisms. Such mechanisms would allow programmers with existing applications utilizing language-specific and even database-specific ODL mechanisms to produce the interface definitions that would insulate them from the differences between these mechanisms.

Chapter 7

Java Binding

7.1 Introduction

This chapter defines the binding between the ODMG Object Model (ODL and OML) and the Java programming language as defined by Version 1.1 of the Java™ Language Specification.

7.1.1 Language Design Principles

The ODMG Java binding is based on one fundamental principle: the programmer should perceive the binding as a single language for expressing both database and programming operations, not two separate languages with arbitrary boundaries between them. This principle has several corollaries evident throughout the definition of the Java binding in the body of this chapter:

- There is a single unified type system shared by the Java language and the object database; individual instances of these common types can be persistent or transient.
- The binding respects the Java language syntax, meaning that the Java language will not have to be modified to accommodate this binding.
- The binding respects the automatic storage management semantics of Java. Objects will become persistent when they are referenced by other persistent objects in the database and will be removed when they are no longer reachable in this manner.

Note that the Java binding provides *persistence by reachability,* like the ODMG Smalltalk binding (this has also been called *transitive persistence*). On database commit, all objects reachable from database root objects are stored in the database.

7.1.2 Language Binding

The Java binding provides two ways to declare persistence-capable Java classes:

- Existing Java classes can be made persistence-capable.
- Java class declarations (as well as a database schema) may automatically be generated by a preprocessor for ODMG ODL.

One possible ODMG implementation that supports these capabilities would be a *post-processor* that takes as input the Java .class file (bytecodes) produced by the Java compiler and produces new modified bytecodes that support persistence. Another implementation would be a *preprocessor* that modifies Java source before it goes to the Java compiler. Another implementation would be a modified Java interpreter.

We want a binding that allows all of these possible implementations. Because Java does not have all hooks we might desire, and the Java binding must use standard Java syntax, it is necessary to distinguish special classes understood by the database system. These classes are called *persistence-capable classes.* They can have both persistent and transient instances. Only instances of these classes can be made persistent. The current version of the standard does not define how a Java class becomes a persistence-capable class.

7.1.3 Use of Java Language Features

7.1.3.1 Namespace

The ODMG Java API will be defined in a vendor-specific package name.

7.1.3.2 Implementation Extensions

Implementations must provide the full function signatures for all the interface methods specified in the chapter, but may also provide variants on these methods with different types or additional parameters.

7.1.4 Mapping the ODMG Object Model into Java

The Java language provides a comprehensive object model comparable to the one presented in Chapter 2. This section describes the mapping between the two models and the extensions provided by the Java binding.

The following features are not yet supported by the Java binding: relationships, extents, keys, and access to the metaschema.

7.1.4.1 Object and Literal

An ODMG object type maps into a Java object type. The ODMG atomic literal types map into their equivalent Java primitive types. There are no structured literal types in the Java binding.

7.1.4.2 Structure

The Object Model definition of a structure maps into a Java class.

7.1.4.3 Implementation

The Java language supports the independent definition of interface from implementation. Interfaces and abstract classes cannot be instantiated and therefore are not persistence-capable.

7.1.4.4 Collection Classes

The collection objects described in Section 2.3.6 specify collection behavior, which may be implemented using many different collection representations such as hash tables, trees, chained lists, etc. The Java binding provides the following interfaces and at least one implementation for each of these collection objects:

```
public interface Set extends Collection { ... }
public interface Bag extends Collection { ... }
public interface List extends Collection { ... }
```

The iterator interface described in Section 2.3.6 is represented by the Java Enumeration interface.

7.1.4.5 Array

Java provides a syntax for creating and accessing a contiguous and indexable sequence of objects, and a separate class, Vector, for extensible sequences. The ODMG Array collection maps into either the primitive array type, the Java Vector class, or the ODMG VArray class, depending on the desired level of capability.

7.1.4.6 Relationship

ODMG relationships are not yet supported by the Java binding.

7.1.4.7 Extents

Extents are not yet supported by the Java binding. The programmer is responsible for defining a collection to serve as an extent and writing methods to maintain it.

7.1.4.8 Keys

Key declarations are not yet supported by the Java binding.

7.1.4.9 Names

Objects may be named using methods of the Database class defined in the Java OML. The root objects of a database are the named objects; root objects and any objects reachable from them are persistent.

7.1.4.10 Exception Handling

When an error condition is detected, an exception is thrown using the standard Java exception mechanism. The following standard exception types are defined; some are thrown from specific ODMG interfaces and are thus subclasses of ODMGException, and others may be thrown in the course of using persistent objects and are thus subclasses of ODMGRuntimeException.

TransactionInProgressException extends ODMGRuntimeException

Thrown when attempting to call a method within a transaction that must be called when no transaction is in progress.

TransactionNotInProgressException extends ODMGRuntimeException

Thrown when attempting to perform outside of a transaction an operation that must be called when there is a transaction in progress.

TransactionAbortedException extends ODMGRuntimeException

Thrown when the database system has asynchronously terminated the user's transaction due to a deadlock, resource failure, etc. In such cases the user's data is reset just as if the user had called Transaction.abort.

DatabaseNotFoundException extends ODMGException

Thrown when attempting to open a database that does not exist.

DatabaseClosedException extends ODMGException

Thrown when attempting to call a method on a database handle that has been closed or when calling a method on a database ID for which the database is not open and was required to be open.

DatabaseIsReadOnlyException extends ODMGRuntimeException

Thrown when attempting to call a method that modifies a database that is open read-only.

ObjectNameNotFoundException extends ODMGException

Thrown when attempting to get a named object whose name is not found.

DatabaseOpenException extends ODMGException

Thrown when attempting to open a database that is already open.

ObjectNameNotUniqueException extends ODMGException

Thrown when attempting to bind a name to an object when the name is already bound to an existing object.

QueryParameterCountInvalidException extends ODMGException

Thrown when the number of bound parameters for a query does not match the number of placeholders.

QueryParameterTypeInvalidException extends ODMGException

Thrown when the type of a parameter for a query is not compatible with the expected parameter type.

LockNotGrantedException extends ODMGRuntimeException

Thrown if a lock could not be granted. (Note that time-outs and deadlock detection are implementation-defined.)

7.2 Java ODL

This section defines the Java Object Definition Language, which provides the description of the database schema as a set of Java classes using Java syntax. Instances of these classes can be manipulated using the Java OML.

7.2.1 Attribute Declarations and Types

Attribute declarations are syntactically identical to field variable declarations in Java and are defined using standard Java syntax and semantics for class definitions.

The following table describes the mapping of the Object Model types to their Java binding equivalents. Note that the primitive types may also be represented by their class equivalents: both forms are persistence-capable and may be used interchangeably.

Object Model Type	Java Type	Literal?
Long	int (primitive), Integer (class)	yes
Short	short (primitive), Short (class)	yes
Unsigned long	long (primitive), Long (class)	yes
Unsigned short	int (primitive), Integer (class)	yes
Float	float (primitive), Float (class)	yes
Double	double (primitive), Double (class)	yes
Boolean	boolean (primitive), Boolean (class)	yes
Octet	byte (primitive), Integer (class)	yes
Char	char (primitive), Character (class)	yes
String	String	yes
Date	java.sql.Date	no
Time	java.sql.Time	no
TimeStamp	java.sql.TimeStamp	no
Set	interface Set	no
Bag	interface Bag	no
List	interface List	no
Array	array type [] or Vector	no
Iterator	Enumeration	no

The binding maps each unsigned integer to the next larger signed type in Java. The need for this arises only where multiple language bindings access the same database. It is vendor-defined whether or not an exception is raised if truncation or sign problems occur during translations. The Java mappings for the object model types Enum and Interval are not yet defined by the standard.

7.2.2 Relationship Traversal Path Declarations

Relationships are not yet supported in the Java binding.

7.2.3 Operation Declarations

Operation declarations in the Java ODL are syntactically identical to method declarations in Java.

7.3 Java OML

The guiding principle in the design of Java Object Manipulation Language (OML) is that the syntax used to create, delete, identify, reference, get/set field values, and invoke methods on a persistent object should be no different from that used for objects of shorter lifetimes. A single expression may thus freely intermix references to persistent and transient objects. All Java OML operations are invoked by method calls on appropriate objects.

7.3.1 Object Creation, Deletion, Modification, and Reference

7.3.1.1 Object Persistence

In the Java binding, persistence is not limited to any particular subset of the class hierarchy, nor is it determined at object creation time. A transient Java object that is referenced by a persistent Java object will automatically become persistent when the transaction is committed. This behavior is called *persistence by reachability.*

Instances of classes that are not persistence-capable classes are never persistent, even if they are referenced by a persistent object. The value of an attribute whose type is not a persistence-capable class is treated by the database system the same way as a transient attribute (see below).

Nevertheless it is possible to declare an attribute to be transient using the keyword transient of the Java language. That means that the value of this attribute is not stored in the database. Furthermore, reachability from a transient attribute will not give persistence to an object.

For example, a class Person with an attribute currentSomething that must not be persistent must be declared as follows:

```
public class Person {
   public String name;
   transient Something currentSomething;
...}
```

When an object of class Person is loaded into memory from the database, the attribute currentSomething is set (by Java) to the default value of its type.

On transaction abort, the value of a transient attribute can be either left unchanged or set to its default value. The behavior is not currently defined by the standard.

Static fields are treated similarly to transient attributes. Reachability from a static field will not give persistence to an object, and on transaction abort the value of a static field can be either left unchanged or set to its default value.

7.3.1.2 Object Deletion

In the Java binding, as in Java, there is no notion of explicit deletion of objects. An object may be automatically removed from the database if that object is neither named nor referenced by any other persistent object.

7.3.1.3 Object Modification

Modified persistent Java objects will have their updated fields reflected in the object database when the transaction in which they were modified is committed.

7.3.1.4 Object Names

A database application generally will begin processing by accessing one or more critical objects and proceeding from there. These objects are *root objects*, because they lead to interconnected webs of other objects. The ability to name an object and retrieve it later by that name facilitates this start-up capability. Names also provide persistence, as noted earlier.

There is a single flat name scope per database; thus all names in a particular database are unique. A name is not explicitly defined as an attribute of an object. The operations for manipulating names are defined in the Database class in Section 7.3.6.

7.3.1.5 Object Locking

We support explicit locking using methods on the Transaction object.

7.3.2 Properties

The Java OML uses standard Java syntax for accessing attributes and relationships, both of which are mapped to field variables.

7.3.3 Operations

Operations are defined in the Java OML as methods in the Java language. Operations on transient and persistent objects behave identically and consistently with the operational context defined by Java. This includes all overloading, dispatching, expression evaluation, method invocation, argument passing and resolution, exception handling, and compile time rules.

7.3.4 Collection Interfaces

A conforming implementation must provide these collection interfaces:

- Collection
- Set
- Bag
- List

An object database may provide any number of instantiable classes to implement representations of the various Collection interfaces. At a minimum, the database must provide three classes SetOfObject, BagOfObject, and ListOfObject, which implement Set, Bag, and List, respectively.

The collection elements are of type Object. Subclasses of Object, such as class Employee, must be converted when used as Collection elements (Java converts them automatically on insertion into a collection, but requires an explicit cast when retrieved).

Chapter 2 defines a number of collections and the semantics of the operations on them. The following sections specify the Java binding interfaces and methods that map on to these collections. Method names have been chosen to match JavaSoft work in progress on collections where possible.

7.3.4.1 Interface Collection

The remove method returns the object removed from the collection, or null if the object was not present in the collection.

```
public interface Collection
{                                                  // Chapter 2 operations
   public int size();                              // unsigned long cardinality()
   public boolean isEmpty();                       // boolean is_empty()
   public void add(Object obj);                    // void insert_element(...)
   public Object remove(Object obj);               // void remove_element(...)
   public boolean contains(Object obj);            // boolean contains_element(...)
   public Enumeration elements();                  // Iterator create_iterator(...)
   public Object selectElement(String predicate);
   public Enumeration select(String predicate);
   public Collection query(String predicate);
   public boolean existsElement(String predicate);
}
```

7.3.4.2 Interface Set

```
public interface Set extends Collection
{                                                       // Chapter 2 operations
    public Set union(Set otherSet);                     // Set create_union (...)
    public Set intersection(Set otherSet);              // Set create_intersection (...)
    public Set difference(Set otherSet);                // Set create_difference(...)
    public boolean subsetOf(Set otherSet);              // boolean is_subset_of(...)
    public boolean properSubsetOf(Set otherSet);        // boolean is_proper_subset_of(...)
    public boolean supersetOf(Set otherSet);            // boolean is_superset_of(...)
    public boolean properSupersetOf(Set otherSet);      // boolean is_proper_superset_of(...)
}
```

7.3.4.3 Interface Bag

The method occurrences returns the number of times an object exists in the Bag, or zero if it is not present in the Bag.

```
public interface Bag extends Collection
{                                                       // Chapter 2 operations
    public Bag union(Bag otherBag);                     // Bag create_union(...)
    public Bag intersection(Bag otherBag                // Bag create_intersection(...)
    public Bag difference(Bag otherBag);                // Bag create_difference(...)
    public int occurrences(Object obj);
}
```

7.3.4.4 Interface List

The beginning List index value is zero, following the Java convention. The method add that is inherited from Collection will insert the object at the end of the List. The remove method returns the object removed from the List, or null if the object was not present in the List.

```
public interface List extends Collection
{                                                       // Chapter 2 operations
    public void add(int index, Object obj)              // void insert_element_before(...)
            throws ArrayIndexOutOfBounds;
    public void put(int index, Object obj)              // void replace_element_at(...)
            throws ArrayIndexOutOfBounds;
    public Object remove(int index)                     // void remove_element_at(...)
            throws ArrayIndexOutOfBounds;
    public Object get(int index)                        // any retrieve_element_at(...)
            throws ArrayIndexOutOfBounds;
    public List concat(List other);                     // List concat(...)
    public void append(List other);                     // void append(...)
}
```

The Chapter 2 operations defined on List but not explicitly specified above can be implemented using methods in the Java binding List interface as follows:

Java bindingmethod	Chapter 2 operation
add(index + 1, obj)	insertElementAfter(index, obj)
add(index, obj)	insertElementBefore(index, obj)
add(0, obj)	insertElementFirst(obj)
add(obj)	insertElementLast(obj)
remove(0)	removeFirstElement()
remove(theList.size() - 1)	removeLastElement()
get(0)	retrieveFirstElement()
get(theList.size() - 1)	retrieveLastElement()

7.3.4.5 Interface Array

The Array type defined in Section 2.3.6.4 is implemented by Java arrays, which are single-dimension and fixed-length, or the Java class Vector, instances of which may be resized, or by a class implementing the VArray interface, instances of which may be queried and are otherwise compatible with other collection operations. The remove method returns the object removed from the VArray, or null if the object was not present in the VArray.

```
public void put(int index, Object obj);          // void replace_element_at(...)
        throws ArrayIndexOutOfBounds;
public Object remove(int index)                  // void remove_element_at(...)
        throws ArrayIndexOutOfBounds;
public Object get(int index);                    // any retrieve_element_at(...)
        throws ArrayIndexOutOfBounds;
public void resize(int newSize);                 // void resize(...)
```

7.3.5 Transactions

Transaction semantics are defined in the object model explained in Chapter 2.

Transactions can be *started, committed, aborted,* and *checkpointed.* It is important to note that all access, creation, and modification of persistent objects and their fields must be done within a transaction.

Transactions are implemented in the Java OML as objects of class Transaction, defined as follows:

```
public class Transaction {
   // Creates new transaction object
   //       and associates it with the caller's thread
   Transaction();
```

```
    // Attaches caller's thread to this existing Transaction;
    //        any previous transaction detached from thread
    public void join();

    // Detaches caller's thread from this Transaction,
    //        without attaching another
    public void leave();

    // Returns the current transaction for the caller's thread, or null if none
    public static Transaction current();

    // Starts (opens) a transaction. Nested transactions are not supported.
    public void begin();

    // Returns true if this transaction is open, otherwise false
    public boolean isOpen();

    // Commits and closes a transaction
     public void commit();

    // Aborts and closes a transaction
    public void abort();

    // Commits a transaction but retains locks and reopens transaction
    public void checkpoint();

    // Upgrade the lock on an object
  public void lock(Object obj, int mode);
  public static final int READ, UPGRADE, WRITE;
  }
```

Before performing any database operations, a thread must explicitly create a transaction object or associate (join) itself with an existing transaction object, and that transaction must be open (through a begin call). All subsequent operations by the thread, including reads, writes, and lock acquisitions, are done under the thread's current transaction. A thread may only operate on its current transaction. For example, a TransactionNotInProgressException is thrown if a thread attempts to begin, commit, checkpoint, or abort a transaction prior to joining itself to that transaction.

A DBMS might permit optimistic, pessimistic, or other locking paradigms; ODMG does not specify this.

Transactions must be explicitly created and started; they are not automatically started on database open, upon creation of a Transaction object, or following a transaction commit or abort.

The creation of a new transaction object implicitly associates it with the caller's thread.

The begin function starts a transaction. Calling begin multiple times on the same transaction object, without an intervening commit or abort, causes the exception TransactionInProgressException to be thrown on the second and subsequent calls. Operations executed before a transaction has been opened, or before reopening after a transaction is aborted or committed, have undefined results; these may raise a TransactionNotInProgressException.

There are three ways in which threads can be used with transactions:

1. An application program may have exactly one thread doing database operations, under exactly one transaction. This is the simplest case, and it certainly represents the vast majority of database applications today. Other application instances on separate machines or in separate address spaces may access the same database under separate transactions.
2. There may be multiple threads, each with its own separate transaction. This is useful when writing a service accessed by multiple clients on a network. The database system maintains ACID transaction properties just as if the threads were in separate address spaces. Programmers *must not* pass objects from one thread to another one that is running under a different transaction; ODMG does not define the results of doing this. However, strings can always be passed between threads, since they are immutable, and scalar data such as integers can be passed around freely.
3. Multiple threads may share one or more transactions. When a transaction is associated with multiple threads simultaneously, all of these threads are affected by data operations or transaction operations (begin, commit, abort). Using multiple threads per transaction is only recommended for sophisticated programming, because concurrency control must be performed by the programmer through Java synchronization or other techniques on top of the DBMS's transaction-based concurrency control.

Calling commit commits to the database all *persistent object modifications* within the transaction and releases any locks held by the transaction. A persistent object modification is an update of any field of an existing persistent object, or an update or creation of a new named object in the database. If a persistent object modification results in a reference from an existing persistent object to a transient object, the transient object is moved to the database, and all references to it updated accordingly. Note that the act of moving a transient object to the database may create still more persistent references to transient objects, so its referents must be examined and moved as well. This process continues until the database contains no references to transient objects, a condition that is guaranteed as part of transaction commit.

Calling checkpoint commits persistent object modifications made within the transaction since the last checkpoint to the database. The transaction retains all locks it held on those objects at the time the checkpoint was invoked.

Calling abort abandons all persistent object modifications and releases the associated locks.

In the current standard, transient objects are not subject to transaction semantics. Committing a transaction does not remove from memory transient objects created during the transaction, and aborting a transaction does not restore the state of modified transient objects.

Read locks are implicitly obtained on objects as they are accessed. Write locks are implicitly obtained as objects are modified.

Calling lock upgrades the lock on the given object to the given level, if it is not already at or above that level. It throws LockNotGrantedException if it cannot be granted.

Transaction objects are not long-lived (beyond process boundaries) and cannot be stored in a database. This means that transaction objects may not be made persistent, and that the notion of *long transactions* is not defined in this specification.

7.3.6 Database Operations

The predefined type Database represents a database.

```
public class Database {
   // Access modes
   public static final int notOpen = 0;
   public static final int openReadOnly = 1;
   public static final int openReadWrite = 2;
   public static final int openExclusive = 3;

   // Returns the database the name specified.
   //      Opens database if not already open.
   public static Database open(String name, int accessMode)
                throws ODMGException;
   public void close() throws ODMGException;
```

```
    // Named object binding and lookup
    public void bind(Object object, String name);
    public Object lookup(String name)
                throws ObjectNameNotFoundException;
    public void unbind(String name)
                throws ObjectNameNotFoundException;
}
```

The database object, like the transaction object, is transient. Databases cannot be created programmatically using the Java OML defined by this standard. Databases must be opened before starting any transactions that use the database and closed after ending these transactions.

To open a database, use the open method, which takes the name of the database as its argument. This locates the named database and makes the appropriate connection to it. You must open a database before you can access objects in that database. Attempts to open a database when it has already been opened will result in the throwing of the exception DatabaseOpenException. A DatabaseNotFoundException is thrown if the database does not exist. Some implementations may throw additional exceptions that are also derived from ODMGException. Extensions to the open method will enable some object databases to implement default database names and/or implicitly open a default database when a database session is started. Object databases may support opening logical as well as physical databases. Some implementations may also support being connected to multiple databases at the same time.

To close a database, use the close method, which does appropriate clean-up on the named database connection. After you have closed a database, further attempts to access objects in the database will cause the exception DatabaseClosedException to be thrown. Some implementations may throw additional exceptions that are also derived from ODMGException. The behavior at program termination is vendor-defined if databases are not closed or transactions are not committed or aborted. The effect that closing a database has on open transactions is also vendor-defined.

The bind, unbind, and lookup methods allow manipulating names of objects. An object is accessed by name using the lookup member function. The same object may be bound to more than one name. Binding a previously transient object to a name makes that object persistent. The unbind method removes a name and any association to an object and raises an exception if the name does not exist. The lookup method returns null if the specified name is bound to null and generates an exception if the name does not exist.

7.4 Java OQL

The full functionality of the Object Query Language is available through the Java binding. This functionality can be used through query methods on class Collection or through queries using on a stand-alone OQLQuery class.

7.4.1 Collection Query Methods

The Collection interface has a query member function whose signature is:

```
Collection query(String predicate);
```

This function filters the collection using the predicate and returns the result. The predicate is given as a string with the syntax of the where clause of OQL. The predefined variable this is used inside the predicate to denote the current element of the collection to be filtered.

For example, assuming that we have computed a set of students in the variable Students, we can compute the set of students who take math courses as follows:

```
SetOfObject mathematicians;
mathematicians = Students.query(
                "exists s in this.takes: s.section_of.name = \"math\" ");
```

The selectElement method has the same behavior except that it may only be used when the result of the query contains exactly one element. The select method returns an Enumeration on the result of a query.

7.4.2 The OQLQuery Class

The class OQLQuery allows the programmer to create a query, pass parameters, execute the query, and get the result.

```
class OQLQuery{
   public OQLQuery(){}
   public OQLQuery(String query){ ... } // You can construct or ...
   public create(String query){ ... }     // assign a query.
   public bind(Object parameter){ ... }
   public Object execute() throws ODMGException { ... }
}
```

This is a generic interface. The parameters must be objects, and the result is an Object. This means that you must use objects instead of primitive types (e.g., Integer instead of int) for passing the parameters. Similarly, the returned data, whatever its OQL type, is encapsulated into an object. For instance, when OQL returns an integer, the result is put into an Integer object. When OQL returns a collection whatever its kind (literal or object), the result is always a Java collection of the same kind (for instance, a List).

As usual, a parameter in the query is noted $\$i$, where i is the rank of the parameter. The parameters are set using the method bind. The ith variable is set by the ith call to the bind method. If any of the $\$i$ are not set by a call to bind at the point execute is called, QueryParameterCountInvalidException is thrown. If the argument is of the wrong type, the QueryParameterTypeInvalidException is thrown. After executing a query, the parameter list is reset. Some implementations may throw additional exceptions that are also derived from ODMGException.

Example: Among the students who take math courses (computed in Section 7.4.1) we use OQL to query the teaching assistants (TA) whose salary is greater than $50,000 and who are students in math (thus belonging to the mathematicians collection). The result we are interested in is the professors who are teaching these students. Assume there exists a named set of teaching assistants called TA.

```
Bag mathematicians;
Bag assistedProfs;
Double x;
OQLQuery query;
mathematicians = Students.query(
    "exists s in this.takes: s.sectionOf.name = \"math\" ");
query = new OQLQuery(
    "select t.assists.taughtBy from t in TA where t.salary > $1 and t in $2 ");
x = new Double(50000.0);
query.bind(x); query.bind(mathematicians);
assistedProfs = (Bag) query.execute();
```

Appendix A

Comparison with OMG Object Model

A.1 Introduction

This appendix compares the ODMG Object Model outlined in Chapter 2 of this specification with the OMG Object Model as outlined in Chapter 4 of the *OMG Architecture Guide*.

The bottom line is that the ODMG Object Model (ODMG/OM) is a superset of the OMG Object Model (OMG/OM).

The subsections of this appendix discuss the purpose of the two models and how the ODMG/OM fits into the component/profile structure defined by the OMG/OM, and review the capability between the two models in the major areas defined by the OMG/OM: types, instances, objects, and operations.

A.2 Purpose

The OMG/OM states that its primary objective is to support application portability. Three levels of portability are called out: (1) design portability, (2) source code portability, and (3) object code portability. The OMG/OM focused on design portability. The ODMG/OM goes a step further—to source code portability. The OMG/OM distinguishes two other dimensions of portability: portability across technology domains (e.g., a common object model across GUI, PL, and DBMS domains), and portability across products from different vendors within a technology domain (e.g., across ODBMS products from different vendors). The ODMG/OM focuses on portability within the technology domain of object database management systems. The ODMG standards suite is designed to allow application builders to write to a single ODBMS application programming interface (API), in the assurance that this API will be supported by a wide range of ODBMS vendors. The ODMG/OM defines the semantics of the object types that make up this API. Subsequent chapters within the ODMG standard define the syntactic forms through which this model is bound to specific programming languages.

To offer real portability, a standard has to support a level of DBMS functionality rich enough to meet the needs of the applications expected to use the standard. It cannot define such a low-level API that real applications need to use functionality supplied only by vendor-specific extensions to the API. The low-level, least-common-denominator approach taken in the standards for relational data management has meant that real applications need to use functionality supplied only by vendor-specific extensions to the API. Several studies in the late 1980s that analyzed large bodies of applications written against the relational API (SQL) showed that 30–40% of the RDBMS calls in the application are actually "standard SQL"; the other 60–70% use vendor-specific extensions. The result is that the relational standard does not in practice deliver the source-code-level application portability that it promised. The ODMG APIs have been designed to provide a much higher level of functionality and therefore a much higher degree of application portability.

A.3 Components and Profiles

The OMG Object Model is broken into a set of *components,* with a distinguished "Core Component" that defines objects and operations. The theory espoused by the OMG is that each "technology domain" (GUI, ODBMS, etc.) will assemble a set of these components into a *profile*. Figure A-1 illustrates this. Two profiles are shown—the Object Request Broker (ORB) profile and the Object DBMS (ODBMS) profile.

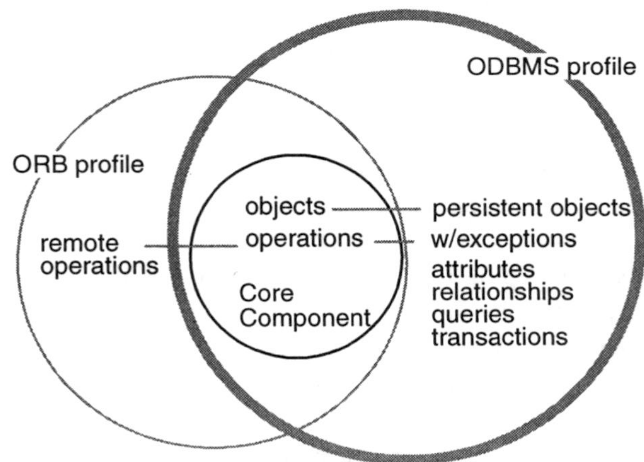

Figure A-1

The ORB profile includes the Core Component plus support for remote operations. The ODBMS profile includes the Core Component plus support for

- persistent objects
- properties (attributes and relationships)
- queries
- transactions

It also strengthens the core component definition of operations by including exception returns.

To date, the only OMG/OM component that has been defined is the Core Component. The additional functionality included in the ORB profile has not been formally specified as a set of named components. Nor are there OMG component definitions for the functionality expected to be added by the ODBMS profile. One of the reasons for making the comparison between the OMG/OM (i.e., the Core Component) is that the members of ODMG expect to submit definitions of each of the items in the bulleted list above as candidate *components*, and the sum of them as a candidate *profile* for object database management systems. Since the submitting companies collectively represent 80+% of the commercially available ODBMS products on the market, we assume that adoption of an ODBMS profile along the lines of that outlined in Chapter 2 will move through the OMG process relatively quickly.

The OMG/OM is outlined below, with indications how the ODMG/OM agrees.

Types, instances, interfaces, and implementations:

- Objects are instances of types.
- A type defines the behavior and state of its instances.
- Behavior is specified as a set of operations.
- An object can be an immediate instance of only one type.
- The type of an object is determined statically at the time the object is created; objects do not dynamically acquire and lose types.
- Types are organized into a subtype/supertype graph.
- A type may have multiple supertypes.
- Supertypes are explicitly specified; subtype/supertype relationships between types are not deduced from signature compatibility of the types.

Operations:

- Operations have signatures that specify the operation name, arguments, and return values.
- Operations are defined on a single type—the type of their distinguished first argument—rather than on two types.
- Operations may take either literals or objects as their arguments. Semantics of argument passing is pass by reference.
- Operations are invoked.
- Operations may have side effects.
- Operations are implemented by methods in the implementation portion of the type definition.

The OMG/OM does not currently define exception returns on operations; it says that it expects there to be an exception-handling component defined outside of the core model. The ODMG/OM does define exception returns to operations.

A.4 Type Hierarchy

The fact that the ODMG/OM is a superset of the OMG/OM can also be seen by looking at the built-in type hierarchy defined by the two models. Figure A-2 shows the ODMG/OM type hierarchy. The types whose names are shown in italics are those that are also defined in the OMG/OM. As in Chapter 2, indenting is used to show subtype/supertype relationships, e.g., the type Collection is a subtype of the type Object-type.

- Literal_type
  - Atomic_literal
  - Collection_literal
  - Structured_literal
- Object_type
  - Atomic_object
  - Collection

Figure A-2

The ODMG/OM is a richer model than the OMG/OM—particularly in its support for properties and in its more detailed development of a subtype hierarchy below the types Object and Literal. The only differences between the two models in the areas common to them are two type names. The type that is called Literal in the ODMG/OM is called Non-Object in the OMG/OM. Although the OMG/OM does not formally introduce a supertype of the types Object and Non-Object, in the body of the document it refers to instances of these two types as the set of all "denotable values" or "Dvals" in the model. In the ODMG/OM a common supertype for Object and Literal is defined. The instances of type Object are mutable; they are therefore given OIDs in the ODMG/OM; although the value of the object may change, its OID is invariant. The OID can therefore be used to denote the object. Literals, by contrast, are immutable. Since the instances of a literal type are distinguished from one another by their value, this value can be used directly to denote the instance. There is no need to ascribe separate OIDs to literals.

In summary, the ODMG/OM is a clean superset of the OMG/OM.

A.5 The ORB Profile

A second question could be raised. One product category has already been approved by the OMG—the ORB. To what extent are the noncore components implicit in that product consistent or inconsistent with their counterpart noncore components in the ODMG/OM? There is some divergence in literals, inheritance semantics, and operations—the latter because the ORB restricts in two key ways the semantics already defined in the OMG core object model: object identity and the semantics of arguments passed to operations. Those battles, however, are not ours. They are between the OMG ORB task force and the OMG Object Model task force. The requirement placed on a prospective ODBMS task force is simply that the set of components included in the prospective ODBMS task force is simply that the set of components included in the ODBMS profile include the Core Component— objects and operations. This appendix addresses that question.

A.6 Other Standards Groups

There are several standards organizations in the process of defining object models.

1. Application-specific standards groups that have defined an object model as a basis for their work in defining schemas of common types in their application domain, e.g.,
   - CFI (electrical CAD)
   - PDES/STEP (mechanical CAD)
   - ODA (computer-aided publishing)
   - PCTE (CASE)
   - OSI/NMF (telephony)
   - ANSI X3H6 (CASE)
   - ANSI X3H4 (IRDS reference model)
2. Formal standards bodies working on generic object models, e.g.,
   - ISO ODP
   - ANSI X3H7 (Object Information Systems)
   - ANSI X3T5.4 (managed objects)
   - ANSI X3T3

It is our current working assumption that the OMG-promulgated interface definitions for ORB and ODBMS will have sufficiently broad support across software vendors and hardware manufacturers that interface definitions put in the public domain through the OMG and supported by commercial vendors will develop the kind of de facto market share that has historically been an important prerequisite to adoption by ANSI and ISO. Should that prove not to be the case, the ODMG will make direct proposals to ANSI and ISO once the member companies of ODMG and their customers have developed a base of experience with the proposed API through use of commercial ODBMS products that support this API.

Appendix B

ODBMS in the OMG ORB Environment

B.1 Introduction

The existing documents of OMG do not yet address the issue of how an ODBMS fits into the OMG environment and, in particular, how it communicates with and cooperates with the ORB. This fundamental architectural issue is critical to the success of users of the OMG environment who also need ODBMSs.

This document is a position statement of the ODMG defining the desired architecture. It explicitly does not discuss the architecture of the internals of an ODBMS implementation but rather leaves that to the implementor of the ODBMS. Instead, it discusses how the ODBMS fits architecturally into the larger OMG environment.

The issues for a successful fit are the following:

- performance—e.g., direct object access
- distribution and heterogeneity—as managed by ODBMS for fine-grained objects
- ODBMS as Object Manager—responsible for multiple objects
- common repository—ability of ORB to use ODBMS as repository
- ODBMS as a user of the ORB—ability of ODBMS to use the services provided by the ORB (including other ODBMSs)

The architecture must support ODBMS implementations and client interfaces to achieve these.

B.2 Roles for the ORB and ODBMS

The ORB and the ODBMS are different. The ODBMS's role in the OMG environment is to support definition, creation, and manipulation with the services of persistence, transactions, recovery, and concurrent sharing for application objects varying from the smallest units (e.g., words in a word processor, cells or formula terms in a spreadsheet) to the largest (e.g., documents, systems). Many applications desire these services to include, within a single vendor product, transparent distribution in a heterogeneous mixture of platforms and other services such as versioning and security.

Note that we define ODBMS according to the services it provides, not according to any particular implementation of those services. Radically different implementations are possible, including not only traditional ODBMS approaches, but also file-based approaches, each offering different levels of services and trade-offs.

The ORB provides a larger-scale set of services across heterogeneous vendors and products; e.g., it allows clients to use multiple ODBMSs. The service it provides is behavior invocation, or method dispatch. In contrast, the ODBMS provides a single-vendor capability and only a specific set of services rather than arbitrary ones; however, those services include more detailed capabilities of high-performance, fine-grained persistence that are used directly within applications to support millions of primitive objects. The ORB, when it needs persistence services, could choose to implement them via use of an ODBMS. The ODBMS services may be invoked via the ORB.

B.3 Issues

Here we describe some of the key issues that this architecture must address. Since the ODBMS supports millions of fine-grained objects used directly by the applications, it must provide high-performance access to those objects. The pertinent characteristic differentiating large- and small-grain objects is access time. If an application is accessing only one or two objects (e.g., open a spreadsheet document), there is little concern for the time to communicate across networks through the ORB. However, if the application is accessing thousands or millions of objects (e.g., formulae and variables in cells in the spreadsheet), system overhead becomes a significant factor as perceived by the user.

In many cases this means access time that is comparable to native in-memory object usage. To provide this, the ODBMS must be able to move objects as necessary in the distributed environment and cache them locally in the address space of the application, if desired, and in efficient format.

Since the ODBMS objects are those used primarily within the application, it is desirable to support an interface that is natural and direct to the user.

Examples of applications and object granularities for which ODBMS services must be available and efficient include spreadsheets; word processors; documents of these; primitive elements within these such as cells, formulae, variables, words, phrases, and formatting specifications; network managers with objects representing machines, users, and sessions; resource allocation schemes; CAD and CAM with objects such as circuits and gates and pins, routing traces, form features, bezier curves, finite element mesh nodes, edges and faces, tool paths, simulation, and analysis support; financial portfolio analysis; and so on. There may be millions of such objects, in complex interconnected networks of relationships.

The interfaces to those objects must be defined in such a way as to allow ORB access when appropriate (e.g., for cross-database-vendor object relationships) or direct use of the ODBMS (e.g., for objects with no need to publish themselves for public use through the ORB). This should be done with a single interface to allow transparency to the client and to allow the client to choose to vary functionality as desired.

The ODBMS acts as manager of many objects, so the architecture and interfaces must allow such assignment of responsibilities. The ODBMS can provide distribution of objects among multiple and potentially heterogeneous platforms, so the architecture and implementation must allow this functionality to be relegated to the ODBMS.

The ORB and other OMG components (service providers, library facilities, service users, etc.) may need the services of persistence, or management of objects that exist beyond process lifetimes, for various kinds of objects, including type-defining objects and instances of these. It is desirable, architecturally, to consolidate common services in a common shared component. The architecture must allow use of an ODBMS for this purpose in order to take advantage both of the capabilities it provides and integration with other OMG components using the same services.

As mentioned above, different ODBMS implementation approaches must be supported. The architecture and the OMG interfaces must provide a single interface (or set of interfaces) that allows use of a wide variety of such implementations. A single interface allows users to choose which implementation to use and when. This should cover not only full ODBMS implementations but other approaches with partial functionality, such as file management approaches.

In addition to direct use of an ODBMS through an interface such as that defined in the ODMG-93 specification, an ODBMS could be decomposed in order to implement a number of semi-independent *services*, such as persistence, transactions, relationships, and versions. The OMG Object Services Task Force is defining such services. This is an area for future work by the object database vendors.

In addition to the ORB and users of the ORB accessing ODBMSs, it is also the case that an ODBMS may be a client of the ORB. The ODBMS may want to use the ORB services such as location and naming (for distributed name services) or may use the ORB in order to access other ODBMSs, thus allowing heterogeneous ODBMS access. Current ODBMSs provide object identifiers that work only within one vendor's products, sometimes only within one database. The ORB object references could serve as a common denominator that allows selected object references and invocations in an ODBMS to span database boundaries (via encapsulating ODBMS object identifiers within ORB object references).

B.4 ODBMS as an Object Manager

The ORB acts as a communication mechanism to provide distributed, transparent dispatching of requests to objects among applications and service providers. The ODBMS acts as manager of a collection of objects, most of which are not directly registered as objects to the ORB, some of which can be very small (fine-grained) application objects, and for which high-speed transparent distributed access must be supported.

If every ODBMS object that an application wanted to reference were individually registered with the ORB or if every request to those objects in the ODBMS went through the ORB Basic Object Adaptor, the overhead would be unacceptable. This is equivalent to saying that every test of a bit of data or change of an integer must invoke the overhead of an RPC mechanism. Instead, the application should have the flexibility to choose which objects and which granularities are in fact known to the ORB, when requests to those objects go through the ORB, and be able to change this choice from time to time.

To achieve this maximum flexibility, we specify that the ODBMS has the capability to manage objects unknown or known to the ORB, to register subspaces of object identifiers with the ORB (to allow the ORB to handle requests to all of the objects in an ODBMS without the registration of each individual object), and to provide direct access to the objects it manages. For the objects unknown to the ORB, this direct access is provided via an ORB request to a containing object (e.g., a database), which then makes those objects directly available to the application. This provides consistency with and participation in the ORB environment and still provides the ODBMS with the ability to move objects around the distributed environment, cache them as appropriate, and provide efficient access.

For objects that the ODBMS has registered with the ORB, it may choose either to let requests to them execute the normal ORB mechanism or request from the ORB that any requests to those objects be passed to the ODBMS, perhaps for some period of time. Requests to such objects, whether through the ORB or directly to the ODBMS, must produce the same effect and be compatible with other users employing both mechanisms. In this way the ODBMS can provide consistency with the ORB and still coordinate with direct object requests.

The currently adopted OMG CORBA document provides for normal object access via the Basic Object Adaptor (BOA). For complete generality, flexibility, and interoperability, it executes via an interprocess mechanism (RPC for short) for every dispatch of every method. An extension is the Library Object Adaptor (LOA) that allows direct, considerably faster access to objects. After the first invocation (via the usual ORB mechanism), or through a compile-time optimization, a direct link is established to the object. Later access by the client to the object is then direct until the client notifies the ORB that it has released the object. We offer a new type of Object Adaptor, the Object Database Adaptor (ODA), to provide the ability to register a subspace of object identifiers and to allow access (including direct access) to the objects as if they had been individually registered.

The ODA provides a mechanism to register a subspace of object identifiers with the ORB rather than having to register all objects in the ODBMS. From the client's point of view, the objects in the registered subspace appear just as any other ORB-accessible objects, with the same interface. The ODA should allow for the use of direct access (as in the LOA) to improve the performance of ORB/ODBMS applications.

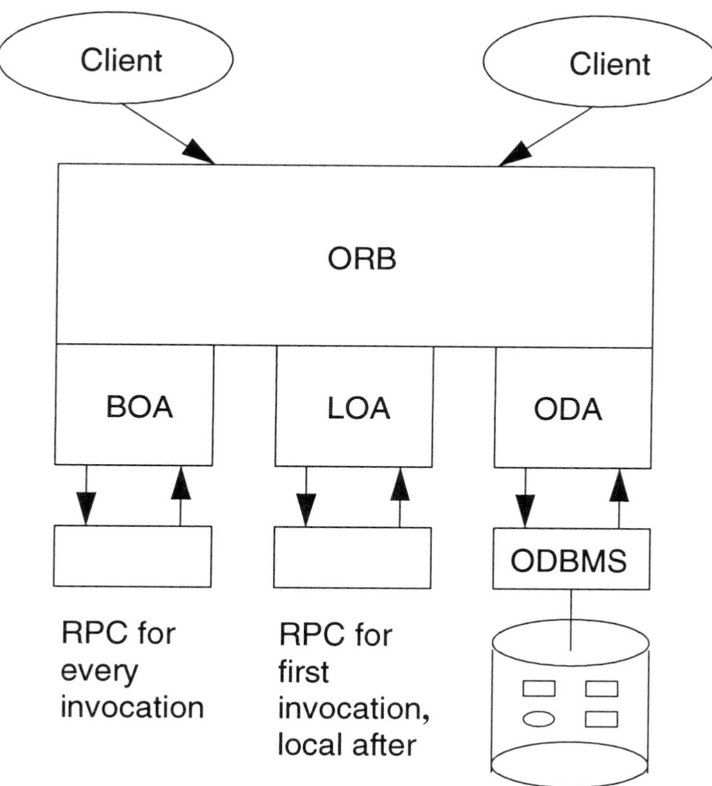

Figure B-1. ODBMS as Object Manager in OMG ORB Architecture

Biographies

Contact information, email addresses, and web sites for the following people can be found at http://www.odmg.org.

R.G.G. Cattell

Dr. R. G. G. "Rick" Cattell is a Distinguished Engineer at JavaSoft, Inc., where he serves as lead architect on database connectivity. He has worked for 12 years at Sun Microsystems in both management and senior technical roles and for 10 years in research at Xerox PARC and at Carnegie-Mellon University.

Dr. Cattell is best known for his contributions to database systems, particularly in object-oriented databases and database user interfaces. He is the author of 40 papers and three books in database systems and other topics. He was a founder of SQL Access, the author of the world's first monograph on object database systems, and the recipient of the ACM Outstanding Dissertation Award. Rick serves as the Chair of the ODMG and the Chair of the ODMG Java Binding Work Group.

Douglas K. Barry

Doug Barry has worked in database technology for over 20 years, with an exclusive focus since 1987 on the application of database technology for objects. As Principal of Barry & Associates, Inc., Doug has focused on helping clients make fully informed decisions about the application of object technology.

Doug is also the author of *Object Database Handbook: How to Select, Implement, and Use Object-Oriented Databases*, published by John Wiley & Sons; the *DBMS Needs Assessment for Objects* and the *ODBMS Implementation Stories*, published by Barry & Associates, Inc.; and the ODBMS column in DOC Magazine. Doug serves as the Executive Director of the ODMG and the Editor of Release 2.0.

Dirk Bartels

Dirk Bartels, founder and CEO of POET Software, Inc., has been working in the software industry since 1983. He holds a Masters degree in Computer Science from the Technical University, Berlin. Dirk serves as the Chair of the ODMG C++ Binding Work Group.

Mark D. Berler

Mark D. Berler is a Senior Principal and Associate of the Center for Advanced Technologies at American Management Systems of Fairfax, Va. He is an architect specializing in the design and development of object-oriented frameworks and services for large-scale distributed systems. He also has experience implementing database infrastructures that manage terabytes of data. Mark holds a Masters degree in Computer Science from the State University of New York at Albany. He serves as the editor for the Object Model and Object Specification Languages chapters.

Jeff Eastman

Dr. Eastman has over 20 years of experience in the computing field, and more than half of this has been focused in the area of object technology. He is the founder of Windward Solutions, Inc., a California consulting firm. Windward was the original developer of DNS Technologies' SmalltalkBroker ORB. Previously, he was a senior architect in Hewlett Packard's Distributed Object Computing Program. There, he led the development of HP Distributed Smalltalk, the first Smalltalk implementation of the Object Management Group's CORBA standard. As a member of HP's Information Architecture Group, he helped to develop and prove many of the key technologies that allowed HP to become a leader in the distributed objects arena. Dr. Eastman has held a variety of management positions in research and development and has managed several object technology projects. He holds a Ph.D. in Electrical Engineering from North Carolina State University. Jeff serves as the Vice Chair of the ODMG, the Chair of the ODMG Object Model Work Group, and the editor of the Smalltalk Binding chapter.

Sophie Gamerman

Sophie Gamerman is Vice President, Support, of O_2 Technology. She is in charge of training, consulting, and hotline services, as well as pre-sales activities. She received her Ph.D. in computer science in 1984 from the University of Paris XI. From 1983 to 1986, Gamerman was teaching at the University of Paris XI and was consultant at INRIA (French National Institute for Research in Computer Science and Control). In 1986, Sophie Gamerman joined the Altair R&D consortium that designed and developed the O_2 object database management system in Rocquencourt, France. In 1991, she was one of the founders of O_2 Technology and has been in charge since then of customer services and pre-sales worldwide. Sophie Gamerman is the technical representative of O_2 Technology at the ODMG and also serves as the editor of the Object Query Language chapter.

David Jordan

David Jordan is a Distinguished Member of Technical Staff at Lucent Technologies. His object technology pursuits began in 1981 with Smalltalk, while he was finishing his masters in computer science. He began using C++ in 1984 and has been designing C++ object models and database schemas for network, relational, and object databases ever since. While employed at Bell Labs, he initiated discussions with Ontologic in 1986, helping them to engineer the first commercial object database for C++. Since then he has used most of the object database vendors' proprietary interfaces, and is now using implementations of the ODMG standard. David is writing a book based on the ODMG C++ and OQL interfaces, titled *C++ Object Databases,* to be published in 1997. David serves as the editor of the C++ Binding chapter.

Adam Springer

Adam Springer is Chief Consultant for GemStone Systems, Inc., where he helps Fortune 500 companies develop and deploy production object systems. He has worked with object systems for 10 years. He has degrees in Computer Science and Economics from the University of California, San Diego. A native Californian, Adam enjoys living in the San Francisco Bay area. Adam serves as the Chair of the ODMG Smalltalk Binding Work Group.

Henry Strickland

Henry Strickland is a programmer at Versant Object Technology. He serves as the editor of the Java Binding chapter.

Andrew E. Wade

Dr. Andrew E. Wade is the founder and Vice President, Corporate Development, at Objectivity, Inc. He previously built DBMSs to support complex, interconnected information at Hewlett-Packard (CAD), Daisy System (CAE), and Digital F/X (Video). He helped found the Object Management Group(OMG), where he co-sponsored the Persistence Service and led the Query Service, helped found the ODMG, and co-authored the book ODMG-93, and many articles. He serves as the Chair of the ODMG Object Query Language Work Group.

Index

E

P

T

U

V

W

X

Related Titles from Morgan Kaufmann:

Object-Relational DBMSs: The Next Great Wave
by Michael Stonebraker, Informix, with Dorothy Moore
Michael Stonebraker, database expert and founder of the object-relational DBMS vendor, Illustra, explores a new and promising class of database management systems—the object-relational DBMS—and demonstrates why it will be the dominant database technology of the future. Stonebraker contends that object-relational technology is ideal for supporting a broad spectrum of data types and application areas, from financial services to the exploding market for multimedia data.
1996; 216 pages; paperback; ISBN 1-55860-397-2

Using The New DB2: IBM's Object-Relational Database System
Donald Chamberlin, IBM Almaden Research Center
An overview of the basic features of DB2 Version 2, including historical notes on the development of SQL. This book offers a comprehensive explanation of the advanced features of the system, including recursive queries, constraints, triggers, user-defined types and functions, stored procedures, and client/server applications. Several complete sample applications are provided, illustrating storage and manipulation of complex objects, design of an active database, and use of stored procedures.
1996; 708 pages; paperback; ISBN 1-55860-373-5

Joe Celko's SQL for Smarties: Advanced SQL Programming
Joe Celko
Joe Celko shares his most useful tips and tricks for advanced SQL programming to help the working programmer gain performance and work around system deficiencies. Addressing real problems that people building real applications face, the author provides new and creative ways to solve and avoid common programming problems.
1995; 467 pages; paperback; ISBN 1-55860-323-9